Conversations with John Gardner

Conversations
with John Gardner

Edited by
Allan Chavkin

University Press of Mississippi
Jackson and London

Library of Congress Cataloging-in-Publication Data

Gardner, John, 1933-
    Conversations with John Gardner / edited by Allan Chavkin.
        p.   cm. — (Literary conversations series)
    Includes bibliographical references (p.).
    ISBN 0-87805-422-7 (alk. paper). — ISBN 0-87805-423-5 (pbk. :
alk. paper)
    1. Gardner, John, 1933- —Interviews.   2. Novelists,
American—20th century—Interviews.   3. Ethics in literature.
I. Chavkin, Allan Richard, 1950-   . II. Title. III. Series.
PS3557.A712Z463   1990
813'.54—dc20   89-27904
                                                              CIP

British Library Cataloging-in-Publication data available

Books by John Gardner

The Forms of Fiction. Ed. John Gardner and Lennis Dunlap. New York: Random, 1962.

The Complete Works of the Gawain-Poet in a Modern English Version with a Critical Introduction. Chicago: University of Chicago Press, 1965.

The Resurrection. New York: New American Library, 1966. Gardner made many changes for the Ballantine edition, 1974.

Le Morte Darthur Notes, Lincoln: Cliff's Notes, 1967.

The Gawain-Poet Notes. Lincoln: Cliff's Notes, 1967.

The Wreckage of Agathon. New York: Harper, 1970.

Grendel. New York: Knopf, 1971.

The Alliterative Morte Arthure The Owl and the Nightingale And Five Other Middle English Poems in a Modernized Version with Comments on the Poems and Notes. Carbondale: Southern Illinois University Press, 1971.

The Sunlight Dialogues. New York: Knopf, 1972.

Jason and Medeia. New York: Knopf, 1973.

Nickel Mountain. New York: Knopf, 1973.

The Construction of the Wakefield Cycle. Carbondale: Southern Illinois University Press, 1974.

The King's Indian Stories and Tales. New York: Knopf, 1974.

The Construction of Christian Poetry in Old English. Carbondale: Southern Illinois University Press, 1975.

Dragon, Dragon and Other Tales. New York: Knopf, 1975.

Gudgekin the Thistle Girl and Other Tales. New York: Knopf, 1976.

October Light. New York: Knopf, 1976.

The King of the Hummingbirds and Other Tales. New York: Knopf, 1977.

The Poetry of Chaucer. Carbondale: Southern Illinois University Press, 1977.

The Life and Times of Chaucer. New York: Knopf, 1977.

A Child's Bestiary. New York: Knopf, 1977.

In the Suicide Mountains. New York: Knopf, 1977.

On Moral Fiction. New York: Basic Books, 1978.

Poems. Northridge, Calif.: Lord John Press, 1978.

Rumpelstiltskin. Dallas: New London Press, 1978.

Frankenstein. Dallas: New London Press, 1979.

William Wilson. Dallas: New London Press, 1979.

Vlemk the Box-Painter. Northridge, Calif.: Lord John Press, 1979.

Freddy's Book. New York: Knopf, 1980.

The Temptation Game. Dallas: New London Press, 1980.

MSS: A Retrospective. Ed. John Gardner and L. M. Rosenberg. Dallas: New London Press, 1980.

The Art of Living and Other Stories. New York: Knopf, 1981.

Death and the Maiden. Dallas: New London Press, 1981.

Mickelsson's Ghosts. New York: Knopf, 1982.

The Best American Short Stories 1982. Ed. John Gardner and Shannon Ravenel. Boston: Houghton Mifflin Company, 1982.

Tengu Child: Stories by Kikuo Itaya. Trans. John Gardner and Nobuko Tsukui. Carbondale: Southern Illinois University Press, 1983.

On Becoming a Novelist. New York: Harper, 1983.
The Art of Fiction. New York: Knopf, 1984.
Gilgamesh. Trans. John Gardner and John Maier. New York: Knopf, 1984.
Stillness and Shadows. Ed. Nicholas Delbanco. New York: Knopf, 1986.

Contents

Introduction

John Gardner's career was a strange one. As he explains in interviews, he began writing before he was an adult. After the accidental death of his younger brother Gilbert, he became guilt-ridden and gloomy and "drifted" into fiction writing.[1] About three decades later, in an attempt to exorcise the demons that possessed him, he presented a slightly fictionalized version of the accident and confessed his feeling of responsibility for his brother's death. As he says in a 1980 interview with Judson Mitcham and William Richard, all of his novels and short stories before "Redemption" (1977) "are shot through with a kind of disguised guilt," but in this story he "decided to take it [the guilt] head-on."

> One day in April—a clear, blue day when there were crocuses in bloom—Jack Hawthorne ran over and killed his brother, David. Even at the last moment he could have prevented his brother's death by slamming on the tractor brakes, easily in reach for all the shortness of his legs; but he was unable to think, or, rather, thought unclearly, and so watched it happen, as he would again and again watch it happen in his mind, with nearly undiminished intensity and clarity, all his life. The younger brother was riding, as both of them knew he should not have been, on the cultipacker, a two-ton implement lumbering behind the tractor, crushing new-ploughed ground.[2]

This fictional account of the accident is very close to what actually occurred in those horrifying moments on that April day in 1945, but Gardner did change some details. Apparently, he wanted to make clear that he could have saved his brother by quickly slamming on the brakes; however, it is probable that there simply wasn't enough time to save Gilbert's life.[3]

Not yet twelve years old on the day of the accident, a despairing Gardner blamed himself for his brother's death; afterward he suffered constantly from nightmares, and even during the day he would experience "flashbacks" in which he would relive the accident. He felt keenly the emotional devastation of his parents, who were unable to console him and relieve him of guilt. He later hinted that this traumatic incident, which haunted him throughout his life, was responsible for his becoming a writer. In *On Moral Fiction* (1978), he writes: "Art begins in a wound, an imperfection—a wound inherent in the nature of life itself—and is an attempt either to learn to live with the wound or to heal it. It is the pain of the wound which impels the artist to do his work, and it is the universality of woundedness in the human condition which makes the work of art significant as medicine or distraction."[4] Gardner then gives several examples of what he means by "wound." In *On Becoming a Novelist* (1983) he gives an example which reveals that his definition of art owes much to his personal experience. Explaining that "what the writer probably needs most is an almost daemonic compulsiveness," he observes: "A psychological wound is helpful, if it can be kept in partial control, to keep the novelist driven. Some fatal childhood accident for which one feels responsible and can never fully forgive oneself. . . ."[5]

Between 1971 (when *Grendel* was published to popular and critical attention) and his sudden death in 1982, the period when he finally achieved recognition after his long "apprenticeship," this driven man proved not only that he was one of those rare writers who could create innovative fiction that was popular with both the critics and the public, but also that he would be prolific. By the end of his career, Gardner demonstrated that he could be a novelist, short story writer, playwright, poet, editor, scholar, biographer, translator, anthologist, critic, script-writer, reviewer, librettist, and writer of children's stories and verse. Of course, as he makes clear in his interviews, he had been building up a "backlog" of unpublished work before the 1970s when publishers were not receptive to his fiction with its unique blend of fantasy and realism. Still, even taking this backlog into consideration, one can only conclude that Gardner was remarkably productive in the 1970s. In fact, by 1976, he had demonstrated in just a few years that he was one of America's most prolific, versatile, and imaginative writers.

By 1978, he had demonstrated also that he could be one of America's most controversial writers. The publication of *On Moral*

Fiction (1978) with its unsparing indictment of the major American contemporary writers became the single most important "event" of his career. The book provoked a prolonged public debate on the health and proper function of modern art, and Gardner's interviews and speeches helped fuel the controversy. Some reviewers agreed with Gardner's contention that the arts had been corrupted; however, others attacked the book in which they found serious problems, including a strident tone, capricious judgments, and self-serving evaluations of rival authors. Gardner focused attention on an important issue and stirred up a great deal of publicity but also hurt his reputation by provoking the hostility of numerous writers, academics, and reviewers, some of whom would savage or glibly dismiss the experimental novel-within-a-novel *Freddy's Book,* (1980), *The Art of Living and Other Stories* (1981), and the ambitious *Mickelsson's Ghosts* (1982).

While Gardner confessed in interviews that the criticism of his later work discouraged him, he had been harshly and unfairly critical of some writers in *On Moral Fiction*. In that polemical book, Gardner had written that "in a world where nearly everything that passes for art is tinny and commercial and often, in addition, hollow and academic, I argue—by reason and by banging the table—for an old-fashioned view of what art is and does. . . ." (p. 5) Seeing himself in the great moral tradition of Homer, Dante, and Tolstoy, Gardner argued that true art should seek to improve and affirm life. On the other hand, "that art which tends toward destruction, the art of nihilists, cynics, and merdistes, is not properly art at all" (p. 6).

An ardent believer in Shelley's view of the poet as legislator of mankind, Gardner felt that the corruption of modern art was a matter of crucial importance because a corrupt art would result in a corrupt civilization. In 1977 he told interviewers Don Edwards and Carol Polsgrove, "if you have one after another—plays, books and so on, which are constantly talking about wife-swapping, people are going to swap wives. Art leads, it doesn't follow." In his interview with Charlie Reilly later that year, Gardner bluntly stated: "the kind of art I write is supposed to be a desperate holding action against the forces of barbarism, which I think are all around us." Unfortunately, Gardner's Messianic belief in his kind of art resulted in overzealous criticism and reductive views of many writers, including, for example,

Saul Bellow, who cogently expresses his own moral vision in "moral fiction." Probably hoping to bring attention to the important issue of the confused state of modern aesthetics, Gardner overstated his case—perhaps he assumed that he could qualify and refine his ideas once he had provoked a debate on the issue.

In fact, Gardner did provoke a debate, and as a result of others, criticism of *On Moral Fiction*, he clarified some of his ideas in interviews. Gardner's interviews are important because, among other things, they help one to understand the controversy on moral fiction. In fact, most of Gardner's interviews, even those that predate the publication of *On Moral Fiction*, contain his ideas on the relationship between art and morality and shed some light on the controversy. (If one considers that all of Gardner's substantial interviews occurred in the 1971-1982 period, and that the writing of *On Moral Fiction* began in the 1960s, then one should not be surprised to find Gardner's views on moral fiction even in his interviews before 1978.) Particularly illuminating interviews on the controversy are those with Thomas LeClair in *The New Republic* (Gardner debates William Gass) and with Stephen Singular in *The New York Times Magazine* (which includes the varied reactions of John Updike, Norman Mailer, Saul Bellow, and some of the other major writers whom Gardner attacked).

It is Gardner's concern over moral fiction which results in a pattern to the interviews. An innovator in narrative techniques but a conservative in values, Gardner was preoccupied with moral fiction in his interviews in the 1970s, and as the decade progressed, he became increasingly critical of such writers as Barth, whom he considered representative of those cynics who had taken modern literature down the wrong path. His proselytizing on moral fiction and his occasionally outrageous remarks on other writers resulted in his being solicited for and his agreeing to numerous interviews around the time of the publication of *On Moral Fiction*. By 1980, however, he was no longer eager to talk about the moral fiction controversy and complained to Judson Mitcham and William Richard, who had asked him about his relations with writers he had criticized: "What I should have said at the start of this is, *On Moral Fiction* was written, published, and debated a long time ago. Why on earth are we talking about all this again?" In their conversations with Gardner in the following years, however, interviewers continued to ask him about the moral fiction controversy, and, at times, Gardner used the interviews to recant some of his opinions.

Undoubtedly, his view of himself as a public figure and as a spokesman for a moral literature upon which the survival of civilization depended resulted in his giving numerous interviews—at least 140 between 1971 and 1982. Unlike many writers who are wary of interviews and who are, at times, reticent, evasive, or hostile when they are being questioned, Gardner seems to have welcomed interviews as an opportunity to promote his ideas and elaborate upon and clarify his stand on issues. In fact, he usually is willing to try to answer any question, even one on such a painful topic as the death of his brother. Usually "scrupulously down to earth," as interviewer John Askins has observed, Gardner talks candidly and responds thoroughly.

While Gardner is usually down to earth and accommodating, during the course of an interview he can be alternately brilliant and blusterous, cocky and modest, argumentative and agreeable. Interviewers usually react favorably to Gardner; they are respectful and often sympathetic. Gardner possesses a knack for establishing good rapport with his interviewers. Believing Gardner to be "America's best working novelist," Larry Swindell comments: "we had an extraordinarily pleasant lunch-and-conversation that stretched to three hours with a lot of grinning and nodding." But not all interviewers react as sympathetically as Swindell. Ed Christian challenges Gardner several times to justify his work and his ideas. At one point during their conversation he scathingly attacks *Grendel* and *The Wreckage of Agathon*, and Gardner responds with a spirited defense of the novels. Stephen Singular during the course of his interview with the novelist is not as confrontational as Ed Christian, but his essay-profile based on that interview is often critical of Gardner, whom he describes in the opening paragraph as looking "something like a pregnant woman trying to pass for a Hell's Angel."

Even Ed Christian would agree that Gardner's vast knowledge of Western culture results in informative, analytically rigorous interviews, in which he speaks eloquently, and at times provocatively, on a variety of subjects, whether it be opera, children's literature, Sartre's existentialism, the teaching of creative writing, or northern and southern "styles of evil." A respected and widely-published scholar on medieval literature who uses some of its techniques and content to enrich his own art, he has a comprehensive understanding of literary history and a rare perspective on modern writing. Gardner can explain not only the intricacies of literary tradition and influence that the scholar studies but also the kinds of practical matters that the creative writer must consider, such as the efficacy of "sprung hexameters" in *Jason and Medeia*. In his interview with Gardner, Alan Burns remarks to him: "One thing that occurs to me as you speak is that you analyse extremely clearly, aptly; you have, it seems to me, an extraordinarily high degree of awareness of what you are doing and that results from that combination in you of the creative person, the novelist, and the academic, critic, teacher."[6] While Gardner often can analyze with clarity and insight the work of writers he admires, he is an especially good critic of his own work. And unlike many writers, he is willing to answer specific questions about the content and techniques of his work and does so at length.

Some probing questions of interviewers stimulate Gardner to ponder in depth more aspects of his life and art than he would have done otherwise. For example, Stephen Singular questions Gardner on why he has written very little about sexual love. Not having recognized this aspect of his writing before, Gardner is "somewhat taken aback by the question," but admits: "That's true. That's the greatest weakness in my fiction—the lack of real sexual love." After pointing out other writers, such as Shakespeare, Chaucer, and Homer, who mastered the subject, he suggests that he has not mastered sexual love in his fiction because of his "puritanical shyness." *Nickel Mountain* is a kind of love story, but he "shies away" from sexual love because he "couldn't handle it." He then suggests that this weakness may be corrected in his future work. He states that his next novel, *Shadows,* will be the "first love story I've ever written flat out. A real love story requires a woman who is the equal of the man. And my women . . . this has been a weakness." In a 1980 interview with Judson Mitcham and William Richard, who ask him about this "weakness" in his fiction, Gardner downplays his remarks to Singular, whom he calls "a very unpleasant, aggressive young man," and states that he "won't be bending over backwards to work in sex scenes" in his future work.

The interviews reveal the man behind the fiction—and the man who is revealed is exceedingly complicated, a man of contrasts and contradictions, as several of the interviewers' physical descriptions of Gardner suggest. Singular seems unpleasantly surprised by the unkempt appearance of the famous writer. "I saw a rumpled gnome of a man descending the long winding staircase toward me. His hair swayed with his steps, and he was wearing a crumpled pink shirt— held together with safety pins—paint-spattered blue jeans and broken shoes. His face was red and swollen with sleep—or the lack of it; he had been writing until 6 A.M., five hours before—and his eyes belonged to someone over 70. He smiled, not welcoming me, but resigned to doing his duty." Critical of the way the novelist dresses, the interviewer asks him why he chooses to appear the way he does. Gardner explains to him that "it's comfortable" and that it serves a practical purpose—his "appearance serves as a wall, so I don't get involved in too many things." Apparently, Gardner believes that his unconventional appearance will discourage people who might think about making demands on him.

In 1982 Stephen Wigler interviews Gardner at his childhood home. The novelist is traveling by motorcycle each week from Susquehanna, Pennsylvania, to Batavia, New York, in order to help care for his father, who has suffered a paralyzing stroke. Unseen by Gardner, Wigler observes the novelist in a field, bending over and planting vegetables, and softly whistling "Someone to Watch over Me": "It's raining. His blue turtleneck sweater, work jeans, and shoes— strangely enough, fashionable tassel-topped loafers—are covered with mud." Wigler then comments: "Here is a man who's a study in contrasts and contradictions."

Curt Suplee describes Gardner as a "bleary juggernaut running on brains, charisma, and gin"—he has "a boyish face somewhere between Prince Valiant and Mickey Rooney with the deep-wrinkled eyes of a Welsh crocodile. A mean red scar from a recent fall cuts across his nose and eyebrow." Bruce Beans also comments on the scar and the tough appearance of Gardner but suggests that underneath is a gentle, likeable man who bearhugs his neighbors and travels long distances to help his ailing father. Beans also compares the novelist searching for his matches to one of his medieval monsters "rooting through a cave" and then adds: "slightly paunchy, with gentle, wrinkled eyes, a soft slightly nasal upstate New York twang, and a pewter-white mane worthy of Merlin, John Gardner was a living engine of ambition who was seen in different ways by different people."

Since Gardner's fiction is usually autobiographical, as he admits, it is useful to know as much as possible about the key events of his life and what Gardner thought about them. He had his share of problems, and, unlike many writers, he was willing to discuss them with interviewers. How accurately Gardner recounted his life to his interviewers will not be clear until his biography is published. But until a biography appears, the interviews are the best source of published information on Gardner's life.

After his premature death in 1982, Joyce Carol Oates stated that Gardner "was an extremely complex personality, almost like a character out of a Dostoevski novel" (Beans). The comparison is apt; in fact, Oates's statement, more than any other, best describes Gardner. Like Ivan Karamazov or some of Dostoevski's other characters, he pondered with not only his mind but also his soul the great philosophical problems of good and evil, of God and his absence. He was capable of sudden changes of mood, from exultation to despondency, from self-doubt to supreme egotism. "He brought to everything he did a passion that at times bordered on madness," remarked Bruce Beans.

In the absence of Gardner's autobiography, these interviews are useful because collectively they become the work in which Gardner talks at greatest length about both his life and his work. The Gardner who emerges by the end of the book is a complex man who contradicts himself at times. The novelist seemed both amused and surprised when he noticed in 1980 that he could be "a bundle of confusion," enthusiastically praising a book in one interview and later in another interview dismissing the book as fraudulent.[7] At least some of the contradictions in the interviews may be the result of Gardner's aesthetic in which writing and thinking were regarded as a process of continual revision of ideas in the search for the truth. Like Norman Mailer, Gardner sometimes discovered what he believed in the act of writing or conversing.

While Gardner was contradictory at times, he was not "a bundle of confusion" on what mattered to him the most—his art. In explaining to Stephen Singular the reason why he continued to teach creative writing even though it was a burdensome task, he stated: "Fiction is the only religion I have. If I don't teach and get my point of view across to younger writers, I will burn in hell for a thousand years." When Singular questioned Gardner on the reason for this Messianic complex about art, the writer explained: "It's made my life, and it made my life when I was a kid, when I was incapable of finding any other sustenance, any other thing to lean on, any other comfort during times of great unhappiness. Art has filled my life with joy and I want everybody to know the kind of joy I know—that's what Messianic means." In his autobiographical story "Redemption," Gardner had presented vividly the devastating despair of his guilt-ridden protagonist who attempted through art to heal his psychological wound and to free himself from emotional and spiritual bondage. Seeking redemption through art was the driving force in the life of John Gardner.

Robert A. Morace has noted the weird twist at the end of Gardner's strange career—his literary battle over "moral fiction" "helped change the face of contemporary American fiction," but this triumph resulted not in the increase but in the decline of his standing as a writer.[8] Yet Gregory L. Morris concluded in his book on Gardner that *The Sunlight Dialogues* "will eventually stand as one of the great books of the twentieth century,"[9] and other scholars who have studied Gardner's canon consider him to be a major writer.[10] In any case, his place in twentieth-century literature requires more study and evaluation; it is my hope that this book of conversations will help prompt such activities and will help scholars assess the quality of Gardner's work and thought.

The interviews selected for inclusion in this book occurred between 1971 and 1982, a period in which Gardner gave all his important interviews. I have arranged the interviews according to the dates on which they took place. As with other books in the Literary Conversations series, the previously published interviews are reprinted here without substantive emendation. Some of the headnotes have been shortened or omitted to eliminate unnecessary repetition. I have also done some minor editing, such as printing titles of Gardner's works in italics. Inevitably, interviewers focus on favorite topics, such as moral fiction, and ask some of the same questions, which, of course, results in some repetition. Gardner's responses to the same questions sometimes vary, however, and comparing responses can be illuminating. Moreover, Gardner's repetition reveals his preoccupations and indicates what he considers important.

My principle of selection has been to choose the most informative and thereby the most important of the numerous interviews which Gardner gave before his sudden death. The conversations included in this book focus on his diverse interests and achievements. The majority of the interviews are in the question-answer format, but I have included interviews in the essay-profile format because they contain important biographical information and reveal the complexity of Gardner's personality. I am pleased that I am able to include previously unpublished conversations with Gardner in which he makes some thoughtful observations on his work. Only part of Charlie Reilly's interview was previously published. Gregory L. Morris's interview is published for the first time in this collection.

Gardner has been fortunate that a number of first-rate scholars have examined his fiction, and some of their names can be found in my "Notes." I am particularly indebted to Robert A. Morace and John M. Howell for their indispensable bibliographies—I found Howell's superb chronology of Gardner from 1933-1979 helpful in writing my own chronology. I would like to thank Fritz Oehlschlaeger, Lisa Lundstedt, Paul Cohen, Bob Randolph, David Cowart, Gregory L. Morris, Robert A. Morace, Paula Chavkin, and my wife and colleague Nancy for offering suggestions for improving this book. I am indebted to the National Endowment for the Humanities for a 1984-85 Fellowship to work on another project on modern American literature but which also gave me the time to read Gardner's work and acquire the knowledge and develop the interest that would eventually result in this book. I also appreciate the financial support of both the Graduate Studies/Research Office and the Development/ Alumni Affairs Office of Southwest Texas State University; my thanks to Nancy Grayson, G. Jack Gravitt, Paul Fonteyn, and Michael Willoughby who helped me in various ways to obtain financial assistance for this project. I owe thanks, too, to the hardworking library staff of the university who provided assistance numerous times. I am grateful to Associate Director Seetha Srinivasan and Assistant Editor Ginger Tucker of the University Press of Mississippi for their excellent advice. Finally, I appreciate the support and encouragement of my parents, Gilbert and Sylvia Chavkin, and my daughter, Laura Michelle Chavkin—all enthusiastic readers of good literature.

AC
August 1989

1. Curt Suplee, "John Gardner, Flat Out," *Washington Post*, 25 July 1982, reprinted in this collection. Subsequent quotations from interviews in this collection will not be cited in the "Notes." Instead, either the name of the interviewer will be cited parenthetically, or it will be clear from the context which interview is the source of the quotation.

2. "Redemption," in *The Art of Living and Other Stories* (New York: Knopf, 1981), p. 30. "Redemption" was originally published in *The Atlantic Monthly*, 239 (May 1977), 48-50, 55-56, 58-59. John M. Howell, "The Wound and the Albatross: John Gardner's Apprenticeship," in *Thor's Hammer: Essays on John Gardner*, ed. Jeff Henderson (Conway, AR: Univ. of Central Arkansas Press, 1985), pp. 3-5, indicates that the story was "in progress" in the fall of 1976 and may have been completed in 1976 or 1977. A similar description of the accident (probably written in the spring of 1975) appears in Gardner's autobiographical novel *Stillness*. In his excellent essay, Howell observes that Gardner "explored the accident and its metaphysical implications from the beginning of his career to its violent end, using many different masks and parallel actions" (pp. 2-3).

3. See Howell, "The Wound and the Albatross: John Gardner's Apprenticeship," pp. 1-4, and "A Conversation with Priscilla Gardner," *MSS* 4 (1984), 233-235.

4. *On Moral Fiction* (New York: Basic Books, 1978), p. 181. Subsequent references will be cited parenthetically in the text.

5. *On Becoming a Novelist* (New York: Harper & Row, 1983), p. 62.

6. "John Gardner," in *The Imagination on Trial: British and American Writers Discuss Their Working Methods*, ed. Alan Burns and Charles Sugnet (London: Allison and Busby, 1981), p. 44.

7. "Afterword," in John M. Howell, *John Gardner: A Bibliographical Profile* (Carbondale: Southern Illinois Univ. Press, 1980), p. 145.

8. *"Stillness and Shadows,"* in *Magill's Literary Annual 1987, Vol. II*, ed. Frank N. Magill (Pasadena, CA: Salem Press, 1987), p. 822.

9. Gregory L. Morris, *A World of Order and Light: The Fiction of John Gardner* (Athens: Univ. of Georgia Press, 1984), p. 230.

10. See, e.g. these books: Beatrice Mendez-Egle and James M. Haule, eds., *John Gardner: True Art, Moral Art* (Edinburg, TX: Pan American Univ., 1983); Robert A. Morace and Kathryn VanSpanckeren, *John Gardner: Critical Perspectives* (Carbondale: Southern Illinois Univ. Press, 1982); David Cowart, *Arches & Light: The Fiction of John Gardner* (Carbondale: Southern Illinois Univ. Press, 1983); Leonard Butts, *The Novels of John Gardner: Making Life Art as a Moral Process* (Baton Rouge: Louisiana State University Press, 1988); and Morris.

Chronology

1933   John Champlin Gardner, Jr.: born in Batavia, New York on 21 July; the first child of John Champlin and Priscilla Jones Gardner.

1945   On 4 April, JG witnesses the accidental death of his younger brother Gilbert.

1951-53   After graduating from Batavia High School, JG attends DePauw University in Greencastle, Indiana, where his initial interest in chemistry eventually shifts to literature, writing, and philosophy.

1953   On 6 June, he marries Joan Louise Patterson, a cousin, and then transfers to Washington University in St. Louis where he works on an early version of part of *Nickel Mountain*.

1955   He graduates from Washington University with an A. B. degree, having been awarded a Woodrow Wilson Fellowship for 1955-56 and having been elected to Phi Beta Kappa.

1955-58   JG attends the University of Iowa to study creative writing. For his M. A. thesis he writes four short pieces of fiction: "Darkling Wood," "One Saturday Morning," "Peter Willis, Resting," and "Nickel Mountain." For his Ph.D. dissertation he writes a novel entitled *The Old Men*.

1958-59   As a lecturer, JG teaches at Oberlin College, Oberlin,
           Ohio.

1959-62   JG teaches at Chico State College, Chico, California. He
           edits a new journal, *MSS*, which gains recognition when
           such writers as Joyce Carol Oates, William Gass, John
           Hawkes, and W. S. Merwin appear in its three issues
           (1961, 1962, and 1964). In 1962 Random House pub-
           lishes *The Forms of Fiction* (edited with Lennis Dunlap).
           During his years in Chico, his son Joel is born (31
           December 1959) and then his daughter Lucy (3 January
           1962).

1962-65   JG teaches at San Francisco State, where Mark Harris
           and Wright Morris are also on the faculty.

1965   University of Chicago Press publishes *The Complete
           Works of the Gawain-Poet*. As Associate Professor of
           Anglo-Saxon and Medieval Studies, JG joins the faculty
           at Southern Illinois University, Carbondale, in September.

1966   New American Library publishes JG's first novel, *The
           Resurrection*.

1968-69   By March 1968, JG completes *The Sunlight Dialogues*,
           but by April 1969, Farrar Straus & Giroux, Houghton
           Mifflin, and Macmillan have rejected it.

1970   JG is Distinguished Visiting Professor at the University of
           Detroit. He is awarded a Danforth Fellowship. Harper &
           Row publishes *The Wreckage of Agathon*.

1971   JG's request that Knopf allow his novels to be illustrated is
           granted. Knopf publishes *Grendel*, which *Time* and
           Newsweek list as one of the year's best novels. Southern
           Illinois University Press publishes *The Alliterative Morte
           Arthure*.

1972   JG is awarded a National Endowment for the Arts grant.
            Knopf publishes *The Sunlight Dialogues*, JG's first novel
            to be fully illustrated, and the first of his novels to be a
            bestseller.

1973   JG teaches at Northwestern University, in Evanston,
            Illinois. Having been awarded a Guggenheim Fellowship
            for 1973-74, he is able to make substantial progress on
            his scholarly studies and his creative writing. Knopf
            publishes *Jason and Medeia*, an epic poem, and the
            popular *Nickel Mountain*.

1974   In August, for the first time, JG teaches at the Bread Loaf
            Writers' Conference, where he will return in later years.
            Southern Illinois University Press publishes *The Con-
            struction of the Wakefield Cycle*. Under the sponsorship
            of the United States Information Service, JG tours Japan
            (8 September-5 October). He is awarded a Hadley
            Fellowship at Bennington College for the 1974-75 aca-
            demic year. Knopf publishes *The King's Indian*.

1975   Southern Illinois University Press publishes *The Con-
            struction of Christian Poetry in Old English*. On 21 May
            JG is elected to the American Academy of Arts and
            Letters. He writes radio plays for National Public Radio.
            Knopf publishes *Dragon, Dragon and Other Tales*,
            selected as "*The New York Times* Outstanding Book for
            Children 1975."

1976   In August JG resigns his position at Southern Illinois
            University, and in October he separates from his wife
            Joan. Knopf publishes *Gudgekin the Thistle Girl and
            Other Tales*, a book for children. At colleges and univer-
            sities, he gives controversial speeches on the moral
            bankruptcy of contemporary writing. Knopf publishes
            October Light, and the novel receives enthusiastic re-
            views; it not only becomes a bestseller but also wins the
            National Book Critics Circle Award for Fiction in 1976.

1977   During the spring semester, JG teaches at Skidmore
           College, Saratoga Springs, New York, and at Williams
           College, Williamstown, Massachusetts. On 21 January, in
           Lexington, Kentucky, he attends the performance of the
           opera *Rumpelstiltskin,* on which he and Joseph Baber
           collaborated, with JG writing the libretto. By early April
           Knopf publishes *The King of the Hummingbirds and
           Other Tales* and *The Life and Times of Chaucer.* Sou-
           thern Illinois University Press publishes *The Poetry of
           Chaucer.* In the fall, JG teaches at George Mason
           University, in Fairfax, Virginia, and Knopf publishes *In the
           Suicide Mountains* and *A Child's Bestiary.* Beginning on
           10 December, JG is hospitalized for cancer of the colon;
           he stays about a month and a half at the Johns Hopkins
           Hospital.

1978   Basic Books publishes *On Moral Fiction,* which JG had
           begun writing in the 1960s. Prompted by Sumner Ferris's
           expose in *Speculum* (October 1977), Peter Prescott in
           Newsweek (10 April), accuses JG of plagiarism in *The
           Life and Times of Chaucer.* Dick Cavett interviews JG
           about his ideas on "moral fiction" *(Dick Cavett Show,*
           PBS-TV, 16 May). In the fall, he begins teaching at the
           State University of New York at Binghamton, where he
           will direct the writing program until his death in 1982.
           Lord John Press publishes *Poems.* On 26 December, the
           Opera Company of Philadelphia performs *Rumpelstilt-
           skin,* and New London Press publishes the libretto.

1979   In July *The New York Times Magazine* publishes a cover
           story on Gardner and the moral fiction controversy. JG
           completes two film treatments and New London Press
           publishes two libretti, *Frankenstein* and *William Wilson.*
           Lord John Press publishes *Vlemk the Box Painter* (a tale).

1980   JG marries Liz Rosenberg. Knopf publishes *Freddy's
           Book.* New London Press publishes *The Temptation
           Game* (a radio play) and *MSS: A Retrospective* (edited
           with L. M. Rosenberg).

1981   JG revives *MSS* to publish new writers. New London
        Press publishes *Death and the Maiden* (a play), and
        Knopf publishes *The Art of Living and Other Stories.*

1982   Houghton Mifflin publishes *The Best American Short
        Stories: 1982* (edited with Shannon Ravenel). Knopf
        publishes *Mickelsson's Ghosts.* Divorced from Liz Rosen-
        berg, he plans to marry Susan Thornton but dies in a
        motorcycle crash near Susquehanna, Pennsylvania, on
        14 September. He is buried next to his brother Gilbert in
        Batavia's Grandview Cemetery.

Conversations with John Gardner

Medievalist in Illinois Ozarks

Digby Diehl/1971

From *Los Angeles Times Calendar*, 5 September 1971, p. 43.
Reprinted by permission.

CARBONDALE, ILL.—If you drive 10 or 20 miles from the University of Southern Illinois where John Gardner teaches medieval literature, you arrive in the green rugged foothills of the Illinois Ozarks. This area has the largest contingent of Weathermen and the largest group of Ku Klux Klan in the U.S.A. The county where Gardner has his 300-acre farm has the highest homicide rate of any county in the country. Moreover, floods from the convergence of the Mississippi and the Ohio Rivers purge the area annually, as well as a seasonal invasion of tornadoes. Tough, violent country.

Perhaps knowing this, it is not so difficult to understand why Gardner has written a novel retelling the Anglo-Saxon heroic epic of *Beowulf*—in which the Scandinavian prince slays a monster—from the viewpoint of the monster. The author of *Grendel* (Knopf: $5.95) explains, "Like the world of Beowulf, southern Illinois is a mixture of primitive and Christian symbolism. (Although it is excellent grape-growing land, the Baptist farmers refuse to grow sinful wine-producing grapes.) These are people full of violence and, in a simple way, full of despair about the human character and civilization. Right now all of society is where Chaucer and Malory were: staring at the abyss. In 14th and 15th-century literature there is nothing but one long gasp of despair. Chaucer saw the grotesque collapse of everything (as did the author of the Wakefield cycle) and saw that it was black and funny. Malory's *Morte d'Arthur* is the most 20th-century book you'll ever read."

In *Grendel* Gardner has a beautifully written, alternately funny and moving philosophical statement. "I teach *Beowulf* all of the time and think that it is the most undersold poem in the language. But I don't really like the value system, the concept of heroism. Really, the hero is a guy who kills a lot of people and grabs a lot of gold. These are Bad Guys. Grendel the monster is sort of a Sartre anarchist who kills

3

himself over a momentary failure of ideals. Sartre is sick and evil, psychotic in fact, as Camus pointed out."

Gardner places *Beowulf* in the context of a dialog that has gone on through the centuries, in which all of the great epics talk to each other: "Homer argues a Bob Dylan point of view in the *Odyssey*. Odysseus becomes a man of passion: total love, total commitment. Virgil refutes him with the *Aeneid*, saying that law and order will hold life together. Virgil's view is really a very sophisticated development from the same roots as Richard Milhous Nixon's. Then the *Beowulf* poet works from the commentaries on the *Aeneid* and comes up with the notion that you have to make heroic sacrifices for law and order. He basically says that life offers no felicity by either the Christian or Pagan routes.

"And finally Dante brings it all together by following Virgil around until he hits *Paradiso* where he refutes him. The opening line of the *Paradiso* is from Homer, and by a complicated argument he shows that Dylan at least has a chance to save his soul, but Nixon never will. As a true epic it is a staggering study in the individual vs. the total society. Of course after Dante's answer, there was nothing left to say. Milton knew that but he took a full swing anyway."

For all this academic structuring, Gardner insists that *Grendel* is pure style. "I have nothing to say, except that I think words are beautiful. I'm a stylist; for me, everything is rhythm and rhyme. There are a handful of other stylists like Gass, Elkin, Barthelme, Barth and Ralph Ellison who have nothing to say either. We just write. I guess Samuel Beckett is the model for all of us, which is ironic since he descends from Joyce, who still thought he could save the world with literature."

Beginning by writing would-be novels at the age of 8 on his father's farm in western New York, Gardner worked his way toward the Iowa Writers Workshop, "where I didn't learn anything from the faculty, but all the best young writers in the country were there and we taught each other." For eight years, Gardner did nothing but writing exercises and imitations of other writers for practice.

In 1961, when he was teaching at San Francisco State, he wrote *The Resurrection*, in imitation of Tolstoy's book by that title. He also has translated the complete works of the *Gawain* poet and wrote another novel, *Wreckage of Agathon. Sunlight Dialogues,* a book based on experiences with his grandfather in New York, arrives next year.

Meanwhile, he will travel from his Southern Illinois farm this fall with his wife and two children in order to follow the route Jason took up the Caucasus. "I'm working on an epic poem called *Jason*, based on the classical figure with the golden fleece in the Medea legend. He was the first wheeler-dealer in literature and his is the story of the first time the East is had by the West."

A noted critic wrote to Gardner telling him that he liked *Grendel*, but that it contained ". . . a disturbing philosophy." To which Gardner replied: "There are no disturbing philosophies left any more. We've hit the bottom and we're just bouncing."

John Gardner
Joe David Bellamy and Pat Ensworth/1973

From *The New Fiction: Interviews with Innovative American Writers*, ed. Joe David Bellamy (Urbana: University of Illinois Press, 1974), pp. 169-93. Copyright © 1974 by the Board of Trustees of the University of Illinois. Originally published in *Fiction International*, 2-3 (Spring-Fall 1974), 32-49. Reprinted by permission of the University of Illinois Press.

This interview is an amalgamation of conversations held with John Gardner by Pat Ensworth in the spring of 1973 at Northwestern University and by Joe David Bellamy at the University of Rochester on July 10 and 11, 1973.

Pat Ensworth: My association with John Gardner began when he was imported to teach a writing seminar at Northwestern University. A writing class is a unique way to become acquainted with someone; one's critical tastes and philosophical biases become evident more quickly than they might through ordinary social or professional contact. One fact became immediately clear: in a class where the typical undergraduate literary consciousness resounded with echoes of contemporary writers like Barth, Barthelme, Hawkes, and Pynchon, Gardner's perspective stood out in occasionally violent contrast. While many students tried to give their prose apocalyptical overtones and experimental flourishes, their teacher often reserved his praise for the most traditional (but "affirmative") boy-meets-girl stories. Gardner's references in the college newspaper to certain contemporary authors as "cynical bastards" may have been caused more by impatience with amateur journalism than by critical condemnation. But when this was followed by a plea to the students to strive for "nobility" in their writing, I felt that his unusual sensitivity definitely needed further exploration.

John Gardner has published five novels—*The Resurrection, The Wreckage of Agathon, Grendel, The Sunlight Dialogues*, and *Nickel Mountain*—as well as a collection of tales, *The King's Indian*, and an epic poem, *Jason and Medeia*. He is forty years old, regularly teaches English at Southern Illinois University, lives on a farm, has gray hair, and smokes a churchwarden. His novels employ more-or-less traditional structures in their attention to the development of plot and character; as an epic poem, *Jason and Medeia* returns to an even earlier technique. Classical and medieval concepts abound in both the subject and the style of his work. In an era of explosive experimentation with the art of fiction, questions about this author's perspective are inevitable.

Joe David Bellamy: Hearing that John Gardner would be in upstate New York teaching at the University of Rochester Writers Workshop, I drove down on a sunny, hot afternoon and met Gardner and his wife, Joan, after a reading (by Judith Rascoe) that night. Gardner is a well-built man of medium height with light collar-length hair and very light eyes. He was wearing scuffed boots, a red sports coat, and a pink tie. We had a late dinner at a restaurant called Tale O' the Whale, where we were mistaken for a bunch of hippies and got the poorest service imaginable; then we came back to the Towne House Motor Inn, the place we both were staying, a gaudy monstrosity in the S&H Green Stamp tradition. In the room we pulled up a walnut-formica table, improvised some coffee and tea makings in a scaly aluminum pot—while Joan listened from the bed—and talked into my Sony TC120 until about two in the morning.

Bellamy: What fictional modes, would you say, are dead, and which ones are still fertile and worth pursuing?

John Gardner: Before the Beatles, music was one way, and after the Beatles, music has been another way. As a matter of fact, in all the arts, the Beatles are a sort of turning point. With the squares, however much one admires squares—I mean Hemingway, Faulkner, all those guys—the voice is always straight. You know they're telling you this serious thing. Certainly they all have their ironies. But basically Hemingway is going to tell you something true. After the Beatles, it turns out everybody is writing an Elijah Thrush. You can't tell where Purdy is in that because he is so much involved in taking on a voice. Another way of saying this is: the tradition of the short story and the novel as it came to be defined straight across the forties and fifties gives way in the sixties to a sort of tale-and-yarn tradition, where there is a distinct voice, a narrator, a guy talking who is *defi-*

nitely not the writer and who is fun to listen to and fun to watch and who tells you all kinds of things that may be true and may be false.

Bellamy: An unreliable narrator.

Gardner: Right. Sure.

Bellamy: Putting you on sometimes.

Gardner: Right. . . . Robert Louis Stevenson, in an essay, talks about the extremes in art. He sets up Victor Hugo at one extreme and Fielding at the other. Victor Hugo is a guy who gives you the streets of Paris, and you really feel you're there. Fielding, on the other hand, gives you Tom Jones, and every time you start to think Tom Jones is a real boy he throws something at you—like a comic or Homeric simile or a battle in a graveyard or some crazy thing—and you know this isn't real. . . . Up into the forties and fifties we were all doing Hugo. In the middle sixties and now everybody is doing Fielding, suddenly tired of the small-minded seriousness of those novels, their delicate apprehensions, and going instead for big emotions, going for big commitments, or for big jokes. *The Sot-Weed Factor* is, I think, nothing but a big joke. It's a philosophical joke; it might even be argued that it's a philosophical advance. But it ain't like Victor Hugo. You're always aware of a page.

Bellamy: Why did this change come about? Is the idea that writers should imitate nature a bad aesthetic idea?

Gardner: Certainly nobody could say that the imitation of reality is a bad idea. It is true, however, that if you keep imitating a particular aspect of reality over and over, stories start sounding an awful lot alike. Guys like Hemingway and Faulkner can make it because they're so great, but with all those third-rate writers it gets to be a bore. So, writers start finding other ways of getting to the same things, or to better things, or to different things. You're going for the dream-reality, for constructing universes, made-up worlds. But one of the things that makes any novel fun is that there's a world that's really real. It's a convincing dream. If you keep doing the realistic, John O'Hara world, the *Butterfield 8* world, it gets so it's the same world over and over. But when you write something . . . like the novel George Elliott is working on now. . . . A central character is an emperor of ancient Byzantium. You know, what a terrific idea! You can suddenly do all those settings and backdrops, and you can do girls in the way girls have never been done—because, you know, who knows what the girls in Byzantium were like? You can do . . . toys, you know . . . golden birds on a golden bough.

Ensworth: You've taught medieval literature for seventeen years. How has this influenced your writing?

Gardner: I think I use the stylistic tricks of Chaucer more than those of any living man.

Ensworth: In what way?

Gardner: For one thing, in the narrative voice. Often my narrator is a real made-up character who gets involved with the story. Chaucer does this in *Troilus and Criseyde*: the narrator describes a situation and then becomes carried away defending his characters. In the "Nun's Priest's Tale" when Chanticleer does something stupid (because he's only a chicken) the Nun's Priest gives every reason in the world why it isn't as stupid as it looks. In *The Sunlight Dialogues* when the narrator tells about Will Hodge, Sr., he throws out long, parody-Faulkner sentences in parentheses: "Invincible Hodge!" "Ah, Hodge!" He is carried away by his character. I'm not allowed to use these medieval techniques in *Grendel* and *The Wreckage of Agathon* because of the first-person narration, but they are present in *The Sunlight Dialogues* and in *The Resurrection*. I use lots of tricks Chaucer uses.

Bellamy: Do you see any other connections between medieval literature and contemporary literature in terms of common modes that you find especially exciting?

Gardner: Maybe it's just my imagination, but it seems to me we are a play out of the seventeenth century. Seventeenth-century civilization is us. The Middle Ages was the end of a different civilization. Someplace in the sixteenth century the Middle Ages stopped. In the fifteenth and sixteenth centuries all the genres break down. It becomes impossible to write a straight romance, or a straight anything. And everybody who is anybody starts form-jumping. Chaucer, for instance, starts putting together the epic poem. That's *Troilus and Criseyde*—it's a whole crazy different kind of thing. Well, and Malory comes out with *Morte d'Arthur*, which is a freaky new kind of form, a breakdown of all kinds of other forms. The mystery play arises. The literary genres of the Middle Ages didn't work anymore because the metaphysic and social ethic that supported them was no longer believed.

Bellamy: Does your sense of the connection between your medieval work and your fiction encompass any special ideas about myth? Myth seems to interest a number of writers now, and *Grendel*, for instance, certainly seems to have those kinds of dimensions. Do you see that as a fertile direction that you plan to keep exploring?

Gardner: It's very tempting to say, "Yes, I am working with myth because myth is so resonant"—it sounds good. . . . In *Grendel* I wanted to go through the main ideas of Western civilization—which seemed to me to be about . . . twelve?—and go through them in the voice of the monster, with the story already taken care of, with the various philosophical attitudes (though with Sartre in particular), and see what I could do, see if I could break out. That's what I meant to do.

Bellamy: Do you go through all twelve major ideas in that book?

Gardner: It's got twelve chapters. They're all hooked to astrological signs, for instance, and that gives you nice easy clues.

These are ideas which have been around from Homer's time to John Updike's time, and all good men have taken one side and all bad men have taken another side on these basic issues. *Because* they are ideas that go all through history, maybe the book resonates. For one thing, I keep echoing people, borrowing from people. I steal lots and lots of things all the time. If my stuff works at all, it's because there's one fusing vision. But I keep borrowing, so it does have a resonance that goes back into prehistory. I guess that's what myth does. That is, I am making up an organizing feature for a lot of stuff.

Ensworth: Do you have any American models for your writing?

Gardner: Certain passages in Melville are models for me, particularly in *Pierre*—a serious approach which is nevertheless ironic, a peculiar detached tone which is nevertheless able to say real, affirmative things. William Gass reinforced some points of style I had learned independently; I don't know if he is a model, but he's someone of whom I am conscious. And then probably Walt Disney.

Ensworth: Walt Disney? I can see that in *Grendel*; monsters are certainly part of Disney's cast of characters.

Gardner: Yes. In *Grendel* the subject matter is Anglo-Saxon, but the treatment is what Walt Disney would have done if he hadn't been caught up in the sentimentality of smiling Mickey Mouse.

Ensworth: What about *The Sunlight Dialogues*? That seems to be

a more realistic book; the narrator is more omniscient, more
encompassing than a cartoon figure can afford to be.

Gardner: But if you look at the character of Clumly—hairless,
with a great big nose and perfect teeth—he's a cartoon figure.
Nobody ever looked like that. The three old Woodworth sisters are a
cross between Poe and Henry James and Walt Disney. Think of the
cop and robber going up to the door together, both funny little men,
the cop carrying a box of flowers . . . there's an awful lot of cartoon
in that. The magic tricks may be from real magicians I saw rather than
from cartoons, but they're pretty cartoonish.

I remember when I was a kid and first saw *Snow White* I hid under
the seat when the witch came on. I still hide under the seat when that
witch appears; it's harder now because the seats have gotten smaller.
And I think it's not just me. Everything Stanley Elkin has written from
A Bad Man on, especially his latest unpublished work, is all cartoon.
There isn't a realistic image in it . . . it's really Disney. Disney is one of
the great men of America. He just had a weak streak, a poor silly
sentimental streak. But America's got that too. Huck Finn's got it.
Updike's got it. Some of us hide it better than others.

Ensworth: In *Grendel* and *The Sunlight Dialogues* you create
characters who function as oracles: the Dragon and the Sunlight
Man. Why did you choose this structure?

Gardner: The Dragon looks like an oracle, but he doesn't lay
down truth. He's just a nasty dragon. He tells the truth as it appears
to a dragon—that nothing in the world is connected with anything.
It's all meaningless and stupid, and since nothing is connected with
anything the highest value in life is to seek out gold and sit on it.
Since nothing is emotionally or physically connected you make piles
of things. That is the materialistic point of view. Many people spend
their lives, rightly or wrongly, doing nothing but filling out their bank
accounts. My view is that this is a dragonish way to behave, and it
ain't the truth. The Shaper tells the truth, although he lies. I don't
know that there are any actual oracles in *Grendel*. There are in *The
Sunlight Dialogues, The Wreckage of Agathon, Resurrection*, and
Jason and Medeia.

And the real oracle in *The Sunlight Dialogues* is not the Sunlight
Man. He's crazy; he's not an oracle at all. But there is an oracle;
there's a real ancient sibyl in that novel. When Clumly is at a funeral

one day (as usual, he's always going to funerals), an old Italian
woman falls down and starts speaking Italian. She gives him oracular
statements about the meaning of life and death. Clumly doesn't
understand Italian, and the little boy refuses to translate the final
oracular statement, which has to do with *disanimata*—"disanimated."
But Clumly comes to understand it at the end. He uses it in his mind
during the last speech.

Yes, there are oracles in my novels. They are only partly metaphorical. Partly they are a metaphor for one who sees the totality, the
connectedness, and is able to communicate it to other people, to
make people see relationships. Partly it is a real mystical touch in me.

We have known for a long time that there are an enormous
number of cases of apparent psychic response. For example, Baxter
connected a polygraph to a gladiola on which a spider was living [see
Harper's, November, 1972, p. 90]. He took away the spider, and the
plant worried about its friend. Dogs have the ability to go thousands
of miles to find the families they love. There are slightly less authenti-
cated tests, like the alleged Russian experiment using a submarine
and a family of rabbits. The mother rabbit was connected to an
electrocardiograph; her baby rabbits were put on the submarine and
killed. At every synchronized moment when one of her babies died,
the mother rabbit's heart went kachoong. In other words, over a
distance a radio can't reach, these impulses reached the mother
without any time gap.

I don't believe or disbelieve things like this. I don't believe or
disbelieve flying saucers or the alternate universe or antimatter or
anything which can't be proved. Maybe they're true and maybe
they're not, but it's good material for art. There are enough indica-
tions that these possibilities might be true that I don't mind affirming
them, at least in a novel. In any case, they ought to be so.

Bellamy: You indicate that the nihilistic dragon in the middle of
Grendel is there to be repudiated; and now that you've brought this
up, I see examples of other philosophies that you offer, in a sense, to
repudiate. I wonder if you are able to state what philosophy, if any,
you are advocating? In your essay, "The Way We Write Now," for
instance, you say: ". . . it's in the careful scrutiny of cleanly appre-
hended characters, their conflicts and ultimate escape from

immaturity, that the novel makes up its solid truths, finds courage to defend the good and attack the simpleminded."

Gardner: That is hardly the description of a philosophical novelist, right? But I agree with that.

Bellamy: In this essay you seemed very wrought up about moral values. I had the sense that you feel it is the writer's responsibility to perpetuate only what you see as "positive" moral values.

Gardner: Yes, as long as those aren't oversimplified—like don't commit adultery, nonsense like that. . . .

Bellamy: Right. But what would that be?

Gardner: Generosity, hope, you know. . . . The ultimate moral value, the moral value I really look for beyond anything else, is to be exactly truthful—seeing things clearly, the *process* of art. Art is the absolute morality, because a good writer won't go to the next sentence until *this* sentence is perfect and says what's true. Then there are other kinds of things that value is related to—the sort of life-affirmation.

We're always at the mercy of critical fads. There was a period, a long period, when art was tied to moral statement. It was expected of any medieval artist, any Renaissance artist, that he would stand up for good principles—you know, support the queen. Then we got past that. It was clear that art doesn't really have to do that. You look at Chartres cathedral now, and it's just as beautiful as it ever was—you have the same holy feelings in it. But you don't know what all those little symbols are. What you know is about arches and light and expanses and rhythm. I think it still means the same thing as when it was built, but we don't talk about it in the same terms.

In more recent times, critics who had this sort of bias that art is supposed to be philosophy became uncomfortable with, say, Christianity—because it didn't seem to hold as a philosophy—or with nineteenth-century German idealism—because it didn't seem to hold as a philosophy. They began to love what are called "troubling visions." So I write a book in which there is a dragon who says everything a nihilist would say, everything the Marquis de Sade would say; and then at the end of the book there is a dragon who says all the opposite things. He says everything that William Blake would say. Blake says a wonderful thing: "I look upon the dark satanic mills; I shake my head; they vanish." That's it. That's right. You *redeem* the world by acts of imagination *every* time you pick up a baby. So that's a simple thing really.

You can't say *Grendel* is a peering into the abyss—nothing of the kind. It has none of that dignity. I am not Nietzsche, nor was I meant to be, nor would I want to be. I do *much* simpler things. I do the same thing guys who make sand castles do. I'm going to make damn good sand castles. That's really all. But, of course, at the same time, my sand castles make any little shanty that some guy builds on the beach look pretty silly.

Building sand castles is like the sculpture of Henry Moore. There's nothing profound about Henry Moore's sculpture. He does manage to find the rhythms of nature in stone or wood or bronze. He does manage to get the essence of a lady and her child—in bronze. In his old age he manages to build arches that look like pelvic bones in their flight against the sky in Florence. Magnificent things—but they're very simple. They don't refute Nietzsche or improve upon Kierkegaard. They're there, and you look at them, and you say: "Thank God for Henry Moore."

Ensworth: Why do you think the writer should be an affirmer of life?

Gardner: I really do believe Shelley's idea about the poet as the legislator for mankind. My dream of the poet is a sort of African shaman, a poet-priest. Imagine a tribe has to go and hunt a tiger, and they're scared of the beast. A man stands up with his helpers and says a poem about how they're going to kill the tiger while his helpers play drums. By the time they've finished their one-day ritual, the poet makes them believe they can kill the tiger and the drummers make their hearts beat fast. The tribe goes out with their spears and that poor tiger's got trouble.

America has moved in the direction of the moving picture. You remember the days of *On the Waterfront*—the tipped-up collar, the cigarette hanging out of the mouth. A whole generation grew up tipping up their collars and hanging cigarettes out of their mouths. That's why we've got so much cancer in middle-age people now. Movies and comic books are the main popular art forms of our moment, and they do change the way people behave. As a writer, once you know this, or at least believe this, then you've got to ask,

"Should I write *Straw Dogs* or should I write something else?" I think the answer is emphatically something else. Nobody's ever proved that television causes violence or that dirty movies cause dirty behavior. But if there's the vaguest suspicion, the least danger that it might be true, then a writer ought to think about it. I don't mean there should be no sex and no violence, and I certainly don't mean anyone should ban books. But a writer must decide how to treat these matters with a responsible concern.

People often say things they may or may not believe, like, "If I only had something that would make me get up in the morning." Most people do get up in the morning, but this kind of statement is popular. If writers reinforce it, pretty soon people are actually going to wonder why they do get up in the morning. And that's dumb. I'm most concerned with the trivial heroic acts of everyday life. These are the actions I want to remind readers of.

Ensworth: Shelley's view of the poet seems to be in conflict with the role you present in *Grendel*. The Shaper incites his community to war; Grendel sees him as a liar and a destructive force.

Gardner: The Shaper comes along in a meaningless, stupid kingdom and makes up a rationale. He creates the heroism, the feeling of tribal unity. He makes the people brave. And sure, it's a lie, but it's also a vision.

Grendel is seduced by the Shaper: he wants to be a part of that vision. Unfortunately, he can't get in because he's a monster. But at the end of the novel Grendel himself becomes the Shaper. Beowulf bangs his head against the wall and says, *feel*. Grendel feels—his head hurts—so Beowulf makes him sing about walls. When the first Shaper dies, a kid is chosen to succeed him, but the real successor is Grendel. In the last pages of the book Grendel begins to apprehend the whole universe: life and death, his own death. Poetry is an accident, the novel says, but it's a great one. May it happen to all of us.

Ensworth: Then Grendel understands that the role of the Shaper—the role of the poet—is to apprehend, to feel, the whole universe?

Gardner: Yes.

Bellamy: Do you agree with Vonnegut then that the artist is the most important person in a society?

Gardner: I guess all artists think that. I think all Xerox men think

that the most important people are Xerox men. But I think that the
most important are artists. They remind you of things that are obvious: human dignity, the terribleness of death, simple things.

Bellamy: Is that your description of what a "philosophical novelist" should be doing too?

Gardner: Stated in a slightly different way, this is my whole
program. This is what I believe. I believe that the art of the thirties,
forties, and fifties was fundamentally a mistake, that it made
assumptions that were untrue about art, basically wrong assumptions
that went wrong in the Middle Ages, too. They went wrong every
time they were formulated as basic assumptions. And I think that
their effect was to cut off readership.

When you think that art is a sophisticated way of thinking out
problems and coming to understandings of things, then for one thing
you start a story in the way that Jean Stafford starts a story—as if the
story were happening inside the reader's consciousness. That kind of
art makes you feel as if you ought to read stories because they're
good for you; and, in fact, you can tell by the beginnings of those
stories that those writers were assuming, "You will read this story
because it's good for you." I don't think that has anything to do with
it. That's not art; that part is just the sermon. The art is the arches and
the light. What art ought to do is tell stories which are moment-by-
moment wonderful, which are true to human experience, and which
in no way explain human experience.

In the past there was a fundamental requirement that a writer was
supposed to meet. Like, you read in the newspaper: "Henry shot
Charlie." And you think: "*Why* did Henry shoot Charlie?" And the
writer's program for a long time was to show you gradually how the
moment came about that Henry shot Charlie. Then one day Kafka
wrote: "As Gregor Samsa awoke one morning from a troubled
dream, he found himself changed in his bed to some monstrous kind
of vermin." You don't find out why he did that; you don't care why
he did that. That's not the point. Barthelme writes: "An aristocrat was
riding down the street in his carriage. He ran over my father." This is
a sort of ringing affirmation of Kafka's rightness. In Bob Coover's
story, "A Pedestrian Accident," a man is run over by a truck and
thinks "Why me?" But then he thinks, "But that's a boring question,"
and the story goes on from there. We are not supposed to be doing

psychology; psychology is not important. We are not supposed to be explaining motivation. Motivation is not important, and it never was important, for example, in those stories when some jinni would enter a person and do something. Motivation is the last thing from the Indian writer's mind in *Tales of Scheherazade*. That is, the motivation is always convincing—the characters always do what you think they're going to do—but it's not a study.

In American movies, for instance, you have this business of every time you have a mean lady in a movie, a lady who pretends to love a guy but she's willing to sacrifice his life for money, sooner or later there comes this boring part where she has to explain that she had a rough childhood—as if there were no other reason a lady would be a mean bitch. Sometimes people have wonderful happy childhoods and they still become mean bitches; but that's not the writer's business.

I don't think any of this is the writer's business. I think that we should not try to be sociologists, although it's fun to use sociology in a novel because a novel is a place where you use anything that's decorative, anything that seems true. You don't have to be a psychologist, and you certainly don't have to be a painter of landscapes.

What you have to do, I think, is tell an interesting story. That means a plot that's kind of neat and that's got characters who are kind of neat and it happens in places that are made by the writer's imagination into "kind of neat." A plot that is kind of neat really is a plot that exercises the emotions of the reader and reminds him of his goodness or of his badness—you know, how *really* wicked he is. Any writer who pretends he's not a bad person, at least in some ways, is going to write pale stuff. To be Tolstoy you've got to be capable of writing the worst characters of Tolstoy with complete understanding as well as the best. That, I think, is what it is, and I don't think it's anything else. I think it has nothing to do with philosophy, although fiction uses philosophy as it uses everything else. And that's the break between contemporary writers whom I admire and earlier writers.

That's what I think fiction now is about. It's about creating circus shows. I *don't* think they're trivial. I think anybody who writes the way us guys write is going to be at the mercy of the critics—because we're going to be misunderstood.

Bellamy: Who's "us guys"?

Gardner: I think . . . guys who are storytellers—postsixties writers. I mean Stanley Elkin, Bill Gass, Donald Barthelme. . . . I don't know if they would be happy to be linked with me; so, you know, all apologies to them for my putting myself in their company. But I think they are fundamentally people making sideshows—but good, serious sideshows, because they raise you to your best, *not* philosophically, *not* morally.

Bellamy: How does that jibe with your statement about the moral qualities that you would like to impart?

Gardner: The moral qualities I want to keep are emotional qualities. The sense of courage that a reader shares vicariously with a character—when he goes out into the world he carries a little of that. . . . Remember your own personal emotion when you finished *Anna Karenina* the first time? You walk around for about two weeks in Russia, no matter what you're doing in Brooklyn or wherever you are. You're living in Tolstoy's world, and you're living by Tolstoy's values—good art does that.

Bellamy: Why all the philosophical meanderings then?

Gardner: I think I'm a philosophical novelist, but that doesn't mean a philosopher. That is to say, I'm a novelist, one of whose main materials is the philosophical ideas of the twentieth century.

Bellamy: But you don't see your purpose as working out the right ideas in the end. Ultimately, you're not offering a system.

Gardner: What I think is "right" is implicit in drama. So, I'm not answering, say, Kant; I'm dramatizing Kant. My business is drama. I can write a novel that doesn't have any philosophy in it at all.

Bellamy: A novel, then, according to your definition, would become a kind of program for emotional experiences for the reader? If the story is told well, and if the form is constructed with proper elegance, and if the moral values are right, then the reader will have this therapeutic experience—almost in the Aristotelian sense?

Gardner: Sure. Absolutely. I would say it's very much in the Aristotelian sense.

Ensworth: You stated in your July, 1972, article for the *New York Times Book Review*, "The Way We Write Now," that "after a period of cynicism, novelists are struggling . . . to see their way clear to go heroic." How do you know the period of cynicism is over?

Gardner: With a few notable exceptions, the things people are writing lately have changed tone completely. Joyce Carol Oates is one writer who is now reassessing her whole career. She's thirty-five, she's gotten the National Book Award, she's published novel after novel, millions of stories—but it was always the same Joyce Carol Oates. In her fiction the world seemed terrifying; she dealt with this feeling by recording it and eliciting sympathy. Suddenly, for mysterious reasons, she has flown up above that world and has begun to look at it from very high up. She sees more beauty, more compassion among characters, and she's turning quasi-mystical. Joyce is a model of the writer who is finding a different attitude, a more heroic and responsible approach. Stanley Elkin is another example: he used to write funny, cynical pieces, and now his work verges on a noble sort of sentimentality.

Most writers today are academicians: they have writing or teaching jobs with universities. In the last ten years the tone of university life and of intellectuals' responses to the world have changed. During the Cold War there was a great deal of fear and cynicism on account of the Bomb. Cynicism is a reaction to fear, a way of covering it. That atmosphere has gradually moved out in recent years. The Vietnam War is a terrible event, but it isn't a cause for cynicism. A very large, solid part of America which we thought was moneygrubbing and cynical was strongly against the war, and it becomes hard to maintain your cynicism when the people around you are all working hard to make the world better.

Notable exceptions to this are writers who very carefully stay out of the mainstream and therefore can't be influenced by the general feeling of people around them. For instance, Thomas Pynchon believes we're on our way to apocalypse. He jokes about this in *Gravity's Rainbow*. The whole novel becomes a huge, whinnying laugh about inevitable destruction. Pynchon stays out of universities. He doesn't know what chemists and physicists are doing; he knows only the pedantry of chemistry and physics. When good chemists and physicists talk about, say, the possibility of extraterrestrial life, they agree that for life to be evolved beyond our stage, creatures on other planets must have reached decisions we now face. That is, they must have seen their way past war, they must have dealt with their own hostilities and aggressions, and so on. These kinds of things were not said by scientists ten years ago when Pynchon was in close contact with them.

If a writer is around people (which is his business, because they're his subject matter) and if he lives in this age, then he has to see that all the worrying and whining we did in the last generation was futile and wrong-headed.

Ensworth: I don't understand the basis of your optimism. Certainly there have always been people working to improve the world, to do away with war. What makes this generation different from any other?

Gardner: What happens in the modern world, in any period of progress, is not that some great man comes along with a grand solution. Not some great man, but a bunch of little people working on a bunch of little problems. Think of the issues we yelled about in the thirties, the crises which made intellectuals communists. None of these issues is still around; for example, everyone is unionized now, and it's no longer a problem. Every single one of these issues was solved not by a grand political overthrow, the kind of change intellectuals hoped for then. They were solved by gradual breakthroughs, little by little, by unknown people. I think we have to recognize that the age of great genius is over. We hoped John Kennedy was a great man, but during his administration we were becoming mired in the worst war we've ever fought. On the other hand, something much more stable is emerging: an informed public. Sometimes the informed public says stupid things, and sometimes it elects leaders who represent its worst interests, but when things are stabilizing it becomes ridiculous to be a man crying wolf.

So, I think we're free to do what art ought to do, which is to celebrate and affirm. Obviously one can't turn one's back on dangers. We have to fight any tendency for the United States to become again the kind of monster it was for a while. After Vietnam we do have to worry about the evil which can come from isolationism and complacency. We must worry above all about righteousness, the kind of cheap righteousness which asserts that all crime is a terrible evil and all law-abidingness is a high virtue. One mentions these dangers in novels. Of course, a beautiful affirmation is meaningless if it doesn't recognize all the forces going against it.

Ensworth: How does the novelist "go heroic"?

Gardner: He becomes an affirmer of life instead of a whiner against it. He takes responsibility and recognizes responsibility in other writers and in other people. He sees through complacency and righteousness. No hero is ever righteous: a hero makes mistakes, recognizes them, says, "I made a mistake," and tries to do something about it. He affirms the goodness of life and the badness of thinking you've got the whole answer.

Ensworth: Who are your heroes?

Gardner: Homer is a hero, and so is Chaucer. Then there are some writers working right now to change their ways of writing, to enlarge their vision. John Updike is an example of this; John Cheever is another. A number of writers at this moment are doing a good job of reassessing themselves.

Bellamy: In that same essay, "The Way We Write Now," you claim that current writers are "doomed by indifference to novelistic form." Many writers feel there is a great deal of consciousness of form right now—perhaps more than there has been for a long time. What do you mean by "novelistic form"? How can you possibly argue that current writers are indifferent to it?

Gardner: You're right to ask: What do I mean by "novelistic form"? I think the novel is a different thing from a lyric, okay? I think that novelistic form is fundamentally plot form, development of a story, the Aristotelian *energia*, the actualization of the potential which exists in character and situation.

Grendel, for instance, is indifferent to novelistic form. I think that's okay—you can get away with it as long as you keep it short—but there are a number of problems in *Grendel*. At about Chapter 8 there is a section in which you are no longer advancing in terms of the momentum toward the end. It's just holding a slow movement, but it's a fake slow movement. We have now developed the whole position of Grendel, you know; it jells when Grendel meets the dragon. At this point, nothing more happens to Grendel. He's just waiting to meet Beowulf. Chapters 8, 9, 10—it's just the wheels spinning. That is *not* novelistic form; it's lyrical form.

Bellamy: So, novelistic form is inexorable plot development working itself out—present action always progressing toward the outcome? Rising action, climax, and denouement?

Gardner: Yes. When I say that people are doomed by an indifference to novelistic form, I'm thinking of some specific failures. Bill Gass and Stanley Elkin, for instance. I'll talk about them because they're my heroes. It seems to me that in *Omensetter's Luck* you have this wonderful beginning, and this wonderful denouement, and then you have this middle, which is the Jethro Furber section. It just goes on and on, self-congratulating and telling dirty jokes and doing things that are not moving Furber anyplace. You need that section, but you need about one-third of it, really. Of course, Gass isn't interested in putting in the break and moving to the next thing. He's just going.

Stanley Elkin has a different kind of problem, I think. He doesn't have any glue in his stories. His stories are one stand-up joke after another—wonderful, you know, brilliantly built lines and sentences and situations, but no glue going from situation to situation. That is to say, there is no novelistic theme which inevitably pushes you through the plot. His plots are the ultimate in existential whimsy—what new funny thing can I think of to say? And since he's so funny, and since he's so special, I say, "Okay, Stanley, go ahead," and I keep reading. But it doesn't have the impact, doesn't have the weight, the solidity, the force, that it would have if you feel yourself slowly being bulldozed.

Ensworth: *Grendel* and *The Sunlight Dialogues* demonstrate the struggle of mighty adversaries: Grendel and Beowulf and the Sunlight Man and Clumly. Do you feel there are any mighty adversaries left in the world?

Gardner: Faith and despair have always been the two mighty adversaries. You don't have to see it in the way of a Christian, Hindu, Buddhist, or any other system. A healthy life is a life of faith; an unhealthy sick, and dangerous life is a life of unfaith. If you're going to drive from here to downtown Chicago you get in your car and assume that the cars coming at you are going to pass, not hit you head-on. They assume the same thing about you. That's called faith. It doesn't work all the time; that's why faith can never be codified. On the other hand, if you assume that everything's out to get you, it's going to get you. You're going to be so worried which direction it's coming from that you're not going to be looking in the right direction. Faith is a physical condition, a feeling of security which enables you to think about what you're doing and yet be subconsciously alert. Whereas unfaith, paranoia, is a total concentration which makes it impossible for your psyche and body to be alert. You concentrate on what's going to happen to you and there's nothing floating underneath. I don't know if that's medically sound, but I believe it.

Ensworth: Why is it that in both *Grendel* and *The Sunlight Dialogues* the characters with the most imagination are defeated or killed by men of lesser vision, mere functionaries like Beowulf or Clumly?

Gardner: That question is not the center of *Grendel*, though it is of *The Sunlight Dialogues*. The Sunlight Man does have imagination; he imagines all the possibilities of the world. These possibilities are disparate and atomic, in the sense of particles not related to other particles. The Sunlight Man can see into all sorts of crazy alternatives, but he finds no order, no coherence in it. He's a wild, romantic poet with no hope of God. The two characters who have the most imagination in the novel are Clumly and Mrs. Clumly, because they can see into other people's minds. With his little mole's intelligence, Clumly stares at the Sunlight Man and tries to understand him. He really tries to understand the principle of evil by empathizing with it.

During the novel, the Sunlight Man, because of his experiences, sees fire around him. He knows that's crazy, but he keeps on seeing fire. Just before his last speech, Clumly looks through a door and sees it's burning inside: he's gotten inside the Sunlight Man's emotions. He fully understands even though he can't make sense of it. At least he has compassion, which is a kind of imagination.

At one point Clumly and Mrs. Clumly are lying in bed together. He thinks of her as a chicken—he wouldn't be surprised to see her feet sticking in the air. Later, Mrs. Clumly lies in the bed trying to sense what she looks like. It comes to her in a great flash: she looks like a chicken. Mrs. Clumly is the Beatrice of *The Sunlight Dialogues*. She guides everybody because she loves. This is the kind of imagination which holds the world together.

The ability to be patient, to be tolerant, to try to understand and empathize, is the highest kind of imagination. The ability to make up grand images and to thrill the reader is a nice talent, but if it doesn't include love, it's nothing—mere sounding brass.

Ensworth: What are your writing habits? When, where, and how do you write?

Gardner: I write as much as I can. I get up early in the morning,

stay up late at night, and write all the time. When I have nothing
else to do, I write. Luckily, because of my university, sometimes I can
go someplace far away where I'm protected from my own weaknesses. Not that I consider writing a duty—but since I have a family of
whom I am very fond, and a teaching job with students of whom I
am very fond, and we have friends who visit us, I often don't get
much writing time in. When I go somewhere I don't know, it takes us
two or three months to build up a circle of friends and thus interrupt
my work.

I work from rhythms more than anything else—the way a sentence
sounds in terms of rhythmical structure and the words you choose
because of that structure. If a character isn't convincing, if a lady in a
novel says something you think she wouldn't say, that's bad. If an
action doesn't seem inevitable, that's bad. But the real heart is nevertheless the rhythm.

If I have any doubts about what a character would say or what a
room would look like, I ask my wife. She has the ability to go into a
room where she doesn't know anyone and tell you the first names of
several people because they seem the Raymond type or the Sheila
type. My writing involves these two imaginations in a very deep way,
page after page after page. My own imagination is poetic and philosophical. I'm concerned with the rhythms of sentences and paragraphs
and chapters, and with ideas as they are embodied in characters and
actions. Joan's imagination is a very close psychological and
sociological one. It informs everything I do. Perhaps I should have
used "John and Joan Gardner" on the titles all along; I may do this
in the future. But in modern times such a work is regarded as not
really art. The notion that art is an individual and unique vision is a
very unmedieval and unclassical view. In the Middle Ages it was very
common to have several people work on one thing; the thirteenth-
century Vulgate cycle of Arthurian romances had hundreds of writers.
I feel comfortable with this approach, but I haven't felt comfortable
telling people it's what I do. As I get more and more into the medieval
mode, I'll probably admit how many writers I have.

Bellamy: You leave it sounding as if your wife is a collaborator.
Has she actually written parts of your books?

Gardner: Frieda Lawrence did the same thing for D. H. Lawrence. It's not new. To have the attitude toward writing that I have at

this moment is unfashionable, but I'm a medievalist, and in the Middle Ages they go in for the object, right? If you're making a cathedral, you don't worry about the abbot getting all the credit. You get the best mason you can, and so forth. I use a lot of people, Joan in particular. She hasn't actually written any lines, because Joan's too lazy for that. But she's willing to answer questions. The extent of her contribution doesn't quite approach collaboration in the modern sense.

Bellamy: How do you manage to be so prolific? I see there are two more of your books scheduled for publication next year.

Gardner: It's not because I'm prolific. For a long period of time, my writing was not liked. It was very difficult for me to get published; it was a very long period of time before I did. Finally people began to publish my things. Actually, *The Wreckage of Agathon* broke it, and I got a sort of mild reputation—although it's a kind of terrible book. Then after that *Grendel* got a sort of underground reputation, and then people were willing to risk *The Sunlight Dialogues*—although nobody had any confidence in it. In fact, I had sent it to every publisher there is. Nobody would touch it. One guy wrote the only encouraging thing, "We'll take it if you cut a third." I wrote back and said, "Which third?" I *have* written hard. I have worked on techniques hard. I have done exercises for years in sentences—working full days, paring sentences, learning to do things with sentences. People talk about my pyrotechnic stuff as if it was some little funny skill I have, but it's something, maybe the only thing, I've worked very hard for. Anyway, I wrote this stuff all the time. I've written lots and lots of novels. Some of them were conscious exercises to see if a certain thing could be done with form, because, I admit, I do love experiments in form. Anyway, I'm not fast. I work very hard and very long, and eventually I inch out a novel. But when you've been sitting writing for fifteen years, and nobody liking you, you do build up a backlog. I've been publishing an early work, a late work, an early work—it's kind of weird. *The Sunlight Dialogues* is an early work; *Grendel* is a late work; *Nickel Mountain*, coming out next year, is a very early work. Right after that comes my newest thing, *The King's Indian and Other Fireside Tales*, a very jazzy technical thing. That and *Jason and Medeia* are my two newest things.

Bellamy: Could you actually set out again to write a book like

The Sunlight Dialogues, which still seems more or less in the realistic tradition?

Gardner: I don't see *The Sunlight Dialogues* as a book in the realistic tradition. I've always written kind of fabulous, weird stuff. In *The Sunlight Dialogues* I wanted to tell a story which had the feel of total fabulation, total mystery—magicians—strange things and impossible tricks—so that everybody would have the sudden feeling at some point in the novel that he's caught inside a novel, but with streets that can be recognized, houses which are accurately described, and so on. I wanted to tint the stock and photograph Batavia. I wanted to make people in the novel just as much like Batavians as possible and yet create the feeling that the whole novel is taking place in Oz. It may or may not have succeeded. I've talked to a lot of people who have been to Batavia since reading the novel, and the reaction was that it was a dull, drab, kind of colorless town, and yet everything I said was true. That is, the houses are exactly the color I said, everything is just as I said, but it's not like that at all. Okay, that's me again, playing tricks. As long as critics feel that novelists should be these terribly serious people, not at all like people who just make wonderful sand castles, then I'm gonna get killed. But I think wonderful sand castles are terrific; I think they're moral. I think they make you a better person much more than a sermon does. I like Barth's funhouse metaphor. I think it's right. Every writer now is lost in the funhouse—and pretty happy with it.

Bellamy: I suppose this is a question that literary historians will worry about in fifty years, but do you think there is any sense of real coherence among those writers who emerged in the midsixties, who were lost in the funhouse and happy to be there, madly building sand castles and fantasizing to their hearts' content? Is there enough in common among them to start talking about these people as a group or as a "generation"?

Gardner: Yes, there is. There really is, and I don't know what it is. At Northwestern I recently heard Jack Hawkes read from his new book, and I could hardly get my breath. I loved it; it's really fantastic. He does these things. . . . I mean, it's like a jazz musician listening to another jazz musician. There are a lot of differences between us, of course—literary historians will see great differences that we don't see clearly. There are very deep differences from a philosophical point of view between Bill Gass and me, for instance. But at least everybody's going for the same goal.

Bellamy: Except Tom Wolfe.

Gardner: Yep, right. Sure. Sure. There are a lot of good writers who don't have anything to do with the group we've been talking about.

Bellamy: What do you think really happened in the midsixties when so many writers started changing? Is that an impossibly difficult question to answer?

Gardner: Sunspots [laughing]. I don't know. I have no idea why things live as long as they do and then die. Maybe it happened earlier in music and art, and literature, being more complex, caught up late. But it happened in all of the arts, you know, within the second quarter of this century and petering into the third quarter.

Bellamy: What happens next?

Gardner: I think people are going to continue to be fairly conservative about form. People will continue to be hung up on formalism, consciousness of technique. There will, I think, be more Brautigans, and they will be an increasingly raucous element.

Bellamy: What is a "Brautigan"?

Gardner: Brautigan's concern is not with a well-built box. It's with a voice, an intuition, a hypothetical reaction, and making up things in a wingding fashion. . . .

Bellamy: What else?

Gardner: I think that where it's going for a while is where it is. This movement that you're talking about, and tracing, is solidly here and is the darling of the New York literary establishment—and for good reason. The real advances or changes are going to be totally dependent upon individual genius and freakiness. *Nobody* could have predicted Barthelme, you know. He wasn't a possibility. Then, suddenly, here he is!

Conversations with John Gardner on Writers and Writing

John Askins/1975

From *Authors in the News,* ed. Barbara Nykoruk. Detroit: Gale Research, 1976, pp. 168-69. Reprinted by permission of Detroit Free Press. Originally published in *Detroit Free Press/Detroit Magazine,* 23 March 1975, pp. 19-21.

John Gardner is the author of several novels, including *The Sunlight Dialogues, Grendel, Nickel Mountain,* and *The Resurrection.* He has a new book out called *The King's Indian,* which is a collection of several short works.

His books are an unusual combination of lovely writing, fascinating stories, and difficult philosophy. The philosophy has ensured him the sort of favorable critical response accorded writers who are more learned than their reviewers. In his early 40s, Gardner is regarded as being in the first rank of American novelists.

He teaches medieval literature at Southern Illinois University and is presently a visiting professor at Bennington in Vermont. Gardner is the author of several highly respected scholarly works which are never listed under "Other Books by John Gardner" in his novels.

Despite his erudition, Gardner first-hand is scrupulously down-to-earth. His speech is neither colorful nor particularly graceful, and most of what he knows about philosophy he keeps to himself unless you press him to reveal it.

During the following interview he fiddled ceaselessly with a pipe which kept going out. Burnt matches piled up neatly on a tobacco tin beside him. He was born in Batavia, N.Y. and grew up on a farm there. He still has a rural suspicion of sophistication, by which he means decadence, and a directness that perhaps explains the heavy-handed application of uncamouflaged metaphysics in some of his works; that's what he cares about, so that's what he puts in, artifice be damned.

Yet his best-known book, *The Sunlight Dialogues,* the story of a battle of wits between an anarchistic Christ figure

28

and a law-and-order police chief in Batavia, was a best seller despite its 673 pages and a style one reviewer called "overwrought." It wouldn't have happened five or ten years ago but, as Gardner says, readers are changing.

Reporter John Askins found Gardner at Marygrove College where he came to give a reading at the request of Dr. Janice Lauer of the English department there. He and Dr. Lauer are friends from the Fall of 1970 when Gardner was a visiting professor at the University of Detroit.

Detroit: Is it important to you to get people thinking about philosophical questions?

Gardner: I think it's important for people to think philosophically. I think the world is in bad shape, and I think the reason is philosophical. I think people have been believing stupid things for a long time.

For instance, I just read the other day a whiney essay in the *New York Times* literary magazine saying how helpless we are when confronted by our children. That's bad philosophy. We are not helpless. When our children misbehave we can tell them. When our children disappoint us we can show them. Children can be wonderful people. But the sort of general feeling in America is that everything is hopeless. What good philosophy does is fight that, show how bad that bad philosophy is.

Detroit: In one of your books, *The Resurrection,* you had your protagonist, a philosophy professor, talk about "self-pitying existentialists." Do you share that point of view?

Gardner: (Laughs). Well—sometimes. Existentialism, of course, is a very fine thing, but it can be self-pitying. Like, you can choose the best of Jean Paul Sartre and it's very optimistic and brave, very noble. Or you can choose the worst of Jean Paul Sartre and it's stupid.

Detroit: Your hero, at any rate, is an appealing man.

Gardner: I mean for him to be appealing. I mean all my characters to be appealing. I hate books where there are bad guys.

Detroit: But you do need villains, don't you?

Gardner: We're all villains. We're all the robbers as well as the cops.

Detroit: According to one biographical note, you started writing at an early age.

Gardner: . . . I was about seven when I started writing poetry. I wrote really good poetry when I was a kid, but when I grew up I didn't write so well. I also wrote novel after novel, thrillers—probably 20—before I was 15 years old. My cousins all worked on the farm and I used to write a chapter every day and read it to them in the barn at night, and they would all say, 'Ooohh.' Very exciting.

Detroit: You're still reading your work aloud today, although to larger audiences. Do you write with that in mind?

Gardner: Oh, I think unquestionably I'm writing for oral effect. Often when I write I can't think of a word, but I know the rhythm has to go "ba-da-da," so I just write "ba-da-da" there and hope that something will come later.

Detroit: One reviewer accused you of making up words.

Gardner: He's probably right. I have made up words. Like, the Greek word for darkness is "thestare." It's a really lovely word, but the only way it exists now is in old cemeteries, where you might see on a tombstone the name of some girl who was called Thester. So in one of my books I speak of "thestral" things.

Detroit: It has a nice sound.

Gardner: Yeah. You don't have to understand words. Language is texture . . .

Detroit: I notice *The Sunlight Dialogues* everywhere in paperback. Does that mean you have a larger public than one would expect you to have?

Gardner: Oh, yeah. Things are very good for serious writers right now. They're very bad for people who write sort of light, frothy mysteries, love stories, dog stories, things like that. The kind of writers who used to publish in the *Saturday Evening Post* for instance. They can't publish anymore. And the reason is that people like Joyce Carol Oates, who is at the top of the serious market, also writes confession stories, detective stories; you know, everything; whatever there is, she writes. So she pushes these other writers out.

There are a lot of writers like this. The kind of writer who used to publish only in the *New Yorker* and *Esquire* now publishes everywhere. I don't know what it's the result of, but it's been very bad for those others. Even a guy like Ross McDonald, he's trying to write really serious novels now. I loved his plain old detective stories; I don't like his serious stuff as much. But I understand: his market is being invaded and he's reacting. It used to be when you read science fiction that there was one Isaac Asimov for every 100 dumbbells. Now they're all Asimovs. Which means, of course, that readers have changed too.

Detroit: You admire Joyce Carol Oates a great deal as a writer in addition to being a friend of hers, isn't that right?

Gardner: I think she's a wonderful writer, although she's a very different kind than what I am. She has a theory about human beings which I don't share. I really believe there is a human nature, to put it one way. Joyce doesn't, apparently. I believe that a character is a certain kind of thing from one page to another, and I'm going to be able to predict certain kinds of things about that character. Joyce believes that people wander into your life, accidents happen constantly, and there is no sort of "core of being." So her novels are in every case partly a search for a core of being, which turns out to be largely unsuccessful. But we are alike in one thing: Enormous respect for the novel form.

Detroit: Is there an overall theme connecting all your somewhat dissimilar books?

Gardner: I have a single philosophical question that I'm working on in all the books. I don't repeat myself; once I've worked out one aspect of the question, I don't go back over it. The question is about the nature of human experience in the 20th century and what's wrong and how can it be fixed. There are very precise points where I think we've gone wrong, and I think I could name them in terms of philosophical schools of thought. For instance, I think the 19th century Oxford idealists were beaten by bad arguments and showy, flashy stuff and a really important idea was lost. From there we head into contemporary philosophy, which sometimes is just insane.

Detroit: What was the important idea that was lost?

Gardner: To simplify it, one could say that it had to do with the question of what makes people happiest. The idea was that man is happiest when he is behaving well. When he's being faithful. When he knows he has certain duties and he performs them. When he has boundaries.

Detroit: Where else did we go wrong?

Gardner: Well, we keep getting to the edge of very important discoveries and then keep messing them up. One of them that's really important is sexual. In the 20th century we get really healthy about sex, really open about it and valuing it, and then we keep getting mixed up. We go off to the orgy, which is missing the point. Utterly and totally missing the point.

Detroit: *Grendel* is charming, but our favorite of your works is your first, *The Resurrection.*

Gardner: Well, it was the book that I wrote most for myself. In all the others I've been very conscious of an audience. For instance, I now read my stuff to my kids, and if my daughter thinks something is too slow, I change it. But in *The Resurrection* I did everything the way I wanted to do it. As a matter of fact, it did get one good review, from Detroit. Which was one of the reasons I later came here.

Detroit: Some writers claim they don't read reviews.

Gardner: William Faulkner said, "Any man who tells me he doesn't read his reviews is a liar." And he's right of course. Not only do you read them, you read them three times, to see if it's maybe better than you thought at first. And it's so wonderful when somebody gets it . . .

Detroit: Well, if you put things in you know people aren't going to get . . .

Gardner: Yeah, but one hopes to write books like the stories of Chaucer, that people will read and re-read again sometimes and keep getting new things from. I want my stuff to be entertaining, to have exciting plots and so forth, and I want them to be as well-built as anybody's. I don't think we have the romantic idea of writers as Shelley or Keats or Byron anymore; we're just workmen. But I want to make really nice houses, things you can live with forever and ever.

Detroit: Some of your work leads us to believe you occasionally have grander ideas. *The Sunlight Dialogues,* for instance, sounded in places like the work of someone who was consciously trying to write a Great Novel.

Gardner: Mm. Well, you can't do that. Gore Vidal once said very wisely that the reason there are no good novels in America is that everybody wants to write great ones.

Detroit: What's your family life like?

Gardner: We have a boy 15 and a girl 13, and they're both really incredible people. The boy just a year ago started playing the French horn, which I also play, and he's developed into a really wonderful player, plays six-seven hours a day. My wife, Joan, is a composer, and my daughter has started taking harp lessons. So I spend like all night working on fiction and then I sleep a few hours and then my family sits together and plays music for hours and hours. We also work together a lot. I work with the kids on their schoolwork and their instruments. My daughter and I spend hours and hours going over fiction together, hers and mine. She's written a lot.

Detroit: It sounds idyllic. Are there any problems?

Gardner: Well, I worry that things can't possibly continue at this level. But—no. Joan and I spent a lot of years doing work we had to do, that wasn't chosen and wasn't a lot of fun. I, for instance, spent years and years teaching freshman composition. I didn't want to teach freshman composition. Since I've started making money, I do only what I want to do.

We've just bought a house in Vermont, so we'll be living there and in Illinois now. I'm really happy in southern Illinois. I like to ride horses, feed dogs, walk through the woods, look at the rain, all that. But Joan likes to go to symphonies and plays and things. So we sort of do two lives, me for a while and then Joan for a while.

Detroit: When you're writing away all alone at night is it the same person as the one who does all those things with his family, or is it another person?

Gardner: No, it's the same person. Basically it's a playful person. When we go to the beach, for instance, being the type of people we are, we make not only sand castles but sand people as well, full size people sitting there, made out of sand. One time in Italy we started doing that, and at the end of the day, the Italians being the kind of people they are, the whole beach for a mile was just full of sand people. That's what my life is, just sort of very serious playing. And when I'm writing that's what I'm doing too: trying to make really fine sand people.

Our Best Novelist: He Thinks So, Too

Larry Swindell/1976

From *The Philadelphia Inquirer,* 16 January 1977, Sec. F, pp. 1, 13. Reprinted by permission.

This interview was conducted on 23 December 1976.

I had been told that it had changed from flax to silver, but it isn't silver, either. More like pewter. John Gardner's hair is the color of pewter.

Although it was our first meeting I had known I'd have no difficulty spotting him, even in a Manhattan lunch-hour congestion. Besides the triumphant mane, there would be the incessant Gardner pipe. But even without the visibility of either hair or pipe, I would expect almost to sense the very presence of America's best working novelist.

I think he is that, and he thinks so too, so we had an extraordinarily pleasant lunch-and-conversation that stretched to three hours with a lot of grinning and nodding.

His "best" credentials now have some certification, for last week the National Book Critics Circle selected Gardner's *October Light* as the best work of fiction published in 1976 by a living American author. Gardner accepted the award ceremonially on Thursday in New York's Time & Life Building.

It's an award I anticipated with fingers crossed in Gardner's interest, and the anticipation incited my bid for the one-to-one meeting. We got together two days before Christmas at the Chalet Suisse over on the East Side, and the possibility of the NBCC award wasn't avoided in the early dialogue.

"I hope I win it," he said of the NBCC fiction award, for which he was then among five nominees, although only three were counted in serious contention. "I'm not opposed to awards, and I think my time has come."

Indeed it has. On his merits, Gardner's award is overdue. In a crowded decade—1966-76—he has produced half-a-dozen novels of mostly good size, a collection of short stories, a full-length epic poem (*Jason and Medeia*), two books of stories for children, and scores of bylined reviews, feature articles, and other fodder about literature.

During most of those years he was also a professor in Middle English at Southern Illinois University. The legend developed and flourished of a John Gardner who can write books almost faster than they can be prepared for publication. Some of the critics already have suggested that he writes too much.

"I am not really prolific," Gardner explained, while I nodded, bewilderingly. "I work slowly. I read slowly, write slowly. I revise. Sometimes I revise again and again. But I'm always working. I write every day, usually 14 hours a day, and usually 7 days a week. That's the difference."

Without having to get specific about it, John Gardner was articulating his contempt for the present decadent state of the professional writer—the "New York writer," if you will—who'll devote a few hours to his craft in any given week, and spend most of his time being some kind of public person.

Gardner is a throwback to the age of Dickens and Trollope (he might appreciate referral to Chaucer even more), when novelists spent most of their waking time writing novels, or gave it to other literary attentions. He warns that there'll be no slackening of his pace or output. There's much he wants to write, and will—in many fields.

Now he's a full-time writer. "I enjoyed teaching. I was a good teacher, and was making what I believed was a valuable contribution. But I don't miss teaching because I enjoy writing more, and I reached a point where I could earn a good living by full-time writing."

That was when John Gardner bought a farm at Old Bennington, the remote Vermont community that is also the setting for *October Light*. That's his "home" now, although he moved out recently, and has a domestic situation that is not clearly resolved. I was disarmed by his easygoing discussion of his apparently tempestuous marriage.

"I was 19 when I married. (He's now 42.) My wife is Joan Patterson, a musician and composer, a fantastic talent. I think she's a genius. She's the person I love, the one I most admire, and she's a pain in the neck. We fight all the time. There was never a time we

didn't fight. We become unbearable for each other, then can't do
without one another. I frankly don't know what will come of it."

He didn't say if this was their first separation, and I didn't ask. But I
did ask when and how he met his future wife, and Gardner
immersed me in an unusual family story.

"My wife is my cousin. The first time I slept with her, I was two
years old. We fought even before we were married.

"There's a long tradition of incest in my family. My parents were
also cousins. This may have something to do with genius. I know it
has something to do with physical misfitness. My son, for example—
Joel. He's a genius. I'm convinced of that. Joel plays the French horn,
as I do . . . as I've done professionally. He's brilliant. But he can
hardly see. His eyesight is terrible, and he'll probably never be able
to drive a car. It's the result of all this inbreeding.

"That's also the explanation for my hair. It keeps changing color. It
used to be brown, and it has gone from lighter to darker to other
shades, no genetic stability for it."

John Gardner also volunteered his belief that son Joel is miserably
unhappy, primarily because of the domestic intramural warfare. This
may also apply to the Gardner daughter, Lucy, who's another genius.

Gardner bestows genius promiscuously. He applies the term to
William Gass, who, perhaps not coincidentally, was the first "name"
American writer to sing major praises for the young John Gardner,
several novels back.

Gardner's geniuses include Isak Dinesen ("I'm closer to her in my
own writing than to any other"), Andre Biely, Hermann Broch . . .

"Broch's *The Sleepwalkers* may be the greatest novel I've read,
meaning, the greatest for me." (Broch also wrote the prose poem,
The Death of Vergil, and should be a kindred spirit for medieval-
classicist Gardner.) "The greatest living writer in the world today? I'd
say it's Robbe-Grillet."

I was beginning to feel uncomfortable, Gardner was getting into
writers I hadn't read and had barely heard of, and the closest I'd
been to Alain Robbe-Grillet was that I saw *Last Year at Marienbad.*
So I switched the topic to likely American influences on Gardner's
work, which continues an apocalyptic tradition that may be traced
from Brockden Brown through Hawthorne and Melville, right up to
Faulkner.

"Among the moderns, count me with Faulkner, but also with Thomas Wolfe. It may be that I'm still trying to get a lot of Wolfe out of my system, but I think he's marvelous."

Faulkner and Wolfe were southerners, but John Gardner is a product of rural, western New York state, where he is currently in residence until he finishes the novel that now has him occupied. Besides his experiences of living and working in the East and Midwest, he did a turn in San Francisco as editor of a controversial, ground-breaking literary magazine called *MSS.*

What else has he done, or is doing?

"I'm really into opera now. I've written the libretto for an opera based on Poe's short story, 'William Wilson,' with music by Louis Calabro. Then, for Jimmy Yannatos, I've provided a libretto that adapts Tolstoy's 'Ivan the Fool' for the opera stage. I may do more of this. Let's see how they fare in performance. I enjoy it."

There'll be more fiction, of course, and I knew that Knopf has also scheduled Gardner's full-length biographical appraisal of Geoffrey Chaucer for spring publication. Gardner also revealed that, in concert with that book, Knopf will also issue Gardner's own edited and annotated selection of Chaucerian verse.

"But in terms of the things I seek to become," he grinned while I nodded, "at the present time I feel more secure as a literary critic. You'll see. I'm about to take them all on—the contemporary American novelists."

When I asked where "contemporary" begins, he said, "With the death of William Faulkner. Oh, there are still a few dinosaurs walking around—Saul Bellow is one. But now there has to be some new direction for American literature, and I have my own ideas where it should be."

We talked about Gardner's other books. I have read five of his six published novels, and have myself reviewed four of them in *The Inquirer,* plus also reviewing *Jason and Medeia.*

I had reviewed his epic poem with admiration for the accomplishment, but a who-needs-it denouement. Again I suggested that the real allure of old poems is their oldness, but he simply said he loves *Jason and Medeia* and let it go at that. He does not like *The Wreckage of Agathon* ("I now think it's a mess") but retains a fondness for *Grendel* (as I do), his telling of the Beowulf legend from the viewpoint of the monster. *Grendel,* to Gardner's delight, has become something of a cause celebre on university campuses.

So has *The Sunlight Dialogues,* the corpulent novel that gave him his first sustained major attention almost five years ago. Rather apologetically, I told John Gardner that I like it least among his novels, while conceding that it is a whopping performance.

"You're right. It's a better performance than novel, just the opposite of *Nickel Mountain.*"

Ah, that's the title that hits home. I cherish *Nickel Mountain* and told Gardner that it was the best American novel published in 1973. If the NBCC had been in existence then and giving awards, I would have been pushing it.

"Yes, I'd say that was the best novel of its year. But then, *Nickel Mountain* was really my first novel although four others were published sooner. I was in my teens when I began writing it. It has existed in several versions. It's also my simplest novel."

When *October Light* was published, I remarked its similarity in tone to *Nickel Mountain,* and it is perhaps indicative of Gardner's development that from the first novel (set in the isolated mountains of New York state) to the more recent one, located in an equivalent Vermont environment, he has come full circle in his experimentation.

Through the course of the other novels he has indulged himself with what some critics have called a scholarly show-offishness, invoking ancient prose motifs, always revealing a lush stylistic command that meets the measure of his intricate, ambitious fictional designs. At the same time, they have made Gardner a "precious" novelist, a writer for other writers, but not for all those people out there.

With *October Light* he seems to be coming into the mainstream, and he is probably our next household word literary figure.

"My admission is that yes, I do believe I am writing the best fiction that's being produced in America today. But my next thought is, isn't that a sad commentary on things! I feel I'm only beginning, that I'm not the writer I hope to become. Or the philosopher. There's philosophy in all of my books, but it keeps changing as I change and develop."

John Gardner is the product of a Protestant experience, culturally and intellectually, and although he rejects the legacy in a kind of general rejection of "organized" religion, there is a powerful spiritual fabric in his fiction and I wasn't the first person to suggest they're all religious novels.

"Yes," his eyes danced, "but WHAT religion?"

I wouldn't hazard a guess, but the answer was quickly given.

"I think I'm the last person on earth who still believes in the almighty Zeus."

A Conversation with John Gardner

Don Edwards and Carol Polsgrove/1977

From *The Atlantic Monthly,* 239 (May 1977), 43-47. Copyright ©
1977 by Don Edwards and Carol Polsgrove. Reprinted by permission of *The Atlantic Monthly,* Don Edwards, and Carol Polsgrove.

"Art makes no laws, only very difficult complicated suggestions," says John Gardner, author of the recent *October Light* and five earlier novels. Born in 1933, Gardner
grew up on a farm near Batavia, New York, and was
educated at Washington University in St. Louis and at the
State University of Iowa. He is married and the father of
two children. A teacher and a scholar specializing in medieval literature, he has been teaching at both Skidmore and
Bennington colleges this year. He was interviewed in January during a visit to Lexington, Kentucky, for the premier
of *Rumpelstiltskin,* an opera for which he wrote the libretto.

**How do you know when you have a situation or an idea or a
set of characters that you want to use in a novel? How do you
know that you have a novel in the making?**

Because physiologically you get excited. You can think of twenty
plots—sometimes, when I'm teaching creative writing classes or
making lectures, I just spin out plots, because in those lectures I'm
trying to show people what makes a work of fiction, so I quickly
make up story after story, you know, the basics of the story, and any
one of them I could make a salable novel, but one of them catches
you for some reason; it hits you right where you live. Every writer has
particular things that bother him in his life, things that he hasn't resolved. For instance, I am on the one hand a kind of New York State
Republican, conservative. On the other hand, I am kind of a
bohemian type. I really don't obey the laws. I mean to, but if I am in
a hurry and there is no parking here, I park. And that conflict in me is
true of other things. I'm unwilling to go along with the social forms.

When people tell me that something in opera is bad, the polite thing to do is say, "Oh, I'll have to think about that." But I say, "You stupid asinine—." I can't be polite about important things. So every time I find the situation which is a kind of perfect expression of that war in my own personality—because I feel very strongly on both sides, like I really believe firmly, you know, gotta obey the laws, what's going to happen to the society if we let the anarchists take over? And on the other hand, I hate people who are always obeying laws that they don't understand—when a plot comes along and that's the essential feeling in it, that's the one I go with.

Do you have strong feelings about politics or political involvement?

No, just strongly negative feelings. I'm very fond of Jimmy Carter. I told one of my friends in New York, since the New Yorkers all hate Jimmy Carter because he's southern, I told this friend that I really like Carter, that I voted for Carter, and he said, "Oh yes, of course you would, you're a Republican." Basically, I think that politics is not a very useful thing. It's necessary.

You have done some work with government grants. There has been important government support for artists recently . . .

Yes, that's been pretty good. Actually, under Nixon, we got a fair amount of money for the arts, for the simple reason that Nixon is so stupid. In certain ways he is very bright, of course, cunning and also bright, but he believes the arts have no effect, really. He worried about sciences and cut them cold. But the arts—"What can they do?" And of course the truth is, the arts can make or destroy civilization. When you see movie after movie after movie which celebrates violence, you are going to have a violent society; there's no question about it. If you have one after another—plays, books, and so on, which are constantly talking about wife-swapping, people are going to swap wives. Art leads, it doesn't follow. Art doesn't imitate life, art makes people do things. When the courtly love poets started writing about courtly love, they established a way of life for centuries, the elevation of the lady, but at the same time denigration: opening the door for her but making her mop the floors. Kind of weird business. We're still there. And art has put us there. That's not the normal way for human beings to live. Look at any other society.

The Africans don't open doors for ladies; a lady's as strong as a man, she opens the door. But art always sets those things up. And if we celebrate bad values in our arts, we're going to have a bad society; if we celebrate values which make you healthier, which make life better, we're going to have a better world. I really believe that.

William Faulkner used to sidestep questions like this by saying that he wasn't a literary man, he was just a writer. But you are a literary man, and you must have had some thoughts about which group you stand with in American fiction.

Well, I think that Bill Gass and Stanley Elkin and I represent three main positions in modern fiction. And I think both of them are wrong and I'm right. Bill Gass takes the point of view that fiction is an object like a tree, just one more natural object to look at, it's just there. It's beautiful and all kinds of things but it's not apposite to real life. And Stanley takes the point of view that it's an entertainment, a performance. We were arguing one time, the three of us—it was a wonderful evening . . . they're both absolutely devoted, dedicated artists, they wouldn't compromise or cheat on anything. Otherwise they would have come around to my position long ago. And Bill was talking about literature as opaque and all these things he always says; that it's nothing but words. That words mean a different thing when they're in a fiction than they do when they are in the real world and fiction has nothing to do with the real world, it's art for art's sake. So I said I think that's not what it's about. I think that what you should do is you should so completely explain the character and the situation that when that lady lifts the coffee cup, you know precisely why she is lifting the coffee cup. The whole point of fiction for me is to explore the world and to explain it, to understand it. It's profoundly relevant to the world. And Stanley, who believes fiction is performance, said, "I can make a goddamned lady pick up a goddamned coffee cup any goddamned time I want." And that's absolutely true. He can do anything. . . . Anyway, I think those are the three positions going now. I think Barth and Barthelme would be along with Gass—maybe Barthelme belongs with both Gass and Elkin—and hardly anybody belongs with me. Very few people believe in fiction as exploration, as understanding.

Where do you put Bellow?

Well, Bellow does exactly what I do. I have great respect for

Bellow, but I think Bellow cheats all the time. I think Bellow is fundamentally an essayist and not a writer of fiction. Any time he wants to, he leans the chaacters against the door and philosophizes. It's as if he's got his favorite graduate students around him and he's telling them about life. He'll just stop and talk about Spinoza for thirty pages. I believe that in a work of art, all the ideas are changed into people, places, and things. It's true that in my fiction, characters argue philosophy, but as a matter of fact, I don't believe in the philosophy of the argument. They argue that philosophy because that's what's important to them and it expresses their feelings and positions. In *The Resurrection*, I've got a long section which is a paper that a character is writing about the aesthetic opinions of Immanuel Kant, and I actually think I know what went wrong with Kant's theory and I really wanted to say that, but I had a character who was dying of aleukemic leukemia, and one of the things that happens with that is that your mind stops working well. And so what I had to do was—I present the beginning of the argument really well and then, in spite of the fact that I would like the world to know the truth, and I would really like to write that essay, I have to write an essay which imitates the deterioration of this man's mind, and so it ends up a bad philosophical essay and gets worse and worse and more and more inchoate and that's just the way it is, that's the way fiction is. Bellow would have written the essay.

How does writing opera satisfy you in a way that writing fiction does not?

Terry Southern has a definition of writing as "out of the old gut onto the goddamn page." And that's about right. It's very private, and nobody judges it but you. . . . On the other hand, when you write opera, you're working with somebody else, and if it's good, which is the kind of relationship Joe Baber* and I have—I absolutely trust Joe Baber's compositions, I believe he is one of the very great composers of modern time, I believe that history will prove me right, and I believe that I'm one of the really great writers; I haven't proved that yet, but I feel it's coming. And when we work together, we get ideas much more complex than either of us would get alone, because we have more axes to hit with. There are certain kinds of emotions

---

*The composer of *Frankenstein* and *Rumpelstiltskin*, operas for which Gardner wrote the librettos.

that can only be expressed musically. For instance, in *Frankenstein,* a poem occurs at a moment when Frankenstein is suddenly questioning his whole life and the whole value of science and so on, and he is furious at himself and at humanity because, he says, "I make, I make, I make," and doesn't think about what he makes, and now suddenly he looks at it all and what he has created is monstrous, which science sometimes does, not that science always does. And it's a good poem; it would stand in any poetry anthology as a really fine poem about the agony of science, which isn't to say that there's not another side, too. But when you put the music on that—what I've done in the poem is suggest a set of emotions which Joe Baber can deepen and intensify. . . .

Where did your interest in music come from?

I'm half Welsh, that had a lot to do with it. I grew up in churches that sang and sang and sang. . . . And they're storytellers and poets and have been for generations. Also I lived in Batavia, which is near Rochester, so very early I got familiar with real music—we went to concerts and operas. I loved those operas there. My father used to let us off on Saturday afternoons to listen to Texaco opera. A farmer who let his hired hands, and those who wanted to, quit work on Saturday afternoon was risking a lot. But it was worth it. My father had a radio on his tractor to listen to. . . . It was in the days of a lot quieter tractors than we have now.

You are praised for your skillful use of language, and I was wondering how that happened, that you use language so well.

Well, it's really pretty simple. My father, a farmer, who does sermons, goes around to these little churches and preaches. He knows the Bible backwards and forwards, as well as Shakespeare and poetry. He reads that stuff and he loves language. Everybody in his family does . . . it's in the family. So that when I was a little kid, I was writing poetry and, in fact, novels. And my mother is an English teacher. When I was in college I discovered that I was better in English courses than in other things. I was more interested in chemistry than in English, but I kept getting A's in English. I never went to chem labs because I didn't like them, just the theory of chemistry. Finally I just sort of slid into it. But then, of course, what happened was I became a medievalist and classicist. . . . When I discovered Chaucer—I couldn't believe that there was such great literature. And really, it's true, the farther back you go in time (there are reasons for it), the greater literature is.

You use earlier forms and experiment with forms in your writing. I was wondering if you sometimes sat down and said, "I think I would like to experiment with this thing," or if those are just the forms that the thing takes. Like the tale within the tale in *October Light*—**if you thought, "Hm, I think it would be nice to write a novel within a novel, and that's what I'll do."**

The thing is that everything works together to work out the idea. Nothing takes shape by accident. . . . If you have a philosophical idea that you want to work with, you can't just say, here is this philosophical idea. You figure out a way of putting it into action. And when you get a really complicated philosophical idea, like the difference between novels and life, and what novels do to life and what life does to novels, then you've got a problem, and you mess around in your head or on paper until finally you find a form that will do. It may be a strange, "experimental" form or it may be perfectly ordinary so that a hundred years later nobody knows that what you were doing was hard. But it's in working out the ideas that I get to the form.

It's of course true that I've taught medieval and classical literature for a long time and the result is that I have a tendency—since every artist thinks in terms of conventions and traditions, these are his essential vocabulary—and I have a tendency to think in terms of old conventions and old traditions rather than new ones. That's mainly because that's what I'm most familiar with. That is to say, I've read a lot more ancient literature than I have modern, and, I think, quite rightly, because when I do read modern literature . . . it seems to me pretty boring, in comparison with the *Iliad* and the *Argonautica,* at least from my point of view. So I fall into those forms, one or another depending on the philosophical question that's involved. But it is true that I incline to think out so-called modern questions in terms of archaic forms. I like the way archaic forms provide a pair of spectacles for looking at things. Like, it's easy to see how you feel about modern life with your own eyes—you see it every day, you feel certain things, you get mad at certain people and you're pleased by certain things. When you look at your values through the eyes of a medieval courtly poet, then his values and your values are sure to be in some degree of contrast already, so you kind of triangulate the subject of the novel.

Is that basically what you were doing in *October Light*, playing off the two? At its simplest, is that why you put the tale within the tale?

Is which?

Playing off the two perspectives. The one of the larger novel and the other.

Hm. Not really.

I liked it, but I've read at least one review by a critic who didn't understand it.

A lot of people don't understand it and a lot of people don't like it. But when you do fairly serious art, you assume certain people are going to read it two or three times. When Sibelius did the Fourth Symphony, he knew nobody was going to get it. I mean people always want things to have simple schemes, simple messages. I don't know why, because it's wonderful to have something really great to go over and over. But Sibelius sort of sat back and waited for the world to come round to looking twice. . . . I don't care that a particular critic doesn't understand at all how the inner novel works. That's okay. The critic says that it doesn't work. Fine. I think it works, and I've spent years on the thing. I know where every little nut fits. I know exactly where the novels bang on each other. He spends a few hours and doesn't see it. Well, one of us is wrong. You just have to sort of wait for time to referee. Time may not save me, or it may take a long, long time. Lots of good writers don't get caught for centuries. . . .

Are you saying that the critic, if he wants to get the connection, can read the book two or three times and work on it and—

Well, even then he might get it or he might not.

Is it something that cannot be stated or that you can't talk about and analyze, if you wanted to?

I analyzed it when I was writing it, very carefully, in great detail. But the point is, when a writer says, "What I meant was," then from then on—it's like art appreciation courses: the teacher tells you, "Notice the balance in paintings, all paintings have balance." From then on, everybody goes into the art museum and all they see is balance.

They miss the whole thing because they're looking for balance. Sure there's balance, and there's a lot more. It's what's being balanced. Sometimes there's no balance, yet the painting has value. And so on. So that to say in too much detail what I mean to do in the two novels that make up *October Light* is to skew or to simplify the meaning. But there are some sorts of basic things that are obvious. For one thing, I'm parodying a kind of popular form of serious contemporary fiction in the inside novel. For another thing, art does touch life, it has effects on life, and life also goes into art. And obviously, that inside novel has effects on my character Sally Page Abbott and the kinds of ideas that the novel works with are ideas which are important to the battle outside the novel. As you read the inner and outer novels, you begin to recognize that that situation is exactly like this situation, that character is paralleled to this one; you start seeing more and more connections until eventually, I hope, the outside novel and the inside novel just flow together as one thing. But it's certainly true that the first time you look at it, *October Light* is going to seem a little strange.

The tale within a tale didn't bother me, but there was another thing that did. I wasn't sure that James's discovery that his son Richard was possibly the person who scared Sally's husband to death could bear the weight and significance it had at that point, and I thought maybe in your scale of values, accidentally scaring people to death might be more serious than in my personal scale.

Oh, I don't think accidentally scaring people is necessarily a bad thing. In *October Light*, the evils are other than that. After he scares his uncle, Richard is afraid to tell anyone, which is bad, not so much good or evil as simply a bad situation, and it comes from the nature of his father, who has behaved in certain ways all his life out of the noblest kind of ideals, but ideals that cause all kinds of disaster, and that's what's bad. It's always self-righteousness that kills. That's why art has so long been hostile to religion. It's not that artists don't believe in God or in religious principles, particularly—some do, some don't—but that every individual religion has a rigid code, even if it's a loose code, like "Do what Jesus would do"—that's a sneak, because then they tell you what Jesus would do. . . . But the problem is that religions always have simple answers which exclude people. Judaism excludes people who aren't Jewish, Christianity excludes people who aren't Christian. . . . And what art tries to do when it's serious, when it's moral, is give a full and universal view of morality. Art, I think, ultimately tries to support life. That's what I think morality is, what it means when you take it back to its roots. Morality is that which supports life, immorality is simply that which tends to kill. Human beings are healthy in some situations, unhealthy in other situations. Like you take a little kid and every time he comes around you scream at him, he's going to be unhealthy, he's going to grow up kind of crooked. You take a little kid, and every time he turns around you love him or, if necessary, you're stern with him though clearly loving, that makes a strong grown-up, that's healthy.

There are principles in the world, "eternal verities," as Faulkner liked to say, because of our nature, and those principles can be discovered. Artists, insofar as they're concerned with morality, can discover them. And the point of religions is, they make nice, neat laws—"Thou shalt not eat pork." Art never does that. Art makes no laws, only very difficult, complicated suggestions: it says this situation is exactly like this and shows you all the details of it. The overall effect of art is to say, one should have the noble ideals James Page has, one should do an hour's work for an hour's pay and so on, but one should also be aware that by being stern and rigid in pursuit of one's ideals, one can kill everybody around. When you get all through with the complex system of values in *Moby Dick*—or *October Light*—or in any other book that's dealing with values you have something that every religion will for one reason or another condemn. If religions were allowed to burn books, both *October Light* and *Moby Dick* would be sure to be burned by somebody—probably by everybody, in the end—because there are things to offend every inflexible code.

In several of your novels the characters are living in the shadow of death. Did you make a conscious decision to place characters in that position?

Yes. One way or another, my characters are always set against the tragic backdrop, because values have meaning only insofar as they're mutable, we're mutable. If we lived forever, all these values that I keep exploring . . . would be unimportant. Like Homer's gods—they slap each other, kick each other, throw each other out of heaven, they make each other crippled, but they live forever, so it's always comic. But once you've got people that die, once that threat of death is there, as it always is, you don't think about it every day, luckily, but it is always there, and of course life becomes much more intense, much more serious, when you are thinking about it, and the value of exploration becomes much more important. I want my readers to read my stuff not just for entertainment, though it is, I hope it's good entertainment, I hope it whiles away unpleasant hours in the hospital or gives somebody something to think about after his child has died, or any of those things . . . but I don't want it to be just entertainment. I want the sense, the importance of what we're talking about, the reader and I, to come through clearly. I don't mean to come up with messages or morals or anything like that. I'm not preaching. I'm just exploring.

A Conversation with John Gardner

Charlie Reilly/1977

Part of this interview was published in *Classical and Modern Literature: A Quarterly*, 1 (Winter 1981), 91-109. Copyright © 1981 by CML, Inc. The complete interview, which occurred in August 1977, is published here for the first time. Reprinted by permission of *Classical and Modern Literature: A Quarterly* and Charlie Reilly.

Since nothing about John Gardner can be described as "ordinary," it was appropriate that our conversation got off on an extraordinary foot. We were scheduled to meet on the campus of Bennington College on an August Friday in 1977. The weather had been erratic all day, and as our 7 p.m. appointment grew near, the heavens became downright ominous. Skies darkened, thunder roared through the Green Mountains, the locals—familiar with Vermont cloudbursts—were busily sealing windows and gathering up toys.

As 7 p.m. became 7:15 and then 7:30, I grew increasingly worried. The campus was rapidly emptying and the campus-police had already motored by to give me a less-than-congenial scowl. Still no John Gardner. Gardner's descriptions of our northeast "wilderness" (*vide Sunlight Dialogues, Nickel Mountain* and *October Light*) warned me that the ride back down the mountain could be adventurous—especially since my car could have been described as unreliable even before the spare tire blew up.

The long-haired, hippie-ish chap on the front steps, my silent companion for the last half hour, must have been entertaining similar thoughts. Periodically he stalked about the lawn, kicked an occasional stone, frowned at his watch. Finally, he repaired to his motorcycle and rummaged about the carrying case. A beer can, a glance in my direction, a sympathetic smile, another beer can. We sipped quietly, both wincing with each new peal of thunder, both peering first down the road and then at our watches. An odd looking sort this hippie: too old for a student, too unbarbered and be-jeaned for a professor. Finally we conversed. "You waiting too?" he began. Reasoning that since I was about to drown, there was no reason not to drop a name, I replied: "Yeah, I was supposed to meet a writer named John Gardner." The hippie's eyes narrowed; he carefully examined my hair, levis and sneakers; finally he broke out in a grin. "Are you Professor Reilly?" he laughed.

After that it was all uphill—well, downhill behind the motorcycle, and up lanes to John Gardner's modest bungalow. The interview was fast-paced, lively and long (the last not so much because we went on until the wee hours but because Gardner speaks as rapidly as I do). The topics were fairly predictable—the classics, Chaucer, translation, contemporary realism, etc.—but the answers never were. One of the most stimulating aspects of the conversation was that not only did John Gardner know a lot about a variety of subjects, but he had an opinion about each subject as well. When speaking about the classics, for instance, he advanced original theories about the rhythms of Homeric prose, the effect of Homer upon Sappho and the tragedians, and the *real* attitude Vergil had toward Augustan Rome. When we moved on to other topics— e.g., the extraordinary role Edgar Allan Poe played in American literature, the translation problems that burdened medieval Europe, the impact an editor should and should not have upon a work in progress—his thoughts were as intriguing as they were unexpected.

We also discussed his books and the controversial (and to a great extent misunderstood) thinking in *On Moral Fiction*. It is this last topic, Gardner's ferocious insistence that art must be informed by morality and his impatience with any type of art that cannot be measured by a moral yardstick that impressed me most. I did not know at the time about his apparently successful but surely harrowing battle with cancer. And because *On Moral Fiction* had not yet been published, neither of us could have known about the firestorm of criticism and controversy it would engender. I did recognize, however, the degree to which John Gardner reverences life and the extent to which his own life and art and philosophical-moral vision enrich his every word, spoken and published. Regardless of our particular stance in one Gardnerian controversy or another, we are surely indebted to him for that reverence and dedication.

Reilly: I've been contemplating all the works I've read by you and have been trying to place you in some kind of context. It struck me that of all the people I've spoken to I've never encountered anyone quite like John Gardner—I'm thinking not only of your diversity but also of your classical and medieval background and pure narrative style. Do you see yourself in any kind of literary mainstream, say, the school of American fiction or American realism?

Gardner (smiling): That's almost three questions and I'm not sure I've got a satisfactory answer to any of them. As for a mainstream, the people for whom I feel the most affinity as a writer and the authors whom I read for pleasure have been dead for a long time— say, Homer, Euripides, Dante, Chaucer, Shakespeare, and so on. So I don't really see myself in any type of mainstream. Insofar as American fiction goes, I find that a difficult subject to generalize about. At present, there is a lot of theorizing about it, and I feel the theory that places American fiction about twenty years behind European fiction is an important one. European fiction has probably drifted toward American writing recently, and surely there's some wonderful innovation going on here. But it seems to me that some of the most interesting developments in our novels follow experiments that were begun years ago by people like Gide, Camus, Sartre and Beckett. American writers are doing some very important things, and I'm certainly aware of them. But at the same time, I grew up on European fiction; Gide and Unamuno helped shape my style. As for realism, I find it hard to locate myself precisely in a realistic tradition; I find it hard to locate a lot of American fiction in it for that matter. For a long time in this country there was a tendency to think that all really serious art had to be conventional, realistic, and naturalistic. I guess a corollary to the rule was that there had to be some sort of emotion involved—whether it was conscious emotion or not was never pinned down—and the prevailing theory was that democratic art had to appeal to everybody in every place. I don't think that's true any more.

Reilly: I've seen a couple of articles that insist you operate in a realistic tradition similar to Dickens, and there *is* something in the sweep of your plots, your mixture of humor and realism, your social consciousness that remind me of Dickens. How do you feel about Dickens? I noticed you didn't mention him a second ago?

Gardner: Well, I admire Dickens and when I was a kid I read a lot of him. But I haven't read him in a long time and, if I did, I think I'd

find him a little crude. I'm not suggesting he isn't a great writer—
surely he is—but to me he's a part of the "Great Tradition" and I
think our contemporary realistic tradition has to be separated from
that tradition. The Great Tradition, to me, operates in what could be
called a fabulist school of thought—it springs from a tradition of
monsters and allegories and whatever—and one of its merits is its
mixture of what seems very realistic with what is obviously impossible. Now that is certainly something I've worked with. But I guess
what bothers me about the direction your question could lead is my
conviction that it's important. I follow my own impulses as a writer
and avoid honoring any set of guidelines. It's critical that I write about
what I want to write about and refuse to be tied down by the
constraints of realism as it's severely defined. If I don't think it's
important to demonstrate, for example, how a character gets to work
in the morning, I'll leave it out. Probably that violates some sacred
canon of realism, but that sort of thing doesn't interest me.

Reilly: Fair enough, but you once wrote that when a character
picks up a letter in a novel, it's important that the writer convey why
he's picking it up.

Gardner: Okay, but keep in mind that we're talking about fiction
on one hand and realism on the other. Surely I'll agree that when a
dragon picks up a letter, I want to know why he's doing it.

Reilly: I guess I was thinking that since *Grendel* and *Jason and
Medeia* nothing much has happened in your works that strikes me as
being improbable.

Gardner: That's true, there have been changes in my work. For a
time I used to introduce mysticism—in *Nickel Mountain*, for instance,
I brought in ghosts and whatever—but I no longer do things that way.
I feel *October Light* is an even more mystical book in its own way
than *Nickel Mountain* because of the imagery of charms and spells.
But I've domesticated it so the magical world exists comfortably
within the real world because of the nature of the characters. As long
as the characters believe in the magical world, I don't have to use
magic as such in the novel.

Reilly: You have written two books about the ancient world—
Jason and Medeia and *The Wreckage of Agathon*—and you once
said: "the farther back you go in time, the greater you find literature
is; there are reasons for it." What are those reasons?

Gardner: I think the inventors of forms always get the most out of them. When Bach created the *Well Tempered Clavier*, he became involved in a burst of creativity that was simply explosive. Nobody had ever heard music like that before because everyone played on a natural scale; no one had even considered that different keys had different effects. So once Bach had achieved this breakthrough, he produced something that was both unprecedented and unparalleled. It was the same way with the Mozart-Beethoven orchestra: once that orchestra was established, an entirely new kind of music was created. And it happened again with Richard Strauss and the Romantic orchestra. It was a remarkable time: the virtuosi of the orchestra were no longer playing for courts since the courts had all fallen, and their job-hunting had led them to Vienna. Suddenly, instead of the orchestra Mozart and Beethoven wrote for—say, a master violinist and a group of first violinists—there were thirty people, every one of whom could play the most difficult music. It was Strauss' genius to recognize the potential in this development and create what we now know as the Romantic orchestra. He was the one who had the brains to put all those people into a section and write for them. Once Strauss made that invention, his last works were all but inevitable. For a second, it seemed something similar might happen with today's synthesizer, but it didn't—probably because the synthesizer is a lousy instrument.

Now, to answer your question. I feel Homer was the first great poet, and he came along at that rare moment when writing was being reintroduced and was taking hold. He knew, of course, all the "epic fragments," as we call them—even though they were minor epics in themselves, each one as long as one book of the *Iliad*—but it was Homer's genius to have the vision and ability to go over these traditional song/stories and revise them. He was able to notice, for example, that Apollo has a bow and Pandarus breaks the truce by shooting a bow, and by interweaving those and similar events he enriched his work with the "symbol of the bow." It was a whole new invention, a new way of writing, and since Homer was so wonderfully skilled as a writer, he produced two literary masterpieces. Oddly, the type of breakthrough that I'm referring to silences at least as much as it inspires. Since one can never duplicate the achievement of a pure genius, the very occurrence of an artistic breakthrough urges artists to concentrate on something different. So in the centuries after Homer, we see the slipping away of the epic and the emergence of tragedy. The epic tradition collapsed because of the incomparable brilliance of Homer, so now you find artists deciding to confine themselves to a single myth, limiting the tale to a handful of characters, and focusing upon the techniques of dialogue and the psychological/metaphysical relationships that dialogue produces. And—wham!—you've got Aeschylus, Sophocles and Euripides, unparalleled masters. In a similar sense, Homer exhausted the possibilities for poetry, so Sappho had the genius to similarly limit the scope of her writing and invent the lyric.

We can look back over the centuries and see that although every culture had an epic poet, none of them—not even Apollonius or Vergil or Dante or Milton—could touch Homer. Similarly, I don't feel any dramatist has come close to Aeschylus, Sophocles and Euripides, and I feel no lyric poet has equalled Sappho. They're the ones who invented their respective "machines," and, in the midst of that creative burst, they produced masterpieces. "Machine" is a poor term, of course; it's not the type of machine an airplane is, something which by nature invites technological advances. Since art addresses itself to people's feelings and relationships, it's unique, and once the break-throughs and triumphs have occurred, you're reduced to tinkering with the artifact. Throughout the history of literature, writers start varying on the theme. After Homer, Apollonius comes along and demonstrates what happens if you treat the epic tradition ironically. He does so because he lived in a decadent age, an age more like ours than I think any age ever was. In fact, I feel the New York establishment of nihilists and meliorists, of whiners and winers, bears an incredible resemblance to the society Apollonius scored.

Reilly: I don't think it's much of an exaggeration to say you work with a different format almost every time out. Is that consistent with the thoughts you've just expressed? Do you try to come up with something that hasn't been done before? Certainly, your own epic, *Jason and Medeia*, hasn't been done in our time, and I'm not sure there has ever been anything precisely like it.

Gardner: I don't know. I think that what happens is that as a writer I have a tendency always to plan and write with literary forms in mind. In other words, the epic form, as Homer established it for all time, commits the writer to certain things. I'm tempted to say I don't really believe some of the things Homer says—actually I believe them all in a special way—but I must surely admit that some of them don't work in the modern world. Suffice it to say my writing has convinced me that when someone writes about modern life within the form of the Homeric epic, he finds himself able to think in a way that would otherwise have been unavailable—a way that permits him to produce an unusual text. What I'm saying is, I never approach a work with a purely realistic approach—with a conviction that "I want to express some ideas about my childhood." Rather, I begin a work thinking something to the effect that: "I want to write a particular form of tale. I want to fulfill the requirements for that form, and at the same time I want to express my own feelings and, as best I can, suggest my generation's and country's feelings." I suppose the reason why my material is different each time is that I continue to experiment with different forms, seeing where they take me, seeing what I can say inside each one.

Reilly: I'm fascinated by the demands of literacy you make upon your readers. In *Jason* and *Agathon*, for example, the more the reader knows about the ancient world the better off he is. In *Nickel Mountain* it helps to know what a pastoral is, and *Grendel* is surely enriched by one's familiarity with the Old English legend. Do you write with any reader in mind? Do you worry about readers who wouldn't recognize all those literary allusions?

Gardner: No, I write for a reader who is like me, and I assume there are a lot of them out there. I may be wrong, but I would imagine most writers do the same. When I was a kid and then a young man, I knew there were very definite things I liked and disliked, things I was interested in thinking about and reading about. I suppose in a sense I write for that kid or young man; I know I recall vividly what it was that interested me then. To pursue what we were talking about a moment ago, when I was quite young I read the complete works of Charles Dickens and, having finished the last one, was overwrought. I recall that the second I was done I started over, started rereading, almost in a panic. And when I had finished the next author I became really interested in, Dostoyevsky, I immediately started over.

As I think back over that period when I read so earnestly, perhaps desperately, I can see characteristics of a dedicated reader that I'm convinced are shared by large numbers of people. For one, age isn't very important. Certainly as a very young man I could get enough from a tale by Dickens or Dostoyevsky to make me delighted, awed and excited. For another, an author needn't hesitate to be literate or fall back upon his education if the work demands it. Even as a young man, I found works that sufficiently aroused my curiosity to send me scampering off to a library to learn something about the author or topic. To get to the point, I write for *that* type of reader, and I suspect Dickens and Dostoyevsky did something similar. I have heard, of course, authors claim they write only for themselves, but I suspect they really mean something similar to what I'm saying now. It's not that they have no sense of an audience. Rather, they have a feeling, a conviction, that since there are millions of thoughtful and educated readers in the world, there *must* be people out there whose interests and reading inclinations are similar to their own.

Reilly: Do you worry about potential sales? Have you ever found yourself backing away from a theme or subplot because you feared it would hurt the book's sales?

Gardner: No, never. I've had such worries on occasion and "friendly advisors" have conveyed to me their alarm about the direction a work might be taking. But, no, I've never backed away from a topic or held back stylistically for that reason. I never would, either.

Reilly: It's to your credit. I think of things as theoretically unsalable as Greek myth and epic form and . . . How did *Jason and Medeia* do, by the way?

Gardner: It had a very good sale. I'm not much at numbers, but I do know it sold very well.

Reilly: I read somewhere—I think it was in reference to the subplot in *October Light*—that you had spent years working on a single part of a novel. That, plus the fact that you've brought forth an extraordinary number of titles over the last six years, makes me wonder whether you had a number of works "backed up." Did you need, say, the breakthrough of *Grendel* to find a sympathetic editor?

Gardner: No, not really.

Reilly: Were the books written in the order they were published?

Gardner: That's a difficult question to answer because of the way I write. What happens is, I'll keep working on a book until I can't "see"—or stand—it anymore, and then I'll put it away and turn to something else. Then, either I'll finish the newer work, or some scenes in that newer work will give me a fresh perspective on the problem with the earlier one. A by-product of this is that many of my novels become closely related—not thematically or formally, but let's say philosophically. Each novel addresses what impresses me as a metaphysical or philosophical problem of major dimensions. I don't know, maybe I'm kidding myself, maybe it's simply a psychological delusion on my part, but each of my works seems to make an honest and thoughtful statement about a separate problem, and yet the thoughts in one work will be quite relevant to those in another. I've thought quite a lot about what fiction is and isn't, and the more pondering I do, the more impressed I become. In fiction, a writer is always balancing the universal against the particular, and every *real* work of fiction, I think, contains a philosophical inquiry. But it's a special kind of inquiry in that the writer not only considers a philosophical problem, but does so by thinking it through in a concrete situation. That means, to me at least, the fiction ultimately comes closer to the truth than philosophy. Nietzsche, for example, gives us the abstract theory of the Superman; Dostoyevsky tests it and demonstrates its limitations. Although Nietzsche is perfectly logical and coherent, he goes astray because his theory doesn't reflect the way real people behave in real relationships. To me that's what is so admirable about serious fiction, the reason it's so valuable to a culture: it puts philosophic theories through laboratory tests. Think of how wonderfully Marcel Proust tested and used the ideas of Henri Bergson, or how Beckett developed the thinking of Descartes.

So what happens to a novelist is that he thinks out a philosophical problem in concrete terms, and because he's obliged to deal with particular people in a particular place, he gets a truer answer than a Nietzsche would get. I don't want to be simplistic; of course, one can immediately respond that because a writer limits himself to a particular locale and certain individuals, he may come up with a narrow answer. But I do know from my own writing that if a writer carefully selects his characters and conscientiously develops them, he will find that his studies and analyses of everyday life, coupled with the lessons he's learned in the art of developing genuinely realistic

narratives, will result in his arriving at some pretty sensible conclusions. They'll also result in his putting in a lot of hard work.

To get back to the idea of working on a number of books
concurrently, I find there can be a definite benefit to the practice.
That is, when I'm toiling on, say, three novels at the same time, each
of which concerns similar philosophical problems, and when I
perceive that each work is headed toward a similar or at least
consistent answer, I have a sense of confidence that I wouldn't get
from working on just one book. Every now and then I'll have that
pleasant experience from a single work. When I was writing *Sunlight
Dialogues*, which is my longest and possibly my most complicated
book, I decided to develop a number of subplots which all focused
upon the same issue. I felt that not only would such a strategy make
the entire novel more digestible to the reader, it would help me come
up with a true answer to the questions I was raising. Most of my
books aren't of such dimensions, though, so I enjoy working on two
or three at a given time.

Reilly: I wonder, was multiple book-writing an accident of
beginning as a writer? In other words, now that you're established
and can count on a speedy manuscript-to-publication process, are
you still working on a number of texts?

Gardner: At the moment, I'm not working on much of anything.
It's hard to generalize, especially since I'm never sure when anything I
begin will grow into a full–length work. Some tales take a good deal
of time but never develop into something I want to publish. Others
contain the right ingredients but take their own time in growing. I
started *Nickel Mountain*, for example, when I was nineteen and spent
almost two decades bringing it to a point where it was ready.

Reilly: That's interesting since some of the reviews of *Nickel
Mountain* described it as the "logical next step" after *Sunlight
Dialogues*. After I had read both, I felt that *Nickel Mountain* was an
earlier work. I guess I was right?

Gardner: Well, that's one of those pleasant occasions when
everyone is right. As I said, I began the novel when I was nineteen,
but I really got to work on it after the publication of *Sunlight
Dialogues*. *Nickel Mountain* went through an extraordinary amount
of revision; in fact, there were a few episodes which I deleted from

the final draft that were published in various journals—one was the *American Poetry Review*, as I recall. Because the characters' names and whatever were different, no one ever associated the excerpts as being portions of the novel. So, I did start it before all of the others, but I had more trouble "ending" it than I did with any of the others. It was worth the effort, though; I'm very fond of it in its finished form.

Reilly: It's interesting how polished the final text wound up. It has a lovely flow to it; it's so smooth it seems almost effortless.

Gardner: I don't know whether to take a bow or heave a sigh— but, thank you. I agree, it does flow smoothly; still, it was the result of a lot of hard and sustained labor. Writing is an unpredictable business. I'm working on a play right now, and there is a single page that I've been lingering over for six weeks. Six weeks, and it's still not right!

Reilly: Is that typical of the way you write? I ask because Joseph Heller told me he works that way, but most of the others I've spoken to seem to skip around more.

Gardner: Right, one page at a time. I guess it's similar to the way Joe Heller works, but I put in a lot more time than he. He works about three hours a day, he says, and I work as many hours as I can squeeze into a day. A fourteen–hour day isn't unusual. As a rule I'll put in at least ten hours each day writing; sometimes I've kept at it for as many as twenty hours.

Reilly: On a typical day, do you work solely on one piece, or do you skip from one to another?

Gardner: As a rule I'll stay with a single work for the day, or week, or whatever the period is.

Reilly: So, if one arranged your novels in sequence according to copyright date, would he have a fairly accurate indication of the times in which you put the lion's share of effort into them?

Gardner: Almost. The one exception I can recall would involve *Grendel* and *Sunlight Dialogues*. I wrote *Grendel* after *Sunlight Dialogues*, but I sold them both together. It was a strange business. As I recall it, I wrote *Resurrection*, then *Sunlight Dialogues*, then *The Wreckage of Agathon*, and then *Grendel*.

Reilly: That's interesting because the copyright dates would suggest *Wreckage* first and *Grendel* last of the three.

Gardner: Well, an editor figures here—a brilliant and wonderful

human being named David Segal. Although he's since died, I think
he was one of the best editors America has ever seen, far better than
Maxwell Perkins, for example. He was the one who saw the potential
of William Gass—he accepted *Omensetter's Luck* at the same time
he accepted my *Resurrection* for New American Library. When he
moved to Harper he accepted *The Wreckage of Agathon*. A little
while later he went to Knopf, and it was then he took *Sunlight
Dialogues*, which was an earlier work, and *Grendel*, which I had just
completed. I don't know, perhaps I've got them confused; but I don't
think so.

Reilly: You compared him with Maxwell Perkins. As I recall, in a
recent essay in *Modern Times* you more or less shook a fist at Perkins
and suggested he interfered with writers. The suggestion seemed to
be that Perkins should have left a writer like Thomas Wolfe alone,
should have given him the free rein that Proust enjoyed.

Gardner: Oh no. That goes too far.

Reilly: Well, to stay with the issue. If your editor told you to
change a scene or rewrite a chapter, would you do it?

Gardner: Oh sure. If I *know* I'm right, I won't make changes, of
course, but a good editor is a good reader. Typically the chapters an
editor worries about are the ones you yourself feel uncertain about,
and usually the suggestions and directions he offers are invaluable. I
have an editor at Knopf, Bob Gottlieb, who is also superb—I'm quite
fortunate in that respect. But Bob works differently from David.
David would produce a carefully written analysis of everything in the
book; Bob works more from the seat of his pants. His remarks are
incisive and immediate; but they're brief, not elaborately spelled out.

What's invaluable about Bob is that he works exactly by my
standards. We've talked at length about what I should be trying to
do, and in that respect, we agree to the letter. I have some important
principles about my writing. One of them, the most important in a
way, is that when a reader begins one of my books, he should fall
into a sort of trance and nothing in the book should snap him out of
it. Imposing a personal style or in some other way intruding upon the
narrative rhythm—the way John Barth and Bill Gass do—would
destroy the type of narrative I try to construct. What I want my reader
to do is go to sleep and read the book with his soul, as well as his
intellect. I don't ever want him to be dragged up out of this dream-

state by an artifice or a mistake. Let me interrupt: I *do* make
mistakes, my wish is not to make them.

So, when I hand a book to Bob Gottlieb, if anything distracts him
from the overall vision or story, he tells me: "John, *that's* no good; it
ruined the story for me." And since he's reading according to "my
rules," I have to respect what he says. Sometimes I think he's wrong,
but the overwhelming percentage of the time I realize he's right. As I
said, he speaks directly—from the seat of his pants, as it were—and
on occasion I've found him an infuriating editor. But he's a good one,
a damn good one; and, yes, I accept his advice and re-write in
response to his suggestions. I'd be insane not to.

Now, about Maxwell Perkins. Thomas Wolfe was a great writer,
although he did have faults common to writers of the thirties. In
fairness, he got them from a master, James Joyce, but still he had that
idiotic Celtic habit of repeating himself in his narratives—you know,
echoing that one key phrase over and over. Wolfe was carried away
by that and by certain excesses that seemed to derive from Biblical
rhetorical devices, but he wrote a wonderful, wonderful book in *Look
Homeward, Angel*. What Wolfe wasn't was Marcel Proust, who was
doing the same thing at the same time; producing an enormous, fat
novel. But Proust was an arrogant, tough, rich man who had the
goods on Gide and . . .

Reilly: He had what on Gide?

Gardner: The goods. Gide was Proust's publisher, and he was
very susceptible to blackmail because his personal life was imperfect.
So Proust was able to pressure Gide into publishing *A la recherche
du temps perdu* precisely and entirely as he wrote it. Poor Wolfe:
imagine what it was like to try to get something on Maxwell Perkins: I
doubt if he even smoked. I'm exaggerating, but I mean there was
nothing a person like Wolfe could seize upon, no leverage he could
exert, to retain a decisive and confident voice concerning what did
and did not belong in his own writing. Perkins did the best he could.
He published as much as struck him publishable, and to his credit, he
kept a very careful record of the manuscript page numbers so if it
ever became possible for an American publisher to do what a French
publisher could do, Wolfe's original text would be preserved in the
basement of Scribner's someplace. But Wolfe's character as a sort of
womanizing, drunkard American Romantic was such that he could

not push for the book as he wrote it. Perkins was in no position to help Wolfe financially, so they were both caught in a trap. Today I don't think any American publisher is in that position; I think the money and resources are available to permit an eccentric work to be published intact.

Reilly: Most of your works are accompanied by some form of illustration—drawings, paintings, sketches—with the exception of *The Wreckage of Agathon.*

Gardner: Right, I wasn't able to control that one.

Reilly: I think you've anticipated my question. Do you control the selection of illustrations and whatever?

Gardner: I control the fact that they will be illustrated and, fortunately, my editor is in total agreement with me about what I want and whom I want.

Reilly: Does the artist simply take your manuscript, work up sketches and mail them to the editor? Or does he submit them to you first?

Gardner: It varies with the temperament of the artist. My thoughts about illustration are strong ones; I *want* it because I want the book to feel like a book. This may sound like a trite statement, but it surely reflects a major difference between the so-called "moderns" writing today, as Ihab-Hassan calls them, and the rest of us. The hope of the "truly modern" or even "post modern" writer—let me hasten to say I hate such terms—is to entice the reader to fall into the story and enter a subjective world. On the other hand, writers like me want you to be conscious at all times that you're reading a work of art. I never want to distract you from the narrative, of course, but at all times I want you to be aware that you've got an object, a book, in your hands. I'm not alone in this wish; I'm sure Kurt Vonnegut and John Updike have something similar in mind when they include, respectively, personal illustrations or unusual typography. The objective, and it seems to me commendable, is to oblige the reader to be aware of the *fact* of the book and to react to that book directly. It strikes me as ironic that so many writers whom I find myself reading lately have noisily separated themselves from the tradition of realism and yet love the rather old-fashioned idea of an art object *as object.* So with my own work, I want illustrators to read the book and then do pretty much what they want to. I emphatically don't want a situation similar to that which existed between Lewis Carroll and John Tenniel, where Carroll would draw the rough draft and Tenniel would finish the sketch. To me, a more satisfactory and productive arrangement is one similar to the one that existed between Dickens and his illustrator. It amounted to Dickens saying, even though he could draw, "I don't know, you do it."

Reilly: Geoffrey Wolff noticed that, typically, your works describe a tension between freedom and order: a "freedom" that takes the form of a special type of rebellion, and an "order" that seems a special form of restraint.[1] And yet, it seems to me that in at least three examples—the monster's destruction in *Grendel*, the triumph of Lykourgos in *Agathon* and the almost mindless murder of Fred Clumly in *Sunlight Dialogues*—the rebel seems to perish in the face of order. Am I over-reading?

Gardner: That's the problem with general theories about overall bodies of work. Since writers don't begin with the principle and demand that the characters behave accordingly, few generalizations survive every test. I know Wolff's essay, though, and I think it's an intelligent one. Certainly, it's true that "freedom" in its various disguises and "order" in its various disguises figure in every one of my books—and probably constitute a controlling theme. I'm not going to defend someone else's theory, but I would point out that *Jason and Medeia* is one of many examples of the accuracy of the reading. Jason is certainly the master of order, an allegorical stick-figure representing western civilization. And Medeia is a stick-figure more or less suggesting eastern civilization—or at least imagination, intuition, witchcraft and so on. There, Medeia wins hands down—at least I hope she does.

Reilly: Speaking of *Jason and Medeia*, I felt your handling of Medeia's final lines was wonderful. In fact, and at the risk of having a teacup thrown at me, I felt you handled them better than Euripides did. Am I correct in guessing it wasn't a literal translation?

Gardner: That's a story in itself. At first I skimmed through Euripides, shook my head, then decided to drop and add passages to portray Medeia as positively as I could. But I certainly have to step back from the thought that I improved upon Euripides. He's a brilliant playwright; it's just that he's been so poorly translated. You know, back when I was young and stumbling along, it took me a long time to think of Euripides as anything more than a master of soap opera. So in working on my own *Jason and Medeia* I decided to use Apollonius' *Argonautica* as a primary source and I wound up translating line after line, and loving every second of it. Finally, when I as coming to the end and after I had delved so deeply into the myth, I thought I had better at least look at Euripides again. As I recall it, I was at the point of the, well, "kick off," when Medeia was preparing to murder her children and was scheming against Pyripta, and I decided to go back to Euripides in Greek and see if there was anything I could keep. It was awesome, a magical moment. I was knocked off my feet by the sheer brilliance of his play.

Reilly: Was it a matter of simple translation?

Gardner: No translation is simple—there are thousands of decisions to make. And, no, I was operating within the epic tradition and in any epic you have a mirror of the twenty-fourth book in the first book, the twenty-third book in the second, and so forth. Since Euripides was writing a play and not an epic, I had to make changes. But I do feel that most of them were inevitable; they were mandated by my decision to adapt Euripides' play to a different form.

Reilly: Let me compliment you on your translation and ask a question at the same time. I majored in Classics and, accordingly, staggered about in the subtleties of people like Pindar. To me, your translation of Euripides and Apollonius is wonderful, as far removed from a slavish regurgitation as could be. Yet, at least in those passages where I hauled out the lexicon and dug in, your translation honored the narrative rhythm and meaning of the original. When I read Morris Dickstein in the *New York Times* saying that you were "plunk(ing) down large chunks (of the sources) line for line,"[2] I was astonished. Do you feel that's a fair assessment of your translation in *Jason and Medeia*?

Gardner: One of the most interesting things I dealt with as a medievalist was the whole concept of "translation"; in fact, I feel one of the more interesting movements in the Middle Ages was the movement back to original translation. It's a difficult subject to reduce to a few words, but in a nutshell it goes like this. In pre-medieval times when the Romans were sending out their word—their culture, their "Good Book"—to places like Anglo-Saxon England and France, they were interested in presenting it in ways that would be understandable to outlanders. So they didn't use word-for-word translation. Rather, they compressed and expanded and added examples as they saw fit; and the whole art of translation was transformed into the art of making another culture available in a new language. The practice had obvious advantages. When the Old Testament was translated into Anglo-Saxon English, for example, it was translated into alliterative verse; it was changed from a Jewish epic into the type of epic the "comitatus" would understand and identify with. Okay, this went on for years and years and it was a perfectly honest kind of translation, as long as everyone remembered what the original was. But by the thirteenth century, a number of guys like Pierre Abelard started saying in effect, "Wait a minute." Boccaccio and Petrarch were rediscovering the ancient texts and, when they studied them they found out, for instance, Aristotle's *Poetics* had been reduced through "translation" to a formula contrived to support the state: "Tragedy" meant poems praising the state; "Comedy" involved satires against opponents of the state.

So Abelard and people in the Oxford-Rationalist movement—like Chaucer in his translation of Boethius—gravitated toward a translation that reflected a literal honoring of the text. At the same time, a practice developed, one which is directly linked to what we're discussing in my *Jason and Medeia*, which involved using translation for the formation of poems. In this case, the wish was to preserve the spirit of the original, but to apply it to completely different political situations and so on. So, when I "translated" Apollonius and Euripides, I was trying to do something similar to what Chaucer did in *Troilus and Criseyde*. Seventy-five percent of Chaucer is word for word out of Boccaccio, but there are a couple of differences. First, Chaucer changed tenses around and made a number of creative decisions which totally transmogrify the poem.

Second, Chaucer wrote a far greater work; in fact, Boccaccio's work would barely be known if it were not for Chaucer's. I hasten to add that I attempted a "Chaucerian" translation in that first sense, in the use of Chaucerian method. I don't mean to imply I created a better work than Apollonius' *Argonautica*—or that my *Grendel* is in any way an improvement on *Beowulf.*

Reilly: How would you respond to my feeling that you did a better job on the "Medea" myth than Apollonius did?

Gardner: He was working toward a different end; when you think about it, you'll see he had a far different perspective. Apollonius is a cynical, nihilistic bastard. He makes it obvious throughout the *Argonautica* that not only is life a mess but matters have so deteriorated that there is very little left in life of value except things like snakes. Accordingly, every time he works with a snake he's wonderful. Seriously, his cynicism runs deep. An example of the cynical genius of Apollonius is reflected in the fact that the wrong man becomes the hero of the poem. When Heracles gets into the boat and Jason asks the crew, "Who shall our hero be?" they all respond with one voice: "Heracles!" Heracles responds like a contemporary basketball player—saying something to the effect of "Aw, come on, guys, Jason brought us together"—but secretly he hopes Jason will urge him to take over. The beauty of Apollonius is that he has Jason respond: "Okay, if Heracles doesn't want the job I'll have to step in." As the *Argonautica* progresses, you find the only reason the Argonauts survive is that, every time they get into what could be a really difficult situation, it turns out that Heracles—whom they lost on the first island—had been there a week earlier and had killed a snake. So the whole poem is about the wrong guy, which is a typically Apollonian trick. In that sense, I'm not sure my work can be profitably compared to Apollonius' since I'm not a nihilist and I wasn't attempting to make the same kind of sardonic statement Apollonius made. Then again, maybe I go too far in calling Apollonius a nihilist. What I want to emphasize is that his work criticizes the horrible civilization he lived in. It's occurred to me that he winds up talking the way writers like Vico and Barthelme or Hawkes would have.

Reilly: Could we talk about *October Light*? The genesis of "The Smugglers of Lost Souls' Rock" puzzled me. In the preface you said something that suggested you had started out to work on a serious book about James Page and Sally Abbott and, after chatting with your wife, decided to slap in "Smugglers." Were the "halves" of the novel that casually tied together?

Gardner: No, what happened was this. Long before I had even contemplated what became the "outside" novel—the part about James and Sally—my wife Joan teased me, saying: "Why don't you write something *popular*, some kind of garbage-philosophy novel that

will make a lot of money?" This took place at a party when I was
pretty drunk, and so I left the room, went upstairs and hacked out
the first chapter of something I called "The Smugglers of Lost Souls'
Rock." The first draft didn't take long—subsequently I had to go over
it many times to bring it to a level I was satisfied with—and I brought
it down and read it to a few people. Everyone thought it was funny,
and I particularly recall Joan laughing and insisting it would sell. I
think she said: "That's it! You've got Bill Gass by the throat!" I was
struggling with *Nickel Mountain* and the novella that became "The
King's Indian" at the time, so I went back to them the next day. But
every once in a while Joan and I would play with the "Smugglers"
piece. All the sentences of the final work are mine, but she would
suggest ideas and plot developments and whatever. To make a long
story short, we ultimately completed a sort of spoof of a contemporary philosophical novel, and then we didn't know quite what to do
with it. Finally I sent it to my agent and asked him to see if he could
get it published under a pseudonym; I certainly didn't want it under
my name because it dealt with what I absolutely hate in modern
fiction. But I did think it was a good parody of, if not trash-fiction, a
kind of inglorious fiction that is enjoying a lot of popularity these
days. My agent was a kind soul and he said: "Look, John, I'll show
it to a couple of people, but this is really grotesque." So I forgot
about it.

Now what I was doing in that piece—and I'm sure it was at least
partly conscious—was talking about the way bad literature can
destroy a culture. I just published an article in the *Hudson Review*
called "On Moral Fiction," which is one of a number of pieces I'm
going to collect into a book about what is wrong with America in
general.[3] My premise is uncomplicated: evil models in art lead to the
destruction of civilization. I really believe that. Civilization, I think, is
created by art, not art by civilization. For example, I've been reading
a two-volume book about Judaism lately and have been impressed
by the way writing, in this case sacred writing, literally fashioned a
civilization. When you think about it—I'm surely generalizing here,
and I'm just as surely not trying to sound like a smart-aleck—a group
of people contrived tales about the way things were, or ought to have
been, and then wound up believing those tales. Not literally the way
fundamentalists do, but as great stories describing how and how not

to behave. Eventually these people, Semites of various kinds, separated themselves as a group and ended up being called "The Jews." Historically, it turns out they weren't a race as such; they were just a bunch of people in the same part of the world who rejected polytheism and sex-worship and whatever. As it turned out, their stories and beliefs were transformed into something that in turn transformed and even defined one of the most important civilizations in history. At the same time, the process can occur in reverse, that is to say, a morally bankrupt work, or collection of works, can have an awesome impact upon the way we live and think. And it was my intention while writing "Smugglers" to make fun of this type of deficient book. So, when I had settled in Southern Illinois I decided to retain the comic and satiric flavor of "Smugglers" but to transform the book into a serious demonstration of the fact that man's achievements are keyed to models. You can't be a hero, in other words, unless you've heard of heroism; you can't be a great statesman unless you've heard of statesmanship; you can't be a great artist unless you've seen art. At the same time I was writing a very serious novel, set in Southern Illinois, about two cranky old people facing the problems and complexities of old age. Well, two things occurred. One was my decision to include the "Smugglers" parody as a contrast to the serious work; the other was an opportunity that presented itself to me to move back east, where I had grown up. . . .

Reilly: Wait a minute! Do you mean that those wonderful accounts of upper New York state in *Sunlight Dialogues* and *Nickel Mountain* were written from memory?

Gardner: Well, whenever I came back for a visit, I'd drop in on certain families. In fact, I often stopped in for long afternoons with a special group of sisters who became the three sisters in *October Light*.

Reilly: But imagine that. I envisioned you up on a New York state mountain watching the scenes and characters create themselves in front of you.

Gardner: There were similarities that made the writing process a smooth one. Southern Illinois is also a place that's, well, stern, not terribly rich, and Republican. But, anyhow, when I came east and saw that black dirt and those granite marks and those little mountains, I was overwhelmed with memories and knew immediately I had to change the setting of the novel to New York. To get back to the question, having decided to use the inner-novel as a contrast, I began to re-shape the inner-work to complement the larger tale, and what Joan and I wrote originally turned out to be a very rough draft of what became the "Smugglers" in *October Light*.

Reilly: I'm cheered to hear you talk about interweaving "Smugglers" because by the end even I was making connections between the tales and I was wondering if I was over-responding. For one thing, at the beginning I thought the longer novel was quaint and the "Smuggler" business with it. By the end, what with the flying saucers and electric eels, I found myself regarding "Smugglers" as whimsical and the Pages' struggles grippingly realistic.

Gardner: Great! I hoped to achieve that effect.

Reilly: Also, Sally reminded me of Peter Wagner in the way they were both trapped; James Page resembled Captain Fist; each portion had an elaborate trap.

Gardner: Sure, sure; you're right.

Reilly: Perhaps this is pushing your good will too far, but may I ask what you were getting at with these parallels? I can't imagine you did it casually or just to amuse yourself.

Gardner: No, it was carefully planned. The first thing about the inside-novel is what you first said, and I'm glad you felt that way. My favorite living painter in the world is Robert Rauschenberg and perhaps his most famous creation is something called "The Rauschenberg Wren." Fortunately he's written about how it came to be. He said he had been walking to his studio, which was by an old antique shop, for a year and, after seeing an old wren in the window, kept saying to himself: "That's art! If only I could make other people see it, if I could only present it somehow." So he bought it and he let it stand around in a corner of his studio, and then he made a platform for it, and he made a plaque saying "Rauschenberg's Wren." Finally, he put a Firestone tire around it and painted the tred white to show that it was totally useless. Now that wren inside the tire just stares back at whoever is looking at it and seems to be irritated because that "goddamn modern world is in its way." And suddenly the wren is *there*!

So with my inside-novel and outside-novel, the first thing I was concerned about wasn't neatness or parallel plotting but a way of conveying the importance of the story, especially the importance of the seemingly mundane characters in the outside-novel. Now if I had limited myself only to that outside-novel, it would seem to be little more than a variant of some Dorothy Canfield Fisher yarn about Vermont. But with the, to use your phrase, "with-it," jazzy, "modern philosophical" inside-novel to serve as contrast, the importance of the outside-novel comes through, I hope, to the reader.

Reilly: It did. I recall that halfway through *October Light* I found myself becoming engrossed in the outside-novel, becoming wrapped up in the realism of the tale.

Gardner: Good, that's exactly what I wanted. Now there was another reason why I embedded that "Smugglers" tale within the tale proper. When you're writing a novel about plain Vermonters, there's a limit to the types of philosophical debates and statements you can put into the mouths of the characters. People like that aren't going to talk about such issues as a rule and, in direct terms, they're hardly going to think about them. I make a point of just this when, at one point, Sally Page more or less snorts about "the universe"—because, really, people in rural Vermont don't hang around pondering the complexities of the universe. On the other hand, if someone like Peter Wagner uses and worries about the phrase in the paperback ["edition" of "The Smugglers of Lost Souls' Rock"] Sally is reading, I can work the concept into the novel. So because of the inside-novel, I'm able to raise philosophical issues which can be relocated into the outside-novel, even if a character gets the idea all wrong.

Reilly: It's funny, I recall telling my wife that in the second half of the book every time there was a shift to the "other" plot, I got angry and found myself tempted to skip over the new passage to keep the current plot going. I never did, and I'm glad I didn't. Also, as I recall, your focus on the Pages was pretty relentless toward the end.

Gardner: That's a risk I ran; Dos Passos ran it too. When you shift from one story to another—and I don't think Dos Passos solved the problem—you know the reader is going to be irritated. But ultimately you give a little to get a little. One thing I've learned over the years is that the whole art of fiction writing involves an intricate process of payments due: if you want a given effect, you have to pay for it. It's a thin line but it's fun to walk that line.

Reilly: You subtitled *Nickel Mountain* "A Pastoral Novel" and,

although I think I understand part of your thinking, I know I haven't
figured it all out. On an obvious level, there's the rural setting and the
feeling of love and peace. But when I recall Vergil and consider your
book, I find myself puzzled by the degree of violence you introduce
into the world of Henry Soames. At the end when I found him
beginning to eat too much again and almost longing for death, I
wondered, why is this pastoral? Why don't I have shepherds singing
happy songs?

Gardner: It's a fair question. It's funny, but I had been working
and working on that novel, trying to get a good hold on it, and the
day it finally clicked was when I realized I could use at least elements
of the pastoral form within it. As it turned out, it became a
combination of the Vergilian pastoral and the Christian pastoral.

Reilly: There's the problem. I don't think I know anything about
pastorals after Vergil. I think I don't get back on board until Milton's
"Lycidas."

Gardner: Sure you do. You must know Edmund Spenser's *Faerie
Queene*, which is really the culmination of the medieval pastoral. If
you think of *The Faerie Queene*'s allegorical nature and witches and
knights and whatever, maybe you'll get a feeling for what I had in
mind. At the same time, what I wanted to achieve in *Nickel Mountain*
was an effect similar to Vergil's in his pastorals. There is no
fundamental relationship between Vergil and, say, Sidney's *Arcadia*
or Spenser's *Faerie Queene*, but there is an effective relationship.
Vergil talks about complicated urban matters in an extremely
sophisticated way, and it's wonderful because he succeeds in
addressing issues and themes he could have never handled otherwise. So, one thing that attracted me to the pastoral was my
conviction that all the issues I considered important in my own world
could be included in the pastoral in a muted form.

The other aspect that appealed to me, and this is true with Vergil
and the others, is the way it concerns the individual within a given
community—the concurrent needs one has to be part of a
community and, concurrently, to retain his individuality. The way
Vergil solves this problem—discounting dialogue, debate and discussion—is through some kind of ritualistic act; that's what Sidney and
Spenser do too. So when I finally recognized the remarkable
potential of the pastoral in this respect—or, better, linked that

recognition with the problems I was having with my novel in progress—I was able to use that special notion of ritual to bring *Nickel Mountain* to its final state. In the book, then, you see the ritual of courtship, the ritual of the wedding, the rituals of birth and death, and so on. Since I tried constantly to emphasize the business of individual will, or freedom if you like, and the needs of the community, or order if you like, the book had to end with some type of ritualistic burial. It's an ironic burial, a disinterment, but it's a burial nonetheless.

Reilly: The burial of Henry Soames?

Gardner: Well, that's suggested; but for the old people at the end, there's the burial of an old, old war. That kind of thing.

Reilly: *Nickel Mountain* contains some of the most gripping scenes and remarkable characters you've ever created. The birth of the child is wonderfully handled, as is the tension you develop when he's alone in the shed on the mountain. And I think Simon Bale is an awesome creation. Was he based on anyone?

Gardner: Not on any person I ever met. When I was a graduate student at Iowa I had a friend named Jim Cox—a wonderful writer who later killed himself—who had a job as a desk clerk in a small flop house. I had an office next to his and he would frequently bring home stories about this madman out at the hotel where he worked. The guy would frequently hand out pamphlets, a lot of which wound up in Jim's office, and to make a long story short I wanted to combine Jim's stories, the pamphlets and my own experiences to create, in Simon Bale, a portrait of a special kind of narrow-minded Christian bigotry. If I succeeded in that respect, though, I failed in another one. I made a terrible mistake in handling Bale, one which I remain sorry for and will atone for in another novel, by representing Bale's doctrines as those of the Jehovah Witnesses. I was simply wrong. Jehovah Witnesses can be a very offensive group—not always, but they can be—but they're a lot smarter than, say, the severely fundamentalist Baptists. This individual I learned about through Jim Cox was one of the Jehovah Witnesses and there are some Jehovah Witnesses traits about Simon Bale. But I made a mistake when I assigned his particular doctrines to that sect.

Reilly: There were so many strong passages in the novel—the way you handled Callie's mind before the wedding, for instance.

Gardner: I liked that part too and I liked Callie, although I've been advised by some women readers—probably they wouldn't object to being described as "feminists"—that there is a definite "male chauvinist pig" bias to *Nickel Mountain* and that one of my failures is my characterization of Callie. I was saddened to learn they felt that way because I feel Callie is a stabilizing force in the book. Then again, I suppose I should listen respectfully to such criticism since I'll willingly concede that, as a writer, I am not deeply involved with popular causes, no matter how worthy they are. As a writer, I'm not a spokesman for Blacks or women or Jews; I'm concerned only with describing and commenting upon the world as it is at the time I describe it. I guess one of the prices I pay as a novelist is that a character I admire, care deeply about, and worked hard on can run afoul of a particular movement. But if the character "exists" outside the movement, what can you do? Millie in *Sunlight Dialogues* is a wonderful character, a genuinely brilliant woman—at least I hope she comes through that way. But, of course, she's going to be a bitch in that time and place. To me, she's a magnificent bitch and it's only when she's broken by the Sunlight Man that she can evolve into a completely wonderful person. Feminists have objected to my handling of Millie and feminists think I depicted Callie as a stupid woman. But, damn it, Callie is the one who knows how to get things done; she's not very articulate but I feel she's resourceful and intelligent and almost entirely admirable.

Reilly: I certainly admired her. And I felt that sense of impermanence about her prospects with Henry testifies to the genuineness of her character, and the strength. I wonder if those critics assign to Callie their own maturity and forget she's still in her teens through most of the novel.

Gardner: I'm sure they do.

Reilly: Of course, I did ache a bit when she modernized that splendidly sleazy old restaurant.

Gardner: I know what you mean, but she was right: a person with children has no right not to worry about them. Someone wrote in a magazine, critically, that Callie had emasculated Henry, but that's not fair. It's true that Henry wants to continue living his odd kind of life and Callie does make some radical changes to it. But no one has a right to raise a kid in a shanty like that, especially if he's got the money to improve things.

Reilly: The characters in *Nickel Mountain* seem different from the characters in, I think, all your other books in the sense that they seem so much more vulnerable and so much less able to rage and fight back against the world around them. I think that in every other book of yours, the characters will take only so much guff and then will fire a beer bottle at you. Is that an accurate comment?

Gardner: It's true, it's true. But *Nickel Mountain* was the only time I really wrote about simple people. It's not immediately apparent in *Sunlight Dialogues*, for example, but Fred Clumly is a very well-educated man. All those years on the boats in the merchant marine, he read and read—he read all of Dante, for instance. That happens in the merchant marine, believe me.

Reilly: You weren't in them, were you?

Gardner: No, but I knew a lot of people in them and, God, I wanted to join! I used to go up to Buffalo port when I was a kid and watch those ships go out. Ah, those guys with their black sweaters and black hats—free as birds. That's what I wanted! You know, I wore a black sweater all through high school and, to be honest, I didn't realize until this very moment that was the reason. But, to get back to the point, Clumly is a complicated and intelligent person, although he doesn't probe deeply into his unconscious mind. But he does dream and his impulses and memories are those of a well-read man. When he drives into his yard that first time and has a vague sense that some animal is going to be waiting for him, for example, he's thinking about the animals of Dante—it's spelled out in the text. So he knows a lot and he's able to bring it to bear. But he also has a cop's mind. He's an analyzer and he's capable of ruthlessness, and that puts him in a position of strength. Conversely, Henry Soames could be fairly described as someone who doesn't know much more than he's gleaned from a few grade-school books. Callie is even more poorly educated. She was a bad student, her father can barely read, her mother isn't much better off. Limiting my characters that way was a challenge, but it was also a joy. In fact, I came to realize the argument and theme of the book demanded such characters. In the early drafts of *Nickel Mountain*, I depicted Henry as something of a reader, but I ended up with nothing but his bookshelves crammed with his father's books, books he can't and won't ever get around to.

Reilly: You've described such diverse scenes: the bogs of Old

England, the ships of ancient Greece, even a prison in Sparta. How
do you know what such things looked like? When you write about,
say, a prison in Sparta, is it just a matter of letting your imagination
go, or do you find yourself doing an enormous amount of research?

Gardner: I've done my share of looking things up, and I read
incessantly. But, no, I don't write novels from reference books. I do
carry around an awful lot of poetry and fiction in my head. As I
recall, when I was trying to recreate the outside of the Spartan prison
[in *The Wreckage of Agathon*] I found myself thinking about the
prison where Dante sent Cavalcanti. It was a pretty awful place—
plague-ridden, holes in the walls, and whatever. And for the inside of
the prison, I spent most of my time concentrating on a chicken coop:
packed dirt floors, straw, dead chickens here and there. *The
Wreckage of Agathon* was a complex book for me to write because I
was working with a number of issues. Certainly I was thinking of the
classical world, but a lot of the time I was playing with Jean-Paul
Sartre. He's a writer I love and hate. I think he's one of the finest
writers who ever lived, and yet there are so many issues of
consequence where I think he's wrong, wrong, wrong. He makes a
number of individual points that are accurate but. . . . Anyhow, the
idea of a creature lying in the straw reminded me of a dead chicken in
a coop and that in turn provided me with imagery which made the
describing of the prison uncomplicated. I used it again in "The King's
Indian," the same kind of image, although it was slightly different
because by then I had been to Maletesta's castle in Tuscany and had
a better idea of what such a prison might have looked like.

Reilly: I think one of the biggest surprises I've ever had in reading
occurred when I started on *Jason and Medeia* and discovered, first, it
was a massive poem, nearly 350 pages, and then it was an *epic*
poem to boot. I spent so many years plowing through Homer and
Vergil, and my encounters with Dante and Milton were limited to
classrooms. They're all dead now, so is Joyce. But I can ask you: had
you always wanted to compose an epic? Was it a long-standing,
almost obsessive ambition?

Gardner: No. As a matter of fact it was very strange how my
Jason and Medeia came to be. I had just written *Grendel* and was still
getting over a very unpleasant time I had working on the galleys.
What happened was, I had labored over the narrative rhythms of the

book and, unconsciously, had placed a good deal of emphasis upon the way the line-breaks in my manuscript influenced the rhythms of the text. When I got the galleys, of course, I was dismayed to see that the effect had been lost because the typesetter, probably a computer, had arranged "his" line-breaks simply according to syllabication and letters-per-line.

Reilly: I guess the book was printed in that, well, "unsatisfactory" way, wasn't it? I don't recall unjustified margins in it.

Gardner: Correct, it was printed the way the typesetter arranged it, I'm sorry to say. So at that point I decided my next book would not be controlled by typesetters and, after fiddling with a number of forms, I came up with something I call "sprung hexameters." You know, I'm convinced that's what Homer came up with as well, although no classicist will ever agree with me. Believe me, I don't read Homer's lines the way you do. But I found out that when you use sprung hexameters—in other words, when you inch some unstressed syllables "up" a bit, and inch some stressed syllables "down" a bit, as I think Homer does—you're able to achieve a wonderful effect, an effect I feel Homer achieves throughout the *Odyssey*. When he wants to move up into a truly poetic sound, he really hits those dactyls. And when he's concentrating more on functional achievement rather than poetic effect, when he wants to fill in some narrative gaps, he sort of inches down into a form that is quite similar to prose. Just look at the translations. Lattimore realized this and that's why his translation is so brilliant; Fitzgerald missed it and that's why his is so sugary. I'm not denying Lattimore's vices, of course. He wrote "the sound of their mourning moved through the rooms of the house," which is a preposterous translation of Homer's "the two men cried."

Reilly: So you used Lattimore's hexameter form in *Jason and Medeia*; none of Homer's dactyls, in other words?

Gardner: Correct, I felt it was the most manageable form I could find, and it worked—just the way it works for Anglo-Saxon poetry. If you believe Hopkins' theory[4] about Anglo-Saxon poetry, and I absolutely do, it works similarly, with the obvious exception that you're using a six-beat, not a four-beat, line. There are moments when I vary it, of course, but there I do so deliberately, for effect—the way Homer does in his "Song of the Sirens."

Reilly: I have to smile to hear you speak about deliberately inconsistent lines. I recall one of the more frustrating assignments I had as an undergraduate was to finish off the famous "unfinished" lines of Vergil's *Aeneid*. The theory was, as I recall it, Vergil dropped dead before he could finish off certain lines, and the least we could do would be to fill in the gaps.

Gardner: My theory is Vergil didn't finish the poem because the politicians brought him to a point where either he was getting back at them or he didn't want to look at his own text. Recall that he got the job when Caesar Augustus said, "Okay, Professor Vergil, I want you to write a wonderful celebration of me." Vergil did produce a magnificent work of art, but the whole time he was surrounded by ignorant politicians who kept praising the *Aeneid* as a celebration of Roman politicians. It must have been maddening, and I think it's no accident that Vergil keeps slipping in lines that say in effect: "If we had known what we were doing, we probably wouldn't have done it." Recall the Dido episode where Aeneas says if he had thought Dido would have gone through with her suicide, he wouldn't have left.

Reilly: I think one of the finest moments in *Jason and Medeia* is where you have Oedipus lament the horror and waste of Dido's death. I think Oedipus says "Life is a foolish dream in the eyes of the Unnameable," and then he refuses to continue advising people. Beautiful. I guess I'm a softy there, since I've always felt the Dido passages are the finest moments in the *Aeneid*.

Gardner: It's a brilliant moment and, in fairness to my source, Vergil got most of that out of Apollonius' *Argonautica*. Vergil's passages are frequently indebted to Apollonius' writing. He felt the only two poets he would set above himself were Homer and Apollonius and he leaned heavily on each. Oddly, he seemed to have little use for the tragedians—which is a shame since it wouldn't have hurt him to have studied Euripides more carefully.

Reilly: An aspect of *Jason and Medeia* that surprised me was the active—I won't say intrusive because he wasn't—and conspicuous part your narrator played. Was that your own invention? I don't recall such a narrator in Apollonius; did you have some literary predecessor in mind?

Gardner: Sure, the greatest epic in the Middle Ages, after Dante. In *Troilus and Criseyde*, Chaucer's narrator very definitely involves himself in the story, and even cuts into it on occasion. He knows the outcome and knows better, but still he'll get emotional and butt in to excuse someone for doing an awful thing, or he'll frump at Troilus for misunderstanding Pandarus. The only difference is, I pushed it a little farther. It's clear that Chaucer's narrator in *Troilus* is a fourteenth-century Englishman looking back at history. He's in control, he's a good scholar, and so on. The narrator in *Jason and Medeia* doesn't understand Greek as well as he might—I know the feeling. I have to resort to a lexicon every time out—and literally fumbles about in the story. His glasses get stepped on at one point; he frequently frets about the relationship between fiction and reality. Chaucer played with that relationship, of course, but he was kidding, he wasn't terribly worried about it.

A hundred years later he wouldn't have been kidding, though. Oxford was closed and, like a black hole in time, the fifteenth century happened. So much of the wisdom in the fourteenth century was killed, literally killed, in the plague. The Dominicans were the great brains of the century, the first to go out and "minister" because they were good doctors. Then the Franciscans took over, but in a short time they were all wiped out. Things were reduced to a situation in which the church was the only educated body; a Hitler-like fiend was on the throne in Henry IV; every decent mind in the country, like Thomas Malory, was in prison.

I feel strongly that if all this hadn't happened, if the fourteenth century had been allowed to survive, we would have gone right to where we are now. Some of the rationalists were already at the point of understanding that poetry is a way of seeing and that all ways of seeing are limited. Amazingly, the most outlandish thing I've said about medieval literature is the only thing my fellow medievalists have quietly accepted—typically I'm treated to a good-natured crucifixion before anyone gets around to thinking about what I said. What I said was, carry the Chaucer-narrator to its last logical step and you'll find an art form where there is no division between art and reality.

Reilly: Our talking about narration and narrators brings to mind a narrator whom I consider unlike any other you've come up with, the one in "The King's Indian." Perhaps I'm wrong but I felt your novella was a story about the art of storytelling.

Gardner: Well . . . would you settle for a story about art in general?

Reilly: I was thinking about the reversals—the captain becomes the dummy, Miranda seems to become a number of things—and the numerous literary allusions. Coleridge's mariner is in there, Melville's *Benito Cereno* seems to be kicking around. I think at one point you said you wrote the novella with the help of Poe and Melville.

Gardner: Right, Melville, Poe and Twain. Melville was a Yankee who believed the hope of the world rested in machines. But he was also afraid of machines, worried about them, because he was a man who hated slavery of any kind. Poe was a man who was unlike any American in history, but I think he was the greatest genius produced in America. Even though he died young, I think he *created* modern literature. Do you want me to digress and tell you why?

Reilly: I'd love to hear why.

Gardner: He created all the forms. He created what we like to call "Post-Modern Fiction," for example. When Kafka writes in his "Metamorphosis" that Gregor Samsa awakens to find himself transformed into a live vermin—not a cockroach, by the way, that's a poor translation—what he's doing is reopening the "Cask of Amontillado." Poe was the first man in the world to discover that narrative fiction needn't be limited to the Aristotelian task of explaining how things happened. Poe said, "I don't care how things *happened*, I'll tell you what happens now." In "Cask of Amontillado," there is no background for the story, not even an implied background. There's a carnival outside, there's the sealing-off of the guy inside, and that's it. He starts near the end—which is the name of the game in Post-Modern fiction. That's what Bob Coover does all the time, it's what I do part of the time.

Poe invented the pirate story: "The Gold Bug" is the first pirate story in any kind of modern sense. Obviously Smollett and others worked with the idea, but it was Poe who came up with the first truly modern pirate story. Being Poe, he didn't capitalize on it and so he presented a very smart businessman across the ocean, his name was Stevenson, with a chance to cash in on it some forty years later. Poe invented the Doppelgänger story. There had been psychological studies of Doppelgängers, but no one had seen this was a literary possibility until Poe came along—and recall how many years elapsed before Dostoyevsky raised it to similar levels. Again, poor Poe. He produced this brilliant, brilliant tale called "William Wilson" and didn't follow it up. Then in the 1880's Stevenson picked it up and within two months started *Dr. Jekyll and Mr. Hyde*. Poe invented the detective story—virtually out of nothing, although there were some feeble attempts in that direction before he got to work on it. It was only after a few decades that another Englishman, Arthur Conan Doyle, followed his lead and made some money out of it. And think about how "Poesque" Doyle's circumstances were: he was pressed for money, he had a young wife, that wife was dying of consumption, and suddenly he decided to write detective fiction. Poe had such an incredibly fertile imagination. He kept hitting on new forms, each a literary breakthrough in itself, and then moving like lightning from one to the next.

But to get back to the question. The problem with Poe, and this is the quality that thinking people object to in his writing, is that he supported and profoundly believed in a form of human slavery because he was terrified of the slavery of machines. He talks about this at some length in *Eureka*. In Melville, then, you have the best possible Yankee, and in Poe the best possible southerner; and in Mark Twain you have someone who floats in-between and hates them both—particularly the late Mark Twain who, after his daughter died, just scorned all possibilities. He was a madman, but he was right. Twain's wisdom in perceiving the errors of Poe and Melville, then, takes us right into the twentieth century. To be specific, Twain could see that Poe was right where Melville was wrong: machines are pretty dangerous, but still they're a good idea. And he could see that Melville was right where Poe was wrong: slavery is repulsive, and it doesn't matter that slaves might preserve us from the horrors of a mechanistic age.

Now, back to "King's Indian." I thought about these various ideas, especially in their literary embodiments, and I asked myself where did they all come from? My conclusion was they all came from Coleridge. So, using Coleridge as the rock upon which the castles of Melville, Poe and Twain were built, I decided to write a book of my own. Now at the time a very close friend of mine—indeed my best friend, who was a superb sculptor and artist—was dying and I couldn't handle it. I wanted to write about it, though not directly, and because my friend participated so splendidly in the field of art, particularly American art, I wanted to write about art too. The result was this strange novella which is all about literature, but is really a book about literature shoring against the ruins of a beloved friend. Literature is, after all, largely concerned with death, so I gathered together *Moby Dick* and *The Narrative of A. Gordon Pym* and *Life on the Mississippi* and a bit of *Huckleberry Finn*, and I tied in the voice of Coleridge.

Reilly: I don't pretend to have caught all that, although I enjoyed the tale and was deeply stirred by it, and I'm not sure I follow all this now. I can't help but recall, listening to you say all this, the lines in Coleridge's *Ancient Mariner* when the spell is finally broken because the mariner can finally recognize the beauty of any living thing and he "blessed them unaware."

Gardner: Sure, exactly.

Reilly: It's odd but, as we talk, I can perceive and marvel at all that went into that tale, and yet I can still recall being captivated by it on the most mindless level. I was fascinated by Miranda, for example; she was a wonderful creation.

Gardner: That's important too and it's something a writer must never forget: story telling *is* storytelling. I did work very hard on Miranda and I guess she's my ex-wife Joan . . . I *know* she is. All my books are really about Joan, an incredibly brilliant woman.

Reilly: You've done so many things and done them so well. You also seem to have no inclination to repeat yourself. I wonder what's left? Do you have any overwhelming desires for new projects?

Gardner: For better or for worse, my whole life is art. Yes, there are three things I want very much to do. I have a couple of novels that I want to write—they're both more or less in progress, hundreds of pages of drafts—but I don't think I'll finish another novel for a long time. One is about an ocean. The other is about Rasputin—about the sudden crash of all medieval thought at the moment of Rasputin's death. As long as Rasputin lived, Russia was in the Middle Ages—which is a good place to be. But when he died, a couple of weeks later the Czar and Czarina and Czarevitch died—because Rasputin was the only force powerful enough to keep them from being murdered by the Bolsheviks. Shortly after that Russia was making war plans, and that was the end of that. So, the kind of art I write is supposed to be a desperate holding action against the forces of barbarism, which I think are all around us.

The other thing I do is teach, and what I find myself teaching more and more is writing, a very moral kind of writing. I find myself harping and harping on the moral obligations of a writer and how civilization depends on his fulfilling those obligations. In this sense I am trying to attack in the most powerful way I can what I think is corrupt art and to support what I think is healthy art.

It's urgent to me that I can in some way contribute to the teaching and recognition of moral art and, of course, to the recognition of the enormous amount of technique that's an integral part of art's moral nature. The more I live and the more I write, I see that art and morality are critical parts of a whole. If you think about it and interpret it fully, you can see that the ultimate morality is, in a sense, getting the line right.

[1]Geoffrey Wolff, "Trench Warfare on the Borders of Reality," *Book World: The Washington Post*, 24 Dec. 1972, 3.

[2]Morris Dickstein, "Bizarre Invention, a Translation without an Original," *New York Times Book Review* 1, July 1973, 4.

[3]Subsequently published as *On Moral Fiction* (New York: Basic Books, 1978).

[4]Gardner refers to Gerard Manley Hopkins' "creation" of a type of verse he chose to call "sprung rhythm." Reduced to simple terms, a poem in sprung rhythm contains four feet, but each foot may contain any number of unstressed syllables. As Gardner observes, the similarity to Anglo-Saxon verse is unmistakable. Hopkins observed it too and specifically cited *Piers Plowman* as one of his inspirations. A more elaborate description of the intricacies of sprung rhythm is contained in a letter by Hopkins. He describes it as "something like abrupt (rhythm, which) applies to rights only where one stress follows another running, without syllables between." See *The Correspondence of G.M.H. and Richard Watson Dixon*, ed. C.C. Abbott, 2nd ed. (London: Oxford University Press, 1955), p. 23.

Where Philosophy and Fiction Meet:
An Interview with John Gardner
Marshall L. Harvey/1977

From *Chicago Review*, 29 (Spring 1978), 73-87. Copyright ©
1978 by Marshall L. Harvey. Reprinted by permission of the
University of Chicago Press.

This interview was conducted in November 1977.

Marshall L. Harvey: You've said that Whitehead and Sartre have
had a great impact on your writing. How have they influenced
you?—how do philosophers influence novelists in general?

John Gardner: Basically writing is a kind of philosophy. Good
writers see their work as a way of testing abstract ideas in the real
world. What happens—though not all good writers are conscious of
what they do—is that you take an abstract idea, your own or
somebody else's, and then you imagine real characters in a real city
in a real world and you put the characters through kind of a
laboratory experiment testing the idea. For example, Dostoevsky
reads Nietzsche and he's interested in Nietzsche's theory of the
superman—for a lot of reasons. For one thing, Dostoevsky had
inclinations in that direction, a touch of megalomania certainly, and a
touch of the outlaw. He makes up a character who is *exactly* the kind
of student that in the real world of St. Petersburg would indeed be
attracted to those ideas. Raskolnikov would naturally, being exactly
the kind of person he is, have certain friends, relatives, associations,
and Dostoevsky introduces them, makes a kind of perfect laboratory
experiment and then just watches what happens—kind of "oonches"
it from time to time, putting pressure on Raskolnikov, seeing how
he'll react to this and that and setting up an ideal cop, Porfiry. No cop
as smart as Porfiry ever existed, but if he did that would be a test of
the superman idea. A good writer, I think, takes the most important
ideas of his time—a great writer—and pushes them. Melville
obviously is the best novelist we've ever had of that kind. Everybody

in Melville's time was worried about the possibility of a brute existent universe, as Sartre would say. Moby Dick, the whale, was a perfect representative of it, and Ahab is a perfect tester of it.

When I was a kid in college, the most interesting course I ever had, in a way, was a course in philosophy. And the way I really came across it was in Plato. I had read Plato but before the course I didn't understand him. And when I came to Whitehead my head went off because—not so much that he's a great philosopher, although he is, but—I felt he said what I would say. That is to say his world-view, incredibly, was like the world-view I had developed—born with it or whatever—so that a lot of times when I'm working with a philosophical question or problem of some kind, I think, "What would Whitehead say?" and then I try that out, dramatizing it; or "What would Whitehead do with this?" As long as you work with pure philosophy, you work with abstract, logical suppositions and logical necessities coming out of those suppositions. The result, as Aquinas found, is that you prove something but you only prove it abstractly, as in mathematics. What Aquinas discovered, the reason that he dropped his *Summa*—he discovered the horrifying thing the Nazis discovered—that absolutely rigorous argument can lead to mutually exclusive positions. So Aquinas quit on this and turned to mysticism. In the same way Dante, in 1300, after the death of Cavalcanti, quit on reason and decided it meant nothing, and he went to a different basis of knowledge. He remembered that there were certain things that he couldn't say to Beatrice because with her eyes on him, he felt that to say them would feel like pettiness or lying. That's the way modern thought goes. We argue by moral intuitions, because otherwise the only test we have for truth is an untrustworthy one, that it's a part of a theory. Argument by honest feeling can of course be an excuse to cheat in philosophy, as Bradley did perhaps, that is to say, to develop an easy, optimistic philosophy—or think of the wishful, optimistic philosophy of Marxism. But if you're aware of that danger, then I think it's useful to ask, "Would I tell this 'truth' to my kid?" If you wouldn't, then the "truth" may well be an illusion. If you would, then certain or not, you say it. I'm not saying any old truth will do; great novels are important because they test supposed truths convincingly. But looking for tentative truths is important. It seems to me that knowing the truth about the world is a kind of defense, it protects you from all kinds of terrible things that can happen, and maybe will, and so even unpleasant truths have to be told.

The two philosophers that really thrilled me were Whitehead and Sartre because I thought Whitehead was right and because I thought Sartre, for all his popularity, was wrong—though it's true that Whitehead doesn't write very well—he writes good philosophy, but the writing is kind of boring—whereas Sartre writes like an angel. That's the thing that fascinates me. Sartre is my great love-hate, kind of because he's a horror intellectually, figuratively, and morally, but he's a wonderful writer and anything he says you believe, at least for the moment, because of the way he says it. In *The Wreckage of Agathon*, I take one of his most glorious passages, the passage on the brute existent. He talks about a mountain, and the image he uses is so powerful that you believe everything he says, but if you change the image to a mean and kind of crazy elephant, you *don't* believe anything he says. So in that passage I just made the substitution and everything else I translated directly from the French. I use Sartre a lot. What happened in *Grendel* was that I got the idea of presenting the Beowulf monster as Jean-Paul Sartre, and everything that Grendel says Sartre in one mood or another has said, so that my love of Sartre kind of comes through as my love of the monster, though monsters are still monsters—I hope.

MLH: You said that the philosophy you found in Plato was like the kind of world you imagined when you were a child. How was that?

JG: It's just that I grew up in a religious family and Christianity doesn't have any firm metaphysic, just something absolute in the sky—indefinite absolutes, like maybe gold as the ideal material for paving streets, or harps as the ideal instruments. In many ways, it's a historical religion, one thing one day, another thing the next. There have been so many metaphysicians, Augustine to Aquinas—Bishop Pike for that matter. So when you come to Plato you have a firm, well thought-out metaphysic that fits the Christian metaphysical intuition, which of course is the reason that the Christians found out about Plato. The only trouble is that once you see clearly what Plato is saying and you see clearly how it applies to Christianity, I think what happens is you don't whole-heartedly believe in either Plato's system *or* Christianity. This is not to say that you're against God or charity or any other value. It's just that the overall system doesn't convince you.

MLH: Do you write for the sheer pleasure of writing?

JG: Yeah. But it's a very complicated pleasure. My fiction, it's a way of thinking things out. Thinking things out that are interesting. It's fundamentally philosophical fiction, and the joy of it is that I reach discoveries—besides the fact that you imitate characters, people you know. That's a lot of fun, getting exactly the way they talk and what they're really like. But ultimately, the thing that's thrilling about it, the reason that I write kind of slowly in spite of my alleged speed of writing—I discover things I never would have dreamed of. I'm working now, working for the last two years, on a long story, a novel. It's about 130 pages long now. God knows what it'll come to. But I've been working with that old question everybody works with, time and space. The thing that I'm doing is trying to work out the connections between all our human cultures, our immiscible definitions, discordant ideas about time, space, birth and death—you know, modern physicists, the ancient Sumerians, the tump-builders. A tump is this man-made hill with a hole, facing east, and on the 22nd of December, the winter solstice, when the sun breaks, the first ray of sunlight hits a spiral carved in the rock, in the center of the tump. Spirals show up everywhere in connection with time and space. The ancient Indians believed that the universe is a spiral, and modern physics supports them—that is to say if you shoot a ray of light in any direction it will follow the curve of space till it hits where it started, except that space has expanded so that it's a spiral, an infinite spiral. In our various cultures the spiral gets related to sex, death, all sorts of things. What I really want to do, if I possibly can, is understand from inside, intuitively, the relationship between these correspondences—I mean the Tibetan *Book of the Dead* implies a similar universe, the Egyptians had the same images in a funny way, except they locked them in a circle, and so on. What I want to do is write fiction in which characters' actions and what they say and what they know comment directly on the questions that are philosophically engaging, and when I get done I want to really know about time and space—know what human beings have known before me. You know, everybody knows certain things. I'm forty-four. Forty years ago I used to sit and watch the long, long night pass. I still do. It takes as long now as it ever did, in spite of what psychiatrists say, but I can remember those nights forty years ago as if they'd happened an instant ago, which means that my whole life is just an instant, which means that the whole life of the world is just an instant, which means that the whole life of the universe is an instant, which means what's it all for? Right? How do we escape it?—how does the universe escape it? It seems to me that that's exactly what the tump-builders, the pyramid-builders worried about and it seems to me that some of them may have had an answer. William Blake thought he did. Now I don't believe Blake's answers but he certainly did. And I want to break that in a way that I absolutely believe. Not that I want to start a new religion or be known as a philosopher; I just want to understand it and present it in a dramatic way so that everybody in the world understands it, so that the relationship between the spiral and the universe and the fact that it's a male symbol and that the coil is a female symbol—all of those things are perfectly clear, at least to intuition. That's what I do. That's the pure enjoyment of it, and it takes forever to work it out, but when you do work out some idea there's an incredible feeling of satisfaction because you're sure you're right. And when you look at other books, like *The Iliad, The Odyssey, The Divine Comedy,* and you realize that of course they got it before you—it's amazing how all the brilliant people got the same stuff—but I can't get it myself by a process of criticism. I can only get it from inside, intuitively.

MLH: Do you think there is such a thing as a good novel which has no effect on the way people live?

JG: I don't think there is. Some people do, like Bill Gass, and John Barth does, I think. I know what Bill Gass says. I'm not sure what John Barth would say, but I believe absolutely that art always affects life. If a creative work of art has no effect on life, then its effect on life is that it tells the reader that life is not that important. Just making a beautiful object has an effect on life—it makes unbeautiful objects noticeably what they are. But I think it's much more than that. If you believe that art has no effect on life then it's possible to do this: to create a character in a story who is a deep and terrible anti-Semite and never bring up the question of anti-Semitism, take him all the way through the story but never bring him into any problem or confrontation because "it's just a work of art and has nothing to do with life," right? But you know perfectly well that if Sherlock Holmes was a Jew-hater and he never got his comeuppance, there would be more anti-Semites in the world than there are. Every time you set up a character, you set up a model, whether you mean to or not, so that a writer has to be enormously careful what he sets up at that level. I think people consciously and devotedly imitate Kojak. When *On the Waterfront* came out, everybody I knew started hanging a cigarette off his lip. Everyone smoked in the normal ways before, but after that movie everybody in town hung a cigarette off their lip and turned their collar up. After the first movie I saw, when I was about seven, with Roy Rogers, everyone in my school started to squint.

MLH: As a very successful novelist, do you feel any pressure to change each novel you write in subject matter or style? Or is that something a writer shouldn't be worried about?

JG: No, I certainly don't think it's something writers should worry about at all. I do because of the joy of pushing the form. I've tried poetry, I've tried radio plays, stage plays, television, movies, and I'm interested in what you can do, what the different limitations are, what you are allowed to say, what kind of discoveries you can make. It's like when you take some kind of foreign language. When you start thinking in Old French, you start thinking thoughts that you could never have thought in English. Or when you look at Greek, suddenly you have tenses that make you see the world in a way you have never before seen it, so that it's a joy. You learn what a short story can do, what kind of machine it is, what kind of microscope, and then you find out what a novel can do, what a radio play can do. It's a pleasure for me to try different forms. I don't think that it's something a writer *should* do. . . . It's not necessary to experiment. It's true, though, I think, for my personality, that it's important for me not to repeat.

MLH: Why is that?

JG: Well, I like variety, I like constant surprises, not the same old meat and potatoes all the time. Basically, I write for some reader who is just like me, that is, just like me when I was mostly reading. I know that when I realized that I had read the last Dickens novel, I felt absolutely awful, deeply depressed, because it's one thing to read them over, and another to think that there's another one, and I want that kind of reader, if such a reader exists, for my own work. I change my approach from work to work, in the same way that Dickens's

novels change drastically—though there are always certain like-
nesses—so that after years of non-realistic writing I've been through a
phase, for a few years, where I've been playing, flirting with realism.
I'm out of it again because finally it doesn't fit me, but I like trying
different things.

MLH: Do you see any value in classifying your works by genre?

JG: When I called *Nickel Mountain* a pastoral, it was only to call
attention to certain qualities of the work that the reader might not get
otherwise. But I don't think it is necessary. The main reason that it's
not important to classify is that in every highly sophisticated age, like
the thirteenth century, like now, like Alexandria, what happens is that
the good writers do everything they do by genre-jumping. For
instance, Faulkner in "Spotted Horses" writes what would be a
traditional southwest-humor yarn, but it's a short story, because he's
crossing, he's "hybreeding" (I don't know if such a word exists)—he's
giving a mixture of the sophisticated short story and the old-fashioned
yarn, and he's getting new values out of everything—style, characters, events. In the same way Chaucer would take the romance or the
fabliau and cross it with the epic. It gives you a new instrument. It
basically comes to the fact for me that literature, writing, is a way of
thinking about things and when you change your instrument, you see
different things. The result is that when you write a tale and you cross
it with the short story or you write a tale and you cross it with the
yarn or the sketch or whatever, what comes out is something you
never could have dreamed would come out. I mean you know the
plot and the characters, but the genres you're pushing make you see
things where you wouldn't have seen without them. It's like when
you throw a lay of tarot cards in a reading for your sister, and the
Seven of Swords comes up in the position that has to do with
domestic life. You would never have thought that the Seven of
Swords would have anything to do with your sister's domestic life,
but now you think about it and you realize things about her domestic
life that you never would have thought of. In other words, you're
freezing yourself from familiar patterns, and by breaking the patterns
you see things you hadn't seen before. It's similar to the idea that in
some African languages there are more colors than there are in
English, even among painters—there are hundreds of colors because
it's important to know this blue from that blue—maybe one's a
spider, one's a snake, one's a fly, and so on—and when you know

those words, you see more colors. At least that's what neurologists say. If it's true, it suggests that writing in different genres should help you see things you wouldn't have seen before. Every genre you invent is a new pair of spectacles. That's what I do. I keep jumping like crazy.

MLH: Why isn't realism for you? Did you work with it and then get tired of it, or—

JG: Yeah, I think it's just that I got tired of it. The other thing about it is that it's kind of an inefficient form for me. You have to spend so much time in a realistic work documenting that these people really lived in Minneapolis that you can't get to what's important to you. If you think about the opening line of some of Isak Dinesen's stories: "After the death of Leonidas, Angelino Santisillia resolved that he would never sleep again. Will the narrator be believed that Angelino kept this resolve? Nevertheless it is the case." In a tale the writer doesn't have to fill in who Leonidas was, or how Angelino kept himself awake, or anything. The reader just believes it. It's what Coleridge is talking about when he speaks of the "willing suspension of disbelief," as opposed to what Wordsworth was talking about. The non-realistic method is much faster, and you can go so much deeper so much quicker. In *Pierre*, Melville opens up with a parody of the Byronic style because the parody, calling up the conventions it does, frees him to go straight to the psychological. He doesn't have to deal with junk.

MLH: Where did you get the idea for the Goat Lady in *Nickel Mountain*?

JG: There was a Goat Lady that came through western New York when I was a kid, and she was a very strange lady. I more or less borrowed her from life and made her a kind of contrast to Henry Soames. That is, the one thing that's most noticeable about her is that she's a loving mother. The trouble is that she's an idiot, and Henry Soames is very much like the loving mother, and he is in a certain way an idiot, but in other ways he's not. It was meant finally as a symbolic contrast.

MLH: Some of the stories in *The King's Indian*, "King Gregor and the Fool," "Muriel," and "Queen Louisa," seem unlike anything else you've written. Was this just a short experiment, or will you do more of this in the future?

JG: No. There won't be more of that, though that series actually ends with another story published in *Esquire* called "Trumpeter." *In the Suicide Mountains* is slightly related. It's not the kind of thing I'll pursue because the philosophical kind of thing I was working on at that time I worked out, and I needed that form to work with those particular aesthetic questions. I don't anticipate going back to it.

MLH: Could you state the philosophical questions you were working with?

JG: The trouble with doing that is that if you do it, then high school teachers will tell students, and they won't see anything else in the story, so that if I forget to say something, I'm shot down. But basically, I'm sure that everything in *The King's Indian* is about literary form and literary form as a vehicle of vision. The way I think the collection works generally is that the opening stories are fairly dark and each one up to the last one in the first section presents a kind of miraculous or "absurd" resurrection. In "Pastoral Care," the minister is caught up in neo-orthodoxy, the kind of thing John Updike is very interested in, which I think is a bad idea, and in the end he loses his self-consciousness, his priggishness, and he's a minister, which is his resurrection. The last story in the group, "The Warden," is about a man who is a destroyer, and the hopeful guy is his father the artist, but the hopeful possibility is kept muted. "John Napper Sailing Through the Universe" is my fundamental theory of art, which I'm now spelling out in a different, more discursive way in a book which comes out from Basic Books this spring, called *On Moral Fiction*, but what John Napper says is the heart of it: the artist can't just describe the world, "bitter reality"; the artist has to create new and wonderful possibilities. What happens in the Queen Louisa stories is that the princess has died; Queen Louisa has gone crazy; and, having no way to make anything out of the fact that the princess is dead and everything's awful, she in her insanity creates a new world, which gets better and better. When I get to "The King's Indian," I do the whole thing in a more serious and complex way, using the greatest writers of the American tradition along with the one English poet who had more influence on American fiction, I think, than anybody else. I'm not sure American literature professors would agree with me, but I think it's true and I think I could prove it. I think the two most important influences on American literature from the beginning to the present have been Keats and Coleridge, and of the

two the most important was Coleridge. Anyway, "The King's Indian"
uses the Yankee Melville, the Southerner Poe, and the middle-man
Twain as a sort of basis, and Coleridge as a sort of background. It's
an attempt to create a new world—a vision—which at the same time
is a story of the American democracy, a people's self-expression in
their ship of state, "The New Jerusalem." The whole book is a study
in aesthetics—aesthetics I think in the only sense that really counts, as
it expresses people through a theory of beauty. Aesthetics can never
be completely abstract, it has to be derived from the physical
expression of a theory in people's feelings and lives, so that to study it
you make up characters and you show what happens if they shape
their world by this aesthetic standard or by that one—this idea of the
sublime or that one—and hopefully what you come to is true art,
which everybody can share in. It puts all artistic approaches in
perspective. The true storyteller, like Jonathan Upchurch, in "The
King's Indian," is a model for all artists—intuition in the service of
King Reason—therefore the eternal artist, God on earth. So basically
it's a book about aesthetics, a subhead under metaphysics. It *is* my
book about aesthetics.

MLH: What led you to write *Resurrection*? Anything similar?

JG: I was very young when I wrote that, and young writers have a
tendency to be oversubtle. Chaucer did, T. S. Eliot did, a lot of good
people have tended to be oversubtle. I think the book goes by even
the most careful reader, that it's not really all there. I had just read
Tolstoy's *Resurrection* and I thought it was an awful, awful, wicked
book, and I meant to answer it point by point, but the answer is
obscure. Anyway, it was meant to be about a person, but also people
in general who love ideas to the exclusion of people, so that people
become ideas. I like James Chandler, but he never really understands
his wife or even looks at her, he doesn't understand his children,
obviously; and he falls in love with a girl and doesn't have the faintest
idea what that girl is like although he has a fatherly feeling about her.
He abstracts, and as a result what he does is cause total disaster. (I
give him excuses. He has aleukemic leukemia, so he's not thinking
very well, and he writes an essay on art which shows why he's getting
it wrong.) Basically I was answering Tolstoy, and I answered too slyly
to make myself clear. Tolstoy hates rote behavior, including such
behavior as is expressed by duty. Chandler shares his theoretical

distrust of theory, but his body controls him exactly as a good theory would—but with more harmful effect. What I wanted to do is show that a theory against rote behavior and convention can be at least as monstrous as rote behavior, that in fact it leads to the same thing.

MLH: How do you manage three careers, those of scholar, teacher, and novelist? Are they complementary?

JG: Sure. Lately, I've been teaching creative writing. I swore I'd never do that, but I've been working on the theory and technique of it and I've been very happy with my results. A lot of the kids that come out of my classes become professional writers, some with very different standards than those I approve of. Even when I disapprove, they're generally higher than the standards of the magazines I read and contests I judge.

It's useful to think about aesthetic questions with students. When I was teaching medieval literature, I was mainly helping graduate students through theses. When a person is doing his thesis, he's trying to understand a poem or a series of poems. In working with students, I got to understand the structure of *Beowulf, Morte Darthur* and other things, and I find that those are structures which nobody uses anymore because, though they used to be normal and standard, nobody thinks of them now, which means that if you use them in modern novels, you can get some of the same effects they got, but the reader doesn't know where it's coming from; he thinks you invented it. Being a medievalist was really wonderful for me. The last couple of years before I got out of teaching literature and got into creative writing, I was doing a little Greek and that too was helpful to me—when I started working on Apollonios, I had no idea a poet could do all that. I learned a great deal from teaching literature, not to mention the fact that if you work very closely with students you get to know about their lives and you can describe a Nebraska farm because they've told you about it.

MLH: Do you have the entire plot in your mind when you begin writing?

JG: Sometimes what happens is that you poke your pick into a piece of respectable earth and silver shows up in an iron-ore vein and God knows where you're heading. You follow it and you have to revise everything in light of the silver. But usually you know pretty well what's going to happen. I sometimes write a thousand pages of notes for a 200-page novel.

MLH: When you were writing *October Light*, were you working with any philosophical ideas then, or what reading was important to you?

JG: Not so much reading. Lately I work more and more from my own ideas, and less from other people, but certainly I meant to be working with the whole idea of models. I'd been thinking about it and talking about and writing about it—the fact that you can't do anything in the world unless you see someone else do it first. You can't even see the color red unless your father saw and named it except if you're a brilliant visual artist and you suddenly discover the color red, but even a great artist can't discover that many new colors in life. What I was interested in is the way a person's notions—people hear of different notions about how they have to behave—affect his behavior for better or worse. Every character in *October Light* is either a model or the victim of a model or trying to break his way free of a model. The whole reason, of course, for my novel inside a novel is that the greatest model of all in our civilization is art, whether painting or literature, but especially literature. I don't mean only written books, but also legends, even jokes. Every time a person tells a coarse, male chauvinist pig joke about women, he's reinforcing a pattern of behavior.

MLH: Is your theory about life imitating art recent, or recent only in the way you formulate it now?

JG: I thought it was recent, actually. I thought I just came to it in this last book that's coming out, but in a thesis I read by a guy named Byron Hoot, he points out that I've said all these things in the novels over and over, sometimes the very same lines. I never remembered that I'd said them before. Each time it came as a great revelation. In fact some of the lines that came, I worked, worked, and revised and revised until I finally got exactly the right way to say them, and getting that right way to say the thing, I understood it I thought for the first time. Then I discover from Byron Hoot that the Sunlight Man said it in exactly those same words. It's a freaky kind of thing. It's rediscovering what you know, reapplying it.

MLH: Would you write any of your works differently now in light of—

JG: Of course I would write them differently. I certainly wouldn't revise them. I may change my mind at another time, but it would be foolish for me to go back and fix a work. I think what you do if you slip into some kind of cheating in a work is, you write another story and pay it back, in the same way that Shakespeare mocks Polonius in *Hamlet*, and takes it back in *The Tempest*. Because a work really comes out of an age. A twenty-year-old man thinks like a twenty-year-old man. If he's an indecent twenty-year-old man, then he says what he says because that's what he thinks. It may be bad in that it reinforces bad feelings common among twenty-year-olds, but it's good, too, in that it can help the rest of us understand certain twenty-year-olds better. To go back, as Henry James did, and try to cover up all of these unbuttoned flies seems to me a mistake. I wouldn't pass a law, though. John Fowles's revision of *The Magus* is a special case.

MLH: Is there any novel of yours that doesn't have the effect on life you would want it to have?

JG: My novels all say what I still believe. One novel, *The Wreckage of Agathon*, is a mean novel in some ways. I don't like the fact that it's got a couple of mean spots. I wouldn't erase them or suppress them, but—

MLH: Is that concerning Agathon?

JG: What he says about some other characters.

MLH: But not what he does.

JG: No, because he's not a hero. Peeker's the hero. Agathon is a seer, right? And without him there would be no Peeker, but I hope it's a hands-down win for Peeker. Peeker is a wonderful person, Agathon wasn't. Agathon was a son-of-a-bitch, brilliant and interesting, but he didn't finally have the compassion that it takes to be a real seer. He could know the future, but he couldn't know people's hearts really.

MLH: What have you been working on lately?

JG: I've been thinking about breaking up the art establishment, the writing establishment again. When I started *MSS*, it was time to smash the stranglehold of realistic fiction, of European imports. It was very hard for an American writer in those days to do the kind of thing that *MSS* magazine did—stories by Jack Hawkes, Joyce Carol Oates, Bill Gass. I think that writers should pay attention to particular writers in some position of power, but sometimes literary fame is empty, and writers need to be taken down a little. Another thing I'm interested in lately is radio plays. There's a whole new wave of radio plays, and they are nothing like the radio plays of the '40s because now we have stereo—if not quadro. Obviously radio is not going to take away the power of television, but television has established itself, in spite of its pretensions, as a schlock form. With a radio play you can get powerful images because the listener makes up his own. The writer can do absolutely amazing things, have a character walk from the right-hand speaker to the left-hand speaker, or if you have quad you can have somebody say "stick 'em up" from behind the listener. You can get wonderful effects. It's really wide open. It seems to me that we need to write terrific radio plays so that people who want high-level art have alternatives, and we need to pay attention to that in creative writing courses. We also need an opening for the sort of fiction that used to be handled by something like the *Saturday Evening Post* but is absolutely impossible to sell anymore, really first-rate ghost-stories and so on. I'm interested in the politics of literature. I'd like to see writers get paid. I'd like to see magazines start off that are not snob magazines. There are all these people, good writers, who really need the serious writers', the established writers' help in getting off the ground. I think that means a number of things. It means that people have to start publishing annual books of new writers, because publishers aren't as eager to find new writers as they used to be. It's now the case, because of paper costs, warehouse costs, and so on, that a new first novel that used to sell for ten dollars would have to sell for twenty-two. What this means is that the university presses are going to have to start publishing novels because otherwise where are good novels going to come from? What I'm trying to say is that because I believe that writing is a way of seeing, an instrument of perception, and because I think that writing has fallen into certain ruts so that we're getting the same perceptions over and over—and because I think that you're not going to get an *Antaeus* or any of the established magazines to change their ways, because they've been successful doing the same things—something has to be done to shape up the possibilities and open up new kinds of writing.

MLH: What about your latest book, *In the Suicide Mountains*? Does it grow out of your strong concern with literature and morality?

JG: I started that book a couple of years ago. My son had an acquaintance in high school who committed suicide. I suddenly realized how much kids think about suicide. It's a subject they can't talk about really. Then I found out that something like three-fourths of people in the United States who commit suicide are under the age of twenty, and that meant to me that somebody had better talk to people about suicide. I really believe Bettelheim. I don't agree with specific interpretations, but that's a very trivial matter. I felt that the thing to do was to take the subject of suicide and to put it in sort of a faraway land with a dwarf, a princess—a blacksmith's daughter—and say everything you can say about suicide. I have had some experience of suicidal feeling, that is to say I'm a person who sometimes can become very aepressed, and I've known, as all of us do, a few people who have committed suicide. I laid out a scheme of why people commit suicide and of what things can be done to help them. I shaped it in the form of a tale. It's interesting that when I submitted the book, the feeling was that the subject was a little touchy. The publisher wasn't sure that parents would buy a book about suicide for their kids, which may be right, but it's turned out that so far it's been selling fairly well. I think what it says about suicide is true. It's as serious a book as I ever wrote, although it's couched in jokes and tales. Everything I know about suicide is in it, and I don't duck the ugly issues, the painful ones. One of the characters in the novel is a chemical suicidal, a person who by his constitution is that type; one of the characters is a sociopath, and one is a "metaphysicalopath." He just doesn't like the damn world. It's an interesting book, I think. It's of course true that when you write a book like that, although it's just as serious as the heaviest novel you wrote, people won't take it as seriously.

MLH: What do you say about what Camus wrote in *The Myth of Sisyphus*?

JG: I don't remember. I do know that Alvarez's book is an evil one, because he has to have known perfectly well that the people he was talking about were in fact chemically imbalanced, that they were against suicide. It was not a grand, romantic thing; it was a physical-psychological ailment. John Berryman had just been in Alcoholics Anonymous, was between drugs and was desperately trying to find the right one. He just didn't get what he needed in time. There's no possibility that the famous suicides, Berryman, Plath, and Sexton, did it because of some grand, romantic notion about life. It's a terrible lie.

An Interview with John Gardner

Roni Natov and Geraldine DeLuca/1978

From *The Lion and the Unicorn*, 2 (Spring 1978), 114-36. Reprinted by permission of *The Lion and the Unicorn*.

GD: We're doing this issue on writers who write both for children and adults, and I guess a good place to start is by asking why you write for children.

JG: It started accidentally, the way all my writing starts. When my kids were growing up, each year I would give them a Christmas present of a story. I'd always make up the stories. Then one day you make an especially polished one and you get to thinking about how a children's story ought to work to be really classic and especially interesting to kids. You want kids to love the story and to buy the book for their children and their grandchildren and their great great great grandchildren and so on. So, while I was making up those Christmas stories I got to thinking about it. And as I was doing children's stories and enjoying them I got to thinking about all the things that Bettelheim talks about—about the way you really can say things that are very important to kids in these stories. For instance, the book I got my daughter to grow up on was *1001 Nights*. It seems to me that that's a wonderful book on how to be a girl—because you have to be cunning, you have to be graceful, but not weak. That's an amazing book. I feel that that book *is* about how to grow up a woman in a chauvinist society and not lose everything. And I think that the book to buy a boy is Malory's *Morte D'Arthur* so that he'll know he's supposed to be a knight. Anyway, then I started writing to issues. For instance, I heard that a kid in school who my children knew committed suicide, then I started hearing other kids talking about suicide, and I discovered that they think about it a lot. Then I started talking to people and I learned from a psychiatrist friend that an enormous number of people, I don't remember the statistics, but maybe two thirds of the people in America who commit suicide are sixteen or under. Which makes sense, because the kid has this problem, you know. He's too little to beat you up. He's too little to argue. And if you're completely unjust to him, as some school teachers and some parents are, all he can do is run away or put up with it. Anyway it suddenly struck me that it's very important and it's something that nobody talks about. And I thought, all these kids are going around agonizing about it. So then I started writing *In the Suicide Mountains* which has the surface of a story but is really a very close analysis of why a person would want to commit suicide. And why he shouldn't. So it's pretty moralistic I guess. But I think fiction is pretty moral; I think all art is pretty moral.

GD: Do you feel more moralistic when you're writing for children than for adults?

JG: No. And I don't think good fiction of any kind, for adults or children, tells lies. If you tell the absolute truth, it will be difficult and complex, but if you discuss the arguments against suicide, you can't cheat on the arguments that the kid already knows. The fundamental thing about suicide is that anyone who's ever been in that situation or even close to it knows you're so unhappy, so aching with misery, that you can burn your hand with a cigarette and it doesn't hurt. So it's a release from pain more than anything else. And if you pretend that that's not true—if you say, "Well, you should just buck up"—that's stupid. Any kid for whom the book is intended, and it's intended for any kid, knows that's dishonest. Any place where you lie, you lose your credibility and the book becomes worthless. In any children's story, the kid has to know that he's in good hands. It's true for adults too: as soon as you begin to suspect a story, you begin to get a little bored. One of the awful things in adult fiction is the unreliable narrator. I know that it's amusing for the writer and I know that it's an interesting kind of game to play when you're an English professor. But it's basically unsatisfying. It's one thing to do what Donald Barthelme does. Donald Barthelme is very good. He doesn't really have unreliable narrators. His narrators are people who don't know the answers. They're just lost. But the flat out smart aleck unreliable narrator is just a nuisance.

GD: One of the things Roni and I found appealing in your writing is that there seems to be a real sympathy for people in it, a real caring, that you don't find in a lot of modern writers. Maybe it's the issue of reliability you're talking about, and the slickness, the cleverness, that overtakes the basic sympathy for people in some writer's works.

JG: Yes, it's a fad that we're in at the moment with writers. The coldheartedness. It's sort of urbane, cool.

GD: Decadent.

JG: But I think that's going to pass. It seems to me that the young writers, and they're not always so young, who are coming out and getting attention today are a sort of strange, more mature version of the flower children. Toni Morrison is middle-aged I guess, but I think of her as a young writer. She's a wonderful, compassionate person and her work reflects that compassion. I think it's a new development, since Viet Nam. While the country was going down, morally, it was awfully hard. I think a great deal of the fiction that came out of that period was a little black because there was such guilt and anger. If you think about Barthelme, his early fiction is full of anxiety and a kind of ironic detachment, but his newer work is open and full of emotion. That's a really different Barthelme, a more mature writer.

Against that, there's a change taking place in children's books that's curious to me. For example, *The Nightmares of Geranium Street* is a wonderful book but it makes me nervous. It takes an honest look at the ghetto, but it seems to me important that a book give you hope and give you models, how to act and how to think, and that book is very uninspiring. There isn't any sunlight. The only sunlight is the compassion you feel, and at the end one of the main characters, who's a junkie, gets carted off to jail. She had no choice anyway, she is a nice lady, that's the way life was for her, but her daughter is left. You don't know what's going to happen to her and the Nightmares, the gang, are left in the same ghetto and that's the way the world is. It *is* a good book. It just makes me nervous, that's all. If I'm going to write for those kids, I'd rather deal with them in a fantasy world where everything's not bleak or where there's a hint of sunlight in the background. On the other hand, I don't like authors like C. S. Lewis, although my kids loved him. He's a melodramatist. He's got good guys and bad guys. He's a class man. The upper class is good; the lower class is bad. In a C. S. Lewis novel, the kid who's from the lower class is always untrustworthy—devious, sneaky, cockney. I hate that. I think that kids know that that's not so good, yet the story's interesting, so they go on. But if they go on, it undermines something. They don't trust Lewis but then they begin to think, well maybe he's right. And then you just don't have any fun in the story. The fairy tales are different. In the fairy tales, bad is bad but good is also bad. You know, for example, that the good little girl in the fairy tale who knows that the stepmother is going to chop off her head when she goes to sleep will get behind the bad sister and move the bad sister into her place so that the bad sister gets it. That's bad, but it's cunning and it's necessary.

RN: We found that the characters in your books are ordinary; you explore the complexity of ordinary people. You give them so much space and intensity. It's an unusual picture of middle America. In *Nickel Mountain,* for example, there is so much detail—about the restaurant, Callie, etc. Or about the police officer and his work in *The Sunlight Dialogues.*

JG: That's a curious quality when it comes to writing for children, because one of the things I find interesting is applying modern novelistic standards to the original fairy tales. For example, in the traditional fairy tale, Cinderella sweeps ashes but you don't get any description of how to sweep ashes. Whereas in my story *The King of the Hummingbirds* where the kid spends the night working—you know, cleaning pots and pans—I describe it. The focus is different. In traditional fairy tales, the focus is on knights, princes, princesses. But when I write, I use middle class characters; that is, even if they're kings, I make them think in middle class ways. Then I have to deal with the differences between the middle and upper class. The aristocracy always thinks it's right, and if it doesn't think it's right, it's not going to tell you. For example, in Nietzsche there are two moralities: the slave morality of the Jewish man and the true morality of the Prussian officer who's in a position of power. I don't like a single thing Nietzsche's ever said. I don't like his politics. I think he's a Nazi. I like the middle class morality. In *The King of the Hummingbirds,* the king doesn't know how to solve the problem, the knight doesn't know, nobody knows. But the king and the knight, in their middle class way, bungle it up together. In traditional fairy tales, the third son wins because he is in fact a natural aristocrat, he's your true prince in disguise. But solutions in my stories do not come about because of the wonderful power of a true-born aristocrat.

GD: Why do you choose fairy tales for your children's work—what do you find in the genre?

JG: I like the simplicity. In realistic fiction you spend a lot of time documenting things. That's okay if you want to describe what it's like to live in a certain town, but I want to get at the moral side of each tale, and every tale presents some basic idea of how to live with other people. The fundamental issue is that you live in a world in which you're not really sure of what's going on. For example, you're walking down Broadway and you see two guys fighting, a little guy and a big guy, and your impulse is to break up the fight. But it may be that the little guy just slept with the big guy's wife and you don't know that, so any action you might take is likely to be absurd. But you may have to act anyway, and sometimes you make a mistake and you may have to pay for it. It isn't fair. That's why I think cunning is a very fine virtue. That's why I like Odysseus and the other heroes who used it.

GD: Could you explain something about your fairy tale "The Griffin and the Wise Old Philosopher"? How does the wise philosopher know the griffin's going to leave town at the end?

JG: He doesn't. That's a fairy tale that's basically a joke. It's for older kids, which is true of most of my fairy tales. All of them, in fact, with the possible exception of *Dragon, Dragon,* I really meant for kids who have been through fairy tales and are ready for slight variety. A kid at that age has probably heard of the Heisenburg principle because that's one of the favorite principles of modern mathematicians. The Heisenburg principle is the uncertainty principle and the fairy tale takes place in the town of Heisenburg where the griffin, by his nature, sets up uncertainty. So all the philosopher does is just follow the uncertainty principle to its end and as it happens in this case it works out.

RN: We get a sense in the children's stories—although it's quite clear in your adult novels too—that there's a figure who represents chaos who enters the world and sets up a threatening situation. That, in turn, encourages someone to figure out how order is going to be restored. Do you see that as a preoccupation in your work?

JG: Yes. Basically my view of reality is that it's a little chaotic—not completely, but chaotic enough so that you don't know what's going to happen to you. Life is full of improbability and we all have ways of dealing with it. Nice clear codes. I mean, don't slam the screen door and everything will be all right. The problem in my stories usually is that a character has his own nice neat code but he has to abandon it. Then, by abandoning it and sort of rolling with the punches, he's successful. In *Dragon, Dragon,* for instance, the two older brothers know what's right. One of them knows that to kill a dragon you have to use intellect; the other knows you have to use strength. But they both fail. The younger brother simply takes his father's advice which is absurd and he succeeds. And *Gudgekin the Thistle Girl* knows what we all know, that you're not supposed to pity yourself, you're not supposed to go around crying, lamenting your lot. You're supposed to care about other peopple. That's true, but once in a while you do feel sorry for yourself. What happens is she finally gives up the code and she becomes a nihilist. Then she doesn't believe anybody; she thinks that she's the most miserable person in the world. Ultimately she finds a kind of middle ground. I think that that is standard in my fiction. I do it in different ways. Clumly in *The Sunlight Dialogues* is a very clear example of this. By the end of the story, all he knows is compassion. He is incapable of functioning practically, but at least he understands what the codes of his society are about. Henry Soames in *Nickel Mountain* is a man who is capable of moving into the world. Everybody around him has a code; the tension inside the novel centers on one neat code after another breaking down. Henry's influence is kind of redeeming in that he works at things until you're left with nothing except attempts at understanding and compassion.

RN: I liked him.

JG: He's a nice man, isn't he?

RN: There's also something grotesque about Henry, though he's very sweet. For example, in the scene when Henry rubs his lips against the door, Callie says "Henry, you're kissing the door," and there's such mortification. There was a lot of that in your stories. The blurb on the cover of *October Light* mentions a similarity between you and Dickens and I think that's very true. Your work also points out that we *are* a little grotesque, eccentric, unpleasant, for all the compassion. I think that's important. I saw it also in the dwarf in *In the Suicide Mountains.*

JG: Sure.

GD: Are you conscious that you're doing that, that you're creating grotesque characters, characters who in some way are repulsive and yet sympathetic? Do you feel that you focus on the grotesque or is it just used to highlight the fact that people are complex?

JG: Partially it's to highlight character traits. That is to say, Henry is a very sensuous kind of man. He likes food, he likes objects, in a different way from George Loomis, who collects them. So he's fat. If you're really really sensual, I guess you'll be fat. On the other hand, if a guy is really ascetic, if he doesn't really care about things, he'll be out of touch with his body. George Loomis goes around mislaying parts of himself. He loses an arm; he's got a truck with a light that doesn't work. All through the novel that light keeps going on; it finally kills the goat lady.

RN: Aha! Is *that* what happens.

JG: Sure. Everybody asks me, "What happened?" and I think it's clear.

RN: Why does he kill the goat lady?

JG: Just because his lights weren't on. She's up on the hill and he goes over the hill and doesn't see her.

GD: How did you come to write *Grendel?*

JG: I'd been teaching *Beowulf* and Anglo–Saxon literature courses for a long time and had been working on an interpretation of the poem. I finally worked out an interpretation that I believe in where Grendel is a cosmic principle of intellectual disorder. He liked unreason, in the same way that Jean Paul Sartre likes unreason. Sartre fundamentally doubts causality. He thinks that you can change your life just like that. Or that you can change history. It's a very valuable thing to believe when you're working with the French underground and there's not a hope. You can pretend the past doesn't exist, that there's no momentum. But the French underground movement was crushed. It was a hopeless position. Anyway, that gave me the idea of telling the Beowulf story from Grendel's point of view, using Grendel to represent Sartre's philosophical position and showing how it came about. A lot of *Grendel* is borrowed from sections of Sartre's *Being And Nothingness*. The first major experience in Grendel's life, when he meets human beings for the first time, is all from *Being And Nothingness*. For example, in one part of the book when he is looking for his mother, various objects appear to be his mother but they are not really his mother and he has to understand that. Sartre is a marvelous poet. He's wrong as a philosopher but he's a brilliant one. It's funny to hero-worship someone you think is flat wrong. But he writes so beautifully, you almost don't care. Once that idea came, it was easy for the book to organize itself.

GD: You were also talking about heroism in that book, about what it takes to be a hero.

JG: Among other things, sure.

GD: And it's not far from what it takes to commit suicide, to be so clearly directed that you close off all options to yourself. I think one of the things you're doing in the children's books is saying keep your options open.

JG: That's true.

GD: *October Light* deals with suicide also. Were you writing those two books simultaneously?

JG: I wrote them one right after the other but I don't know how suicide got into *October Light*. I think I wrote it before I heard about the kid who had committed suicide. I think I needed it for the plot. I don't know where ideas come from sometimes, it's very strange. I really wasn't very interested in the character who committed suicide; I just needed him to explain the tragedy of the father. But when you're building something up so that you can use it for the climax, you can't fake it and still be convincing. Whenever I'm writing a book, for children or adults, I spend 90% of the time carefully thinking about how to support the main plot. In *October Light* I had to give some reason why James Page is so mean, mean enough to lock up his sister, Sally. I mean, what could be meaner? So I had to make up the character of Uncle Ira who would be a natural reason for James to become mean and defensive. But once you've introduced Uncle Ira, who is such an interesting character, if you never mention him again, the novel feels unfinished, incomplete. The reader wonders, "What happened to Uncle Ira?" You can't just bring him back on and have him stand by a tree. You've got to do something. What do you do? But then you remember, that's not what I want to talk about. I want to talk about Sally. The whole novel is about Sally and James. But in order for the novel to work, you have to construct a plot to explain why these characters are what they are. Increasingly, 90% of this novel just isn't central. For example, I didn't really want all those friends of Sally in there. I just wanted Sally to be a lady who is modern. She's not a feminist, but she takes the modern woman's position. She's got some rights, but she can't get that out of nowhere. She has to have these friends. Horace, her husband, wasn't really important either. But somehow she's got this gentle side to her, this interest in music. So increasingly, Horace becomes very important. Her marriage to Horace is necessary to her development.

GD: But Horace is very important. He is typical of a kind of quietly intimidating man.

JG: Yes. I like it that he's intimidating, that's very important. He's just as intimidating as James.

GD: More so. James is such an outright pig, you know.

RN: Which helps. Sally can emerge as a figure who's been pushed and pulled a lot. She's pretty tough and mean in her own ways.

JG: I really loved Sally, Sally was my favorite character. I got accused by whoever was writing the *New Republic* review of being a chauvinist. But that's all right. He can call me whatever he wants to. But I loved Sally. She was by far the most interesting character in the novel. I loved the way she developed. James is a stereotype. I do a lot with the stereotype, but he's still a stereotype. Sally is not like any woman ever written about in fiction.

RN: And she's old. How interesting to find all that energy behind such an old woman. She's not coming into something. She's not on the verge of becoming something.

GD: And you must have had fun writing the trash novel sections. It reminded me of the kind of book that would be written by a graduate student writing for one of these publishing companies under a pseudonym at fifty pages a day. It was very engaging. You let Sally get angry at the novel just at the right points. You know, I was starting to feel that I hated the doctor just as much as she did. It worked very well because you really did get caught up on it.

JG: It's funny. At a certain point I started to get very bored with it and then I invented the character Pearl. She carried me through the rest of it. You finally can't really write about people who aren't people. That's a problem with a lot of contemporary fiction. For example, I'm really fascinated by what Jack Barth does, but I don't care about his characters except for the early ones, whom I love. Very often I find I just don't care about a character.

GD: Do you know why?

JG: Because they're just not real to me. They're constructions, ideas. After you've gone for a while with characters like Peter Wagner, you want to go on to a real person. Like Pearl. It was very strange to me though, because I hadn't planned her.

RN: What are some of the other surprises that you came across when you wrote the novels, things you hadn't planned on?

JG: They happen all the time. For instance, I was writing a novel about an old alcoholic detective. And then I created a girl character who just sort of happened and took over. Then I decided that the girl was going to be the center of the novel. But she only arrives on page 120, which meant that what I had to do was tear the novel apart and open little doors to let her in. In fact, I think the novel will probably be named after her. The thing you can't anticipate is the emotion. You can have a perfectly good plan in which everything is working logically, but there's still something missing. In this novel about the detective, I found there was no heart, no feeling. You may be interested in the detective, because of the problems he deals with, but he's an alcoholic which means that he doesn't have much free will, which means, of course, that his compassion is limited. And I kept looking around for some place where I could get this emotional component. It's out of that need that you invent.

The Sunlight Dialogues started out as a different novel completely. It was about a murder that takes place in a monastery. And it was interesting philosophically, because of the alleged purity of monks. There's nobody in the monastery but monks, yet somebody killed a monk—so it must have been a monk. So this local detective shows up to investigate. He was immediately interesting to me because he was basically a smart cop but one with potential for real emotional depth. And I kept laboring, trying to see where this stupid novel would lead until finally I just threw out everything but Clumly, the cop. But that was years of work wasted. Then I decided to write a story about Clumly and put every kind of pressure on him that I could think of. And that whole Hodge family evolved out of the fact that Clumly had to have a context. Clumly is just one cop with just one wife and no other family relationships and so he has to be part of the town. And in the modern world we are mostly Clumlys. My parents live far away from me, and I'm not near any of my cousins and so on. We're all kind of isolated. And everything that I needed for Clumly had to be in the novel. It really *is* his novel even though there are other characters. Then of course I developed contrasts for Clumly. That is to say, the character Millie appears. She's a parallel. I really like that portrait. It becomes really interesting letting them evolve. Once I knew that the center was Clumly everything fell into place. Basically I think you need to get the emotion that makes the reader strongly empathetic to the characters, especially to characters you don't like at first. I think the friendships that have been the most interesting and lasting for me have always been friendships where my first reaction to the person was not necessarily all that warm. For example, if someone is very intellectual—which I'm not—or has a violent streak or any kind of thing that puzzles me, it puts me off, until I understand it, and then I come to appreciate our differences. What happens to me is that as soon as I get the emotional pull of the novel, I roll—as long as I have at least an abstract plot. One of the things wrong with current novels now—not including John Updike's, or John Cheever's, or Saul Bellow's—is that they are not even carefully plotted. There are whole scenes that don't do anything, don't go anywhere. I think that you absolutely have to have that hard, logical, driving progression moving ahead. But that alone, even if you can get at it, is nothing. Who cares about the events unless you're worrying about the person who's making them happen?

GD: I agree. I feel that way about Pynchon.

JG: Yeah, I do too.

GD: To what extent are your characters modelled on people you know? At a certain point do you just start creating out of your head and hope that they turn out to be believable portraits?

JG: I think the truth is that every character I've ever done has been consciously or unconsciously modelled on real people. Clumly was not consciously modelled on anybody. I had an uncle George whom I was enormously fond of, a major figure or hero in my life. He was fascinating, full of life, he was an amateur magician, and I've told stories about him a lot. Years after I'd written the novel my son read it and pointed out that both Clumly and the Sunlight Man were modelled on this uncle. As soon as he said it, I realized it was true. With everybody else in the books, I knew exactly who they were modelled on but with those two I didn't. But I'm not always conscious of it. I'm not conscious of any model for Grendel.

GD: Grendel is like all those scapegoats in your novels. He's been told, "You are the darkness and I am the light," and he's very angry. It's interesting that you say you're not an intellectual. There are all those meditative, metaphysical pockets in your books. And I was wondering, are you religious?

JG: Not in terms of any particular religion. Yeah, sure, I believe in God. I believe in all kinds of things but I don't believe in Christianity or Judaism or Hinduism or anything. I'm sympathetic to all of them. When I was growing up in the Presbyterian church, the regular subject matter of the sermons was the dirty Catholics. And when I'd go to the Catholic church with my friends, the regular subject matter was the dirty Protestants. They didn't have any Jews to pick on. I didn't know any Jews in our town, or any Buddhists. But I knew then that there was something really wrong and of course later, when I began reading the Bible and the theology of other religions, it became pretty obvious to me that the only real impressive advance of Christianity over Judaism is that it's not ethnocentric. The rest is all in Judaism. That might offend Jews but the fact is that every doctrine in Christianity is in Judaism. That is to say, what Christ and his followers did was to pick up an idea from the Romans that all people are equal. Anyone could become a Roman citizen. The Romans moved into Ethiopia and they were color-blind. They married Ethiopians. They moved into the Gaza strip and they married Jews. That I think is a very important idea.

GD: How do you see yourself in terms of your involvement with teaching and creative writing? How important is your scholarship in relation to your creative writing?

JG: It's all the same. To me it's absolutely indivisible. When I write, I try to write a book that readers are going to love; whether they understand it fully or not doesn't matter to me. If they love it, that's enough. When you teach, you're working with kids who need what you teach. I was teaching a course in sophomore literature, almost every kid in the class had already flunked once, and they were convinced that they couldn't read poetry and were very stupid. They were all biology students or art students or education students or something. I started out the class—it was Anglo–Saxon poetry to the present—by doing an Anglo–Saxon poem and got these looks and so I decided to do two weeks of Elton John and Stevie Wonder. And we discovered that Elton John is a false poet, I mean he's a fraud, and

Stevie Wonder is a poet. By the time we were done, without even knowing it had happened, they had learned about sprung rhythm, they had learned about voice, they had learned about the development of theme and what you do with a theme. And then after we'd done that, we went directly to Shakespeare and they loved it. They may not have any sense of the history of poetry. They may not know what follows right after Shakespeare, but I don't care about that. I care about their loving poetry. It's the same with novels. You make them real to the reader. Your business is to entertain. And at the same time to bring them something which is of lasting value to their lives.

GD: What kind of response have you gotten to your children's books? From children or from reviewers?

JG: Kind of respectful. There's a problem for writers who are in my position. You don't really get honest criticism. Once in a while someone will say what he really thinks, but mostly they don't. With the last *New York Times* reviews of *In the Suicide Mountains* or *The Child's Bestiary,* for example, it was perfectly clear that the writers of both reviews didn't like the books at all, but they wouldn't say it. I would rather hear that they didn't like them. It's a curious thing. Judged by the standards of entertainment, the adventures in *In the Suicide Mountains* aren't very interesting. The *Oz* books are more interesting. But judged by a different standard, that is to say, that *In the Suicide Mountains* is talking about suicide, then it's a worthwhile thing. But since you've got to start with the premise that this is an entertainment, another wacky Gardner children's book, it wasn't very readable. I think that was the problem, but the reviewer didn't say enough about it. I think that if it is true that it's a boring book for kids, then that's a problem.

GD: Have you had any response from kids?

JG: Yes, I've had a lot of response from kids, but the problem is that all the kids are doctors' and lawyers' children and they really like my stuff. And they know me too. The main thing I discovered is that if you read these stories to children too early, they get bored. If you read *Dragon, Dragon* to a five year old, the kid will go around remembering that verse *Dragon, dragon, who do you do? I've come from the king to murder you,* but the story has too many dead spots for him.

GD: Right, they're ironic.

RN: It's a funny book, very funny. I liked the fact that the king is exposed for being very self-involved and at the end the queen is glaring at him. His flaw is not corrected. He just remains human and flawed. The *Gudgekin* stories didn't move me as much.

JG: Oh, I liked *Gudgekin*.

GD: I did too. One night when I was very depressed, I wrote a poem based on it about withholding from yourself the way she did.

RN: I loved *In the Suicide Mountains*. I felt that it was wonderfully paced. Each character has space. And that's one thing that always troubles me in modern fairy tale writing. The king walks on, the queen walks on. And it doesn't quite work the way it does in traditional folktales. So if you're going to try to write a modern fairy tale, you need to blow open the form a little bit. I felt that Armida was a fully developed character. So was the dwarf. And the whole incident with the abbot and the fingers intrigued me. It had suspense; it had mystery. So I don't feel that it was slow moving. I think there was a lot of action.

GD: And it's such an interesting thing to write about too. You don't see any children's stories about suicide. It was so sweet when the abbot talked about it. He said, "Of course if you're very sick, it may be okay." He qualifies it, he's careful to explain it. And you explain that the dwarf was a scapegoat, which is why he wants to commit suicide.

RN: You also capture the feeling of terror when you feel that nobody feels the way you do. And that really seems like what can lead to one to consider suicide. The only thing that bothered me was that there was a lot of tale telling. I kept getting sidetracked.

JG: Yes, I know. That was a real problem. I don't think it was a good idea. That's the only time in my life I've ever done a tale within a tale. It's very odd, because right after I finished *October Light*, I was talking to Jack Barth who was working on a tale within a tale and I said, "It'll never work; it's a hopeless form." Every time you shift from one gear to another, the reader says, "No, I don't want to read that trash novel now."

GD: It works in *October Light* though. You know what was so beautiful in *October Light*: "Ed's Song"—about unlocking.

JG: That's mostly stolen from Noel Perrin.

GD: You mean the prose?

JG: The prose. I changed the order. I just took all of his good stuff and I put it in one place. Then I added some stuff of my own. It's about 70% his. That doesn't bother me though. I'm a medievalist. If Chaucer took 70% from Boccaccio I can do it with Noel Perrin. Besides, nobody reads Noel Perrin. Now maybe they will. In fact it's a central scene in the novel.

GD: What children's books did you read as a child?

JG: I don't remember. I read a lot of children's books. I never liked Lewis Carroll as a child. I guess you have to be a girl. And it's a sort of mathematical world. I thought I should like it. But I didn't. I liked sentimental slop like *Winnie-the-Pooh*. I loved *Winnie-the-Pooh*.

GD: It's very vintage sentimentality. It is precious but he does it so well. He's so damn witty at being sentimental.

JG: That's true. The characters were real characters. A character like Eeyore is amazing.

RN: And Eeyore is not sentimental.

JG: He's a lot less sentimental. In fact he's got some really good lines.

RN: Do you read children's books now? Did you read them to your kids?

JG: I read a lot of children's books. Sometimes friends write them. Sometimes they're sent to me because somebody liked them. But I don't read anything unless I have to. There are so many books I have to read because people send them to me for comment. Once in a while if you're really lucky, you get someone like John Fowles but most of them are pretty bad.

RN: Have you read *Daniel Martin?*

JG: Yes, I think it's his best work. I think he's the greatest living writer around today. I saw him on television and I was amazed because, even though he's such a deep thinker, and people kept asking him these wonderful questions, he just kept answering like an English gentleman. It was frustrating. He was asked about his character Jenny and he said, "I've always been fascinated by princesses." And I said, "What? Jenny's no princess! I can't understand it."

RN: I think I can. When he describes her, he talks about her beauty and the pain of being a woman in that position. In that sense she is a princess. She's been courted and groomed to be a special person. And she seems a little bit shaky about that. And spoiled. Not in the traditional sense, but burdened with that role. Does that make sense?

JG: Yes it does.

RN: Getting back to the children's books, I noticed that in *Dragon, Dragon* you seem to be dealing with what's traditionally thought of as evil—the dragon figure and giant figure and so on—as if they are funny, amusing. You seem to be saying that instead of being evil, they're messy, chaotic. For example, the dragon is killed because he's laughing and totally out of control. Did you have a preconception, that you wanted to convey that evil is not really dangerous? Did you want to transform things that are generally frightening to children, to make them less frightening?

JG: No, not really. The thing about the oldest brother and the second brother is that they have their dignity. They know how to do things. The youngest brother has no dignity. He just does what his father says; it's silly but he does it. He's wearing this heavy armor and carrying this ridiculous sword and he obviously can't do anything. But he recites the verse and the dragon laughs at him, especially when he says that ridiculous poem. I don't know, it's some complicated thing about dignity. About how on one hand one ought not to have any dignity. It's a silly thing to be carrying around. On the other hand, when somebody really insults you, that's the time to get mad. When the dragon laughs at the youngest brother, that's when he attacks. Which is a reasonable response.

GD: You talk about that in *Nickel Mountain*. George Loomis tells Henry Soames, "The only reason you're feeling responsible for Simon Bale's death is that it gives you dignity."

JG: Yes.

RN: The accident of that death was very disturbing to him. Henry has to feel that, in some way, things *can* make sense.

JG: Obviously he reacts to Simon Blake's coming up the stairs because he now knows the reason for his child's nightmares. It's parental rage. He's completely out of control at the moment, which is not like him. And then he tries to get control and assume responsibility. It's the only point at which he becomes rigid, and it almost kills him. As long as he holds to this foolish notion of human dignity—that he must be responsible for what happens—he's hopeless. What saves him is a miracle, a chaos of accidents. Which is to say a bunch of guys come by, hoping it will rain. They practically do a rain dance. It's very ritualistic. It doesn't work. They go home. It rains. It's a result of that combination of things.

GD: Is that what you meant when you were talking about Sartre and the existentialist's need to accept responsibility for everything?

JG: Partly that. Partly Jean Paul Sartre says that you make up meaning because life is chaotic. But you know you're going to die. Then you discover there's one principle and that's existence. Existence precedes essence. And you do want to exist. Then you go over your life to discover a pattern, something inside, not in the world out there, that is of value. And then you assert it for all time. That is called existentialism and I don't think that's true. I think the fact is that we have a huge history which Sartre denies and which many modern novelists deny. We have a history and history moves on. You recognize you're a mammal. And that all mammals, for example, punish their children, physically. So a human being decides, "I am not going to punish my child physically." But if you decide that, you've got to know that you're going against the law of the mammal and you might have to pay. So what happens in the Spock generation, I guess, is that you punish anyway, only you punish by irony or the double bind. A spank on the fanny might be better. Every time you try to figure out a human value, try to figure out what makes people healthy, what makes them function, I think what you have to do is to look around. Try to decide; what makes mammals work, what makes Americans work, what makes Englishmen work, whatever. And try to find the value in the world, outside of you. This is what Tolstoy does, what Dante does, what Homer does. Everybody tries to find value outside, and I think what existentialism does is turn your eyes away from the very things you have to look at. You can't look in your heart; you have to look out at the world. That's my big objection. The other objection, of course, is that once you look inside, you're pushed against all others. That keeps the French underground alive but it's only good in a crisis situation, and the thing is that most of human life is not crisis. You have to deal with the everyday.

RN: I have one last question about *In the Suicide Mountains*— about the abbot and the baby at the end of the book. Could you say what you meant by having the abbot transformed into a baby?

JG: Well, it's really "being born again." The abbot, in imitating good behavior, is trying to be good. That's what all of us do. Our parents tell us to do that. The murderer murders the abbot and begins imitating him and he likes it. It's a nice way to behave, but it's just an imitation. And as long as he's conscious of it as an imitation, he's annoyed by it, he doesn't trust it. He's full of guilt. But he really wants to do it. And suddenly he's released to just being good in itself. It's a very strange twist on Christianity. Obviously Christianity could say "grace" is what does it; Judaism would say "habit" is what does it.

RN: I also felt that the children's stories were dealing with how you learn to trust what you really think is right when it is not being reinforced particularly in the world. Nothing in the outside world is supporting it. So you form new bonds. In the end of *In the Suicide Mountains* the baby joins up with them. In *Nickel Mountain* Callie, her child, and Henry became a new unit. The problem is finding a sympathetic bond.

JG: Sure. What happens to Chudu, the dwarf, is that he hasn't got any bonds. Once he goes on the trip, he forms a bond. And then what he really is can function because it's functioning for someone. As long as he's thinking only about his own individual dignity, he knows he must never go into a rage. But when you're going into a rage for somebody else, it's different. The romantic ideal, as you see it in Byron or Nietzsche, is that there is virtue in isolation. In fact, the hero is misunderstood because he's virtuous. I don't believe that. I'm very classical, Homeric. I feel the only time virtues really work is when they work socially.

John Gardner
Heide Ziegler/1978

From *The Radical Imagination and the Liberal Tradition.* Ed. Heide Ziegler and Christopher Bigsby. London: Junction Books, 1982, pp. 126-50. Copyright © 1982 by Heide Ziegler and Christopher Bigsby. Reprinted by permission of Heide Ziegler and Christopher Bigsby.

For Gardner, the poet and the priest are clearly related: both are concerned with the search for as well as the promulgation of Truth. But while their fundamental beliefs and aims are identical, their means differ radically: the priest strives to enforce Truth by threatening punishment in case of disloyalty; the poet attempts to persuade through metaphor. In other words, the artist provides the reader or listener or viewer with a dramatic equivalent of the prolonged intellectual process he himself went through in his search for Truth.

The True, the Good, and the Beautiful, each follows from the others. Thus Gardner states in *On Moral Fiction* (1978) that 'the Good is form: morality is function.' For he believes that the Good rests with the old traditional values which constitute the norm from which all subsequent moral actions derive. The artist's duty consists in recognizing and reinstalling these archetypal values by divesting them of the diverse individual or ethnic rituals which attach to and obscure them. As early as his first published novel, *The Resurrection* (1966), Gardner seems convinced that the artist ought to create a new morality, since life, according to Gardner, always imitates art—not vice versa. Beauty, on the other hand, 'is the truth of feeling.' The Beautiful is not a given, but the result of the artist's acceptance of responsibility for the inviolability of the things of nature as well as those of civilization.

By these standards the importance of the artist's role in society leaves little room for play or irony. Even parody becomes the expression of a serious conflict between different *Weltanschauugen* as they are represented by various artists or philosophies. Thus *The King's Indian* (1974), a collection of short stories, sketches, and the title novella, parodies and opposes central beliefs in Coleridge,

Melville, Poe, and Conrad through the appropriation of their respective styles. And in the epic poem *Jason and Medeia* (1973), which parodies the ancient myth, the intellectual aloofness of the West is pitted, through Jason, against the emotional spontaneity of the East, embodied by Medeia.

Gardner's literary effort is ambitiously comprehensive, ranging from the realistic to the fantastic but always centering on values which are typically American: the American dream and the pursuit of happiness. By an interfusion of matter and mind, nature and civilization, these values are then made to appear universal. Thus in *Nickel Mountain* (1973), the unpresuming protagonist ends up with an almost mystical insight into the 'holiness of things.' And the governing tyrant of—historically and geographically removed—ancient Sparta in *The Wreckage of Agathon* (1970), who becomes emblematic of the repetitiveness of evil inhering in any human attempt at political power-mongering, is rhetorically overcome by Agathon and Demodokos, the advocates of individual freedom.

Good and evil in Gardner's fiction appear either in a realistic context as social forces, definable as the pleasurable or painful impact which the actions of human beings have upon one another, or in a fantastic setting as innate attitudes which can be changed only through the magic of art. The novels *The Sunlight Dialogues* (1972) and *October Light* (1976), for instance, belong to the first category, the famous *Grendel* (1971) and *In the Suicide Mountains* (1977), the latest of his books for children and also a tale for adults, to the second. In *The Sunlight Dialogues* memory and compassion are evoked as positive values against the threat of entropy. In *October Light* each individual set of values is shown to become evil when its respective representative believes in his or her own self-sufficiency, and nothing short of the painful clash of these individual values will release the higher value of mutual responsibility. Ultimately, in both novels, it is the protagonists' ineluctable 'mortality that makes morality.' Whereas in *Grendel* which retells the Beowulf legend from the monster's point of view, as well as in the tale *In the Suicide Mountains,* the figure of the dragon represents that indifference towards values which grows out of immortality. The good in both cases evolves as a struggle against this indifference, a struggle that John Gardner himself strives to share in each of his fictions.

Baltimore, 12 February 1978

HZ: It's true, isn't it, that you *are* very much interested in the values that liberalism, as a political and philosophical attitude, has always focused upon, namely responsibility and freedom?

JG: Yes, that's true.

HZ: May I pursue the implications of this question regarding two of your novels, an early and a recent novel, *Nickel Mountain* and *October Light? Nickel Mountain* is subtitled: *A Pastoral Novel,* and the succession of chapters corresponds to the 'natural' stages of life: courtship, marriage, childbirth, temptation, guilt, forgiveness, death. The pastoral dimension seems to be further enhanced by a certain mysticism pervading life and nature, culminating in Henry Soames's understanding of the 'holiness of things' at the end of his life. Yet there is a tension between this pastoral background and Henry's struggle to assert himself as an individual character which might even link up with Bellow's thesis in *The Adventures of Augie March* that a man's character is his fate. Do you think that these opposing laws, the law of character and the law of nature, can ultimately be reconciled?

JG: I think my position is almost identical to Bellow's. People do have free will, yet it's always true too, that a given human being has certain predispositions and inclinations—he has one foot planted in the determined physical universe—so that a man who is genetically a sensualist, say, can kill himself eating, can be greedily selfish, and so on; but he has choices all along the way, his second foot swings free, and by the usual luck of the universe—both bad luck and good—his freedom to choose is likely to be forced to his attention. Let me put it in a different way. Some people are born with an inclination to anger—you know, the adrenalin goes quicker—and some people are born with an inclination toward sloth. Obviously, each person is going to work out his individual fate at least partly in terms of those givens, the angry man slugging, the lethargic man wincing; nevertheless, each man does work it out if he's lucky. In a world of physical mutability luck's important. So Henry Soames can never be anything but a sensualist, but if life pushes him, life and the natural impetus toward love—and if he's lucky in love—he can be a responsible sensualist. He can finally love the mutable world, including physically and morally mutable people, in a way that's merciful, unjudgmental—which is what I think it all comes to in the end. He can learn even to be judgmental toward himself—his past, his faults, his slips. His body's a machine, 'mere nature'; but consciousness doesn't work with the simplicity of a ball on an inclined plane. It attaches to values, it generalizes, it dreams of a spiritual-physical totality whereby each of our important acts takes on meaning beyond itself, becomes not an isolated act but a ritual gesture, an affirmation of universal related-ness. Hence the focus you've pointed out in the novel—courtship, marriage, the ceremonialization of childbirth, and so on. We do the things physical objects and animate but mindless objects do—fall down, grow old, struggle to maintain our physical identity (as Whitehead might put it, even chairs 'concentrate', remaining what they are, insofar as possible, by 'negative prehension'); but in our consciousness that what we suffer is also suffered, in various degrees, by chairs and elephants. We rise above self: our necessary animal acts become ritual; we become knowing and (at our best) willing participants in the universal dance of creation and destruction.

Everybody in *Nickel Mountain* is set up as a kind of type, a vari-ation on the universal archetype. Superficially, George Loomis is very different from Henry Soames, partly because he's been unlucky in love; but he's similar to Henry too. Mainly, both of them have curious relations to physical things, including their own bodies. In these two characters especially, the novel emphasizes the opposition between inanimate objects—all the sorts of things we associate with 'body'—and human spirit, 'consciousness', if you like. One thing I was thinking about as I was writing the novel was, you know . . . a chair can't move an inch without our help. The whole physical universe is the helpless, idiot child of mind, yet without it we're nothing—probably not even conscious. Henry's relation to physical objects is, initially, a sentimental one; he loves them, even caresses them; he especially loves them if they're old and familiar, unthreatening; but he consumes them—drives his old car like a maniac, eats his way to a heart attack. That's not really having a responsible relation to things; and the same is true of his relationship to people. George Loomis is no better. He collects old guns and magazines and so on but doesn't really love them except as curios, valuable antiques—a different, more aristocratic kind of sentimentality. He finally loves as well as he can love an inanimate object, given his predispositions and his luck, but ultimately he kills a half-inanimate sort of person, the Goat Lady, because he doesn't take care of his truck right—fails to fix the lights. He doesn't take care of even the parts of his own body—he loses an arm, a foot, you know—sort of misplaces things. Both George and Henry could be doomed by their relationship to things. Henry comes out of it partly because he has the courage to love, which leads to his sense of community and responsibility; he learns the social importance of objects, including his own body. George doesn't. He's still a member of the community, because everybody else, represented by Henry and Mr. Judkins, accepts George Loomis for all his faults, accepts the mutability that leads to George's guilt; but George himself doesn't accept. He's an idealist, a child of Plotinus.

HZ: If, therefore, *Nickel Mountain* is concerned with responsibility, would it be correct to say that *October Light* is a novel about the longing for freedom? For James L. Page, freedom seems to come with life's 'struggle upward . . . against the pull of the earth,' against gravity; whereas for his sister Sally it is a kind of escapism, a conjuring up and enacting, in her imagination, of the possibilities life has denied her. Her freedom is brought about, and at the same time symbolically represented, by the trashy novel-within-the-novel which she reads. A third approach to freedom appears to be a kind of nihilism, hinted at in Lewis Hick's fleeting wish that his life would change entirely, a wish that at the same time is felt as a desire for death. How can these different concepts of freedom be related to each other? Are they irreconcilable, or do they complement each other?

JG: They're irreconcilable when they come into conflict, but the conflict can lead to a higher idea of freedom, a reconciliation—or anyway that's my theory. I think what happens is that the three pursuits of freedom work fine until accident forces them to lock horns on one basic issue, the extent to which one does or does not tyrannize other people or allow oneself to be tyrannized. Any one of the three characters' ways of acting makes a perfectly acceptable 'reality,' that is to say, you can live and not die by it. All three characters, James, Sally, and Lewis, both evade total reality and struggle to take care of things, certain of reality's components. Lewis is always patching things and fixing things—in fact he's a handyman by trade—but he avoids confrontation with his wife though he knows she's killing herself with cigarettes. He refuses to bully, and he refuses to *be* bullied. He's a dodger, an evader. It's admirable that he's neither a tyrant nor a slave, but the fact is that his solution excludes him from civilization in all its troubled complexity. He's half-Indian, symbolically, a half civilized, half natural man. His nearest approach to civilization, until the moment he faces up, is to civilization's physical objects—the chairs and doors he fixes for the people around him. You'll notice he never fixes anything for himself. His car—like George Loomis's truck—is a four-wheeled disaster. James Page, on the other hand, is a tyrant. His way of working is to force everybody and everything—beginning with his animals—to do what he thinks is good for them, because he has a notion of how life ought to be and, mainly from love and concern, he tries to force everybody into it; but he evades his own emotion—in fact he's forgotten the wife he loved. Sally is known for her 'goodness,' but she's been terribly bullied all her life. She's a strong person, full of loves and hates, but she's been bullied by her husband, although he is a gentle-seeming man who likes Mozart and that sort of thing. In a mysterious way (I hope this is true) this ultra-civilized Horace of a man has suppressed her real character, as James, her brother, has in a different way suppressed her, until finally she says *No!* The three ways of living could run along parallel if the novel allowed everybody good luck. As long as she accepts being bullied and simply lives a fantasy life, secretly loving and hating but doing what other people want her to do, Sally will be OK; she could go on forever with her fantasy life. Lewis Hicks, as long as he escapes intense involvement by patching broken objects, could be fine forever; and James Page, as long as he's a successful bully, with no memory of what he's done, could also get along fine. But a moment comes when suddenly every one of them stops being lucky: their three roads converge. James destroys Sally's television— her escape—and the substitute escape she turns to, the trashy novel, ironically becomes, by the accident of its use at just this moment, not just a device of escape but also a weapon. And so the war is on. When Sally reads the trashy novel, she's not only given a means of passing the time of her rebellion—her 'strike,' in effect—she's also spurred, by the accident of the book's subject matter, to more intense rebellion. She isn't willing to be bullied any more. She has laid back and let Horace set the standards during their marriage, and she's accepted James's standards (up to a point); but when she reads the novel, her potential for rebellion rises: the very escape—the trashy novel—becomes the trigger which fires her desire for something that's her own.

The point is that no matter what mode of action you choose, aggression, submission or evasion, eventually life demands fulfillment—or at least demands that you try for it. In the struggle of human evolution—that is, the soul's struggle for survival—fitness demands that we be supple enough to switch from aggression to submission, evasion and submission to aggression. It's an inevitable implication of our double identity as both individuals and members of a group—ultimately members of the whole cosmic business, the club of Living Things. And it's at this point, when our clashing identities strike together, that Sally fights James, and Lewis begins to assert himself in his role as husband, that is, 'house-bond.' It's at this moment, if ever, that 'alternative life styles' give way to something broader, universal. Everybody has to find common ground, the same principle of behavior: everybody has to be responsible to and for everybody else. Sally can't back off anymore; finally she has to take care of her own psyche and take responsibility for her secret aggressiveness, partly because at last she's acted on it. And finally James is forced to recognize his responsibility *to* as well as *for* everybody else. He has to face up to the fascist element in every well-meaning Gilgamesh or Oedipus. Hero gives way to tragic hero. It's hard to express except in the way I've tried to express it in the novel.

HZ: Could you say that the three kinds of freedom collide, releasing a higher freedom, as soon as you are forced to take responsibility?

JG: Exactly. The thing about the three kinds of freedom is that they all work fine when you don't have to deal with other human beings. With robots—or with stick-figures in a trashy novel—you can take any course you please. As soon as you deal with other human beings then everybody has to face up to the same values—or at least they all have to compromise their values. Ultimately it comes to something beyond that, as it always does in my fiction, not just responsibility for other people but responsibility for all of nature, all of life—you know, bears, trees, cows, chipped bedroom doors, the noises which, rightly organized, make music. What I think happens at the end of the novel is that Sally gives up her fight for good reasons rather than for bad ones. Always in the past she has given up simply because she's given up; she just didn't want to fight. Her fantasy identity has been enough for her. When she comes out of her room at the end of the novel she comes out because of something that has happened to Ginny and to James; she doesn't even realize that she has come out of her room; she does it as a spontaneous gesture, selflessly, *forgetting* herself. And, because she sees that James is distraught, she sees everything from a new point of view which, in a funny way, she learned from the experience of reading her escapist novel. It's made her think of other people as they really are, not as bad fiction presents them.

What happens in the world, it seems to me, is that people come together in moments of crisis, and they all work by the same system for a little while; then they can safely go back to their own systems. Sally will still dream, maybe with the same touch of bitchiness, but the novel's events will have their subtle effect. James can never go back to quite the same bullying he was guilty of before, but you can bet that if Sally talks too much on the telephone two weeks after the end of the novel, James is going to yell like hell about the bill. His character won't change, her character won't change, Lewis Hicks's character won't change; but they at least know how to function with one another now, behave like human beings. I guess what I mean is that it doesn't matter too much what your individual road to freedom is; individual roads to freedom are fine, and it's only when you're with other people that values have to be agreed on. They have to be shared, and they have to be shared emotionally; you can't just decide intellectually. And I guess I think that the only way that that can come about is that the values each person lives by have to backfire badly, so that he recognizes that there has to be a higher value. It's like nature versus super-nature, you know—or raw nature, jungle nature, versus civilization. Ultimately, what civilization does, it seems to me, is to protect nature—individual natures. When civilization is doing its work, everything becomes part of everything, but itself is still *part.*

HZ: Would you say, then, that your liberalism amounts to a desire to reconcile opposites, to work towards harmony in social and political affairs? In *The Sunlight Dialogues* Congressman Hodge *worries* about the *E pluribus unum* principle; he assumes that, in the modern world, the differences in culture and opinion have become so great that any unifying idea would be too simple, a sign of madness in fact. Do you agree that the belief in the process of unification may indeed also lead to its own apocalyptic perversion, to entropy or chaos, a notion which seems to be prevalent in much recent American fiction?

JG: It certainly is true that that has become prominent in American fiction. I think it's come about because, instinctively, unconsciously, a lot of American writers feel that the American ideal—as they understand it—is wrong-headed, or unrealistic. But I think those writers are mistaken. They oversimplify. They secretly want their individuality, and they think they're wrong to want it—antisocial— and so they lash out at the ideal of conciliation that seems to threaten them, claiming that, though we ought to admire it, it's a false hope; or else they misapprehend it, confusing it with such amoral levellers as the international corporation. Some conciliation does occur, after all, and it needn't wreck individuality. I think you have to keep your merely social values to some extent. They give identity. Security. But you must recognize that they're not universally shared. You've simply recognized that we have to have a balance of private values and public values, and that, in the realm of public values, we have to compromise; we have to try to dismiss what our own fraction of the culture calls 'bad manners' and ask only for humane goodness. But if we do that privately, if we abandon all we've come from, what we get is—nothing. We poison our emotions.

The people who write nihilistic books in America, I believe, are pretty often people who have given up their private values and have carelessly thrown out their secure belief in universal values with the same bathwater, believing that all values are nothing but the manners of the brainless herd. What they're really saying—not consciously, of course—is, 'If I can't have my home group's values, nobody can have values.' They declare themselves Nietzschean supermen and strike superior poses—and they feel a great loss, which they then can't help but whine about.

I think the important thing—the thing that I tried to work out in *The Sunlight Dialogues*—is that you have to cling to your rituals, yet develop a powerful sense of empathy for other people through particular relationships with other people. In doing that you get a clear sense of what the universal values are without abandoning your own personal supports, the rituals that differently express the universals. Clumly, at the end of *The Sunlight Dialogues,* still wants law and order, which is mostly ritual, given the stupidity of the laws he enforces; but he knows that law and order doesn't lead to justice, and he wants justice even more. All he can really do at the end of the novel is cry, because he hasn't yet resolved the demands of written law and the demands of love. Nevertheless, Clumly's situation is focal. At the end of the novel, everybody understands everybody else better, except for Benson/Boyle who has lost everything; his failure to resolve the conflict is total, because from the beginning he faked both sides of it.

In other novels, I go past Clumly's position. But basically, all I wanted to do in *The Sunlight Dialogues* was to dramatize—not really 'dramatize,' because I didn't know what I'd be forced to say until I finished the novel; I mean I had to think it out in the process of writing it; but what I think I came to by the time I had finished writing was the notion that whatever values you most prize must come from a deep empathetic sense of what makes other people precious (in the old sense). Whatever values you hold to, you have to hold to because they hold for other people, and whatever values you're inclined to enforce, you have to enforce knowing that you may be doing somebody damage, so you have to think hard about those values. Clumly is in a position where he can't enforce anything because the whole dialogue has broken down. Clumly's state is like that of the nihilists among contemporary American writers except in one important respect: he still feels compassion. And to reach that point is to come to the next step, which is working out the new morality for mankind. At the beginning of *The Sunlight Dialogues,* which of course takes place at the end—that is, it's a moment long after the action of the novel, a moment that serves as a prologue—Clumly is talking to the old judge who doesn't remember people who have died, doesn't remember what happened to Clumly's wife and to Miller and so on. Clumly remembers everything. At the beginning of the novel, the point beyond the end, Clumly is a sort of mass, like a planet, like a physical force resisting entropy, resisting everything's dribbling off. He remembers; he knows what happened. I think what I wanted to do in the process of writing the novel was to get him to that point. The opening value in that book, in other words, is simply knowing what's happening and remembering it—clinging to it; not passing it off and not going off in any crazy direction. From that stage, one can go to further stages. But Clumly is the recorder. In an earlier draft I had a line which I then took out: 'And I only am escaped alone to tell thee'—you know, a Biblical line that Melville had used; but I decided that there was enough quotation of other people quoting other people, and I cut it. Anyway, that's the position that Clumly is in. Clumly is the Muse; he's the voice of memory, epic song, whatever. The next stage of civilization has to deal with that knowledge and make a whole new morality. This is the big thing that I'm always working at—in all my fiction. All the codes we have available to us now seem to me too narrow. We have religious codes: the Jews have a code, the Christians have a code, the Muslims have a code; but they aren't the same code and, as long as they aren't the same code, they can't be right. They are only good as long as the groups don't meet. We have all kinds of ethnocentric codes. We have the Anglo-Saxon versus the Italian, Arabian against Jewish, and so on. The code that we have to get to is one that knows what the universal values are, what's good for people, what's healthy for them, what makes them able to live as individuals and as members of society. The first books I wrote all dealt with the limitations of the codes. In my later books I got more and more to mulling over what might be the right way, the new morality, a morality which would be every bit as palatable to a Hindu or Jew or Muslim as to a Christian, as palatable to a black as to a white, and so on. But I suspect that the only way for cultures to come together, the only way two opposite people come together, is through hurting each other so badly that they stop and cry.

HZ: Susan Sontag, in a recent three-part article, 'Images of Disease,' in *The New York Review of Books,* warns against what she calls 'sublimated spiritualism, a secular, ostensibly scientific way of affirming the primacy of "spirit" over matter.' Out of what seems to me to be a similar attitude, you state in *The King's Indian* that 'it's never required enduring forms to make the world Platonic; it requires only inescapable pain.' But should the belief in a spiritual ideal really be abandoned altogether for a pragmatic notion of morality? Perhaps the Platonic forms do reduce man and his actions to imperfect shadows, but they also make it possible to think of progress positively—as a moral approximation to an ideal—rather than negatively—as merely behavioural avoidance of pain.

JG: What I mean when I said that 'it's never required enduring forms to make the world Platonic'—that is to say, it doesn't require deism or Plato's museum in the sky—is that you don't have to have eternal verities or images or forms, all you have to have is successive generations of human beings who always hurt the same way when you hit them the same way. As long as some particular mode of behaviour causes you pain, generation after generation through the centuries, that mode of behaviour is unhealthy, unfit for survival. As long as people pay attention to their pain and to other people's pain, they can try to avoid it—try not to do the things that cause pain to individuals or sickness to individuals and to the society as a whole. So that, obviously, you don't have to have fixed ideas, you don't have to have concepts of good; all you have to have is a sense of self-preservation which recognizes the importance of the preservation of other people's welfare so that they won't hurt you—the golden rule, except it's a negative version of it. It seems to me that the only eternal verity there is for human beings is what works to make you physically and spiritually well, and the main business of civilization should be trying to figure out what are the healthiest ways of doing things to keep everybody going.

HZ: But might it not sound rather too optimistic when you say that the only thing we have to do is find a new morality? And that you can simply get to it through the experience of pain which, although bad in itself, leads to a better understanding of other human beings?

JG: Yes, I suppose my general argument on the probability of humanity does sound optimistic. But I think it's a matter of evidence that the world does get improved. I think that the present behavior of policemen in America is a result of learning through pain. That is to say, we went through the sixties and the cops beat up the kids, and half a century before that it used to be quite normal for a policeman to shoot. But it's top priority in police departments everywhere now, or everywhere but Philadelphia, that you don't kill—even a crazed sharpshooter you try to take alive. We have to find out what works. I mean we can't solve the problems of the world sentimentally; that would be grotesque. We just have to find out what works. The survival of the fittest is a law without heart, but my bet is that the fittest are the gentle people, the just ones.

I'm not after the spiritualism Susan Sontag objects to. What happens at the end of *The King's Indian* is that they get to the point where they see the world of the spirit clearly and they turn back; I mean they move away from it as fast as they can, back to safety. What Jonathan Upchurch wants at the beginning of the novel—his idea of perfect happiness—is to get to southern Illinois, which is his symbol of the world completely visible: Indians and bluffs and the Mississippi River and complete immersion with the physical and no nonsense of intellect, which he has gotten a bad view of through the minister he works for, and spirit, which he's got a bad view of, and poetry, which he's got a bad view of because his father tells all these lies. He wants to get out of all that. But, by the nature of chance, he's thrown into a world where the conflict is over spiritual matters. (They turn out to be fake spiritual matters—and real also, but a hoax.) But ultimately, when he knows where spirit leads, when he knows the value of spirit and he knows the danger of spirit, he turns the ship around. What he wants is to be in the middle of the world, where you are solidly in touch with the physical and you know the spirit is there.

HZ: This leaves us with the impression that mind and matter are not only opposites but irreconcilable opposites, right? Therefore, does the notion in *The King's Indian* that God may be unparticled matter disregard the question of truth? Or does it mean wanting to have things both ways?

JG: Right. The idea that God is unparticled matter is Poe's, of course, not mine—though one of my characters maintains the point of view. I think that finally what I'd say is that it doesn't matter if it's true or not. There may indeed be no God; the only undetermined thing we know by direct experience is consciousness; the rest is none of our business, it's irrelevant; the whole spiritual world is an irrelevant kind of thing except as a metaphor for values, and those we can get at empirically. The only thing that's fundamentally important in 'the spiritual world' is the notion—perhaps metaphoric, but valid for all that—that every life is one life—you know, the Hindu business—that is to say, the notion that there is one life force that is in everything, that pushes up wherever it can, in an insect or a daisy, in a black or a white or an Indian or a Chinese—it's all one same thing.

From the time I was writing the first novel I ever wrote, that has been the metaphysical promise or metaphor behind all my things—as it is, by the way—or so it seems to me—with Joyce Carol Oates and a lot of contemporary American writers.

If it's all one life force, and if you can get the experiential sense of that, if you can really experience what Jonathan Upchurch experiences with his beloved in *The King's Indian,* that they really are the same person, then it becomes possible to behave in a different way from the devouring wolf. As soon as you know that, as soon as you know that there is this one spirit in everything, that's enough; that's all you have to know. You don't go beyond that, kill yourself to get to heaven, you know, which is what would happen if Upchurch and his ship continue toward that maelstrom at the end of that book. What happens in Poe—in *The Narrative of Arthur Gordon Pym,* which is the base of my novella—is that the events form a progression, from the beginning of the novel to the end, of people disobeying rules. The novel opens with two kids going out in a boat into a storm, disobeying their father, and each later event is a further disobedience or mutiny, one kind of disobedience after the other until finally the great white law consumes them, they get swallowed. I don't think that way; I think the world is much more chancy than that, more balanced, more lucky. But I think that it is certainly true that there *is* a kind of great white law out there that is very dangerous, that is to say, that can kill you. A law of spiritual fitness which means destruction of the unfit. I do have a Collingwoodian notion of history; I think Greece fell because it had a built-in mistake; the Romans corrected that mistake. That is, the Romans were not ethnocentric to the same degree that the Greeks were. The Romans went to Ethiopia and didn't notice the Ethiopians were black, and married them; they went to Jerusalem and married the Jews. They were just, but also Laodycean. That's why Virgil is so sad—Virgil's idea is that only one or two things can happen to such a civilization, a civilization which holds itself up to judgement and which is reasonable and responsible as the Romans were trying to be, I mean to everybody—accepting the gods of everybody, accepting the morals and customs and everything else. They would have to end up either orgiastic— exploding into moral anarchy—or else (he didn't know the word Stoic) they would end up nobly suicidal. *Sunt lachrymae rerum.* His intuition was right; there was a mistake built into the Roman Empire. An emotional mistake, also a moral one. And I think that that mistake got corrected by what started out as the Christian Middle Ages, and then they too made their mistake, too much code instead of too little.

And so I think that there are mistakes we make, both individually and in our religions and social systems, and those mistakes are absolute. They're like Platonic absolutes. That is to say, an individual or a civilization can't work if he or it does so and so, violates the terrible white law. And so, step by step, we survive toward a better way of working or else we perish. It may be that we will make the wrong turn before we find it; you know, a technological society could be the wrong turn and end everything; I hope not.

HZ: For me, the question still remains whether the life force you are talking about—apparently a force that drives rather than leads— can, after all, be sufficient. If every civilization has its built-in mistakes and if these mistakes arise from having either too much code or too little code, isn't that the result of the spiritual and the physical possessing different degrees of gravity? I mean, human consciousness is defined by spiritual needs and goals derived from them as well as by life force, isn't it?

JG: Not if it's wise, I think. Consciousness loves only itself, ideally. Except for happiness—the timeless happiness of a child lost in play— all the goals of consciousness are secondary. Consciousness makes up goals for each game it plays, but the real goal is always the same, not essentially spiritual but existential: everybody wants to be happy. From particular experiences of happiness we abstract forms of happiness (being just, being rich, being admired for our looks); and if we're careless we confuse the secondary goal with the primary one. When a whole civilization does that, we get neurotic displacement on a grand scale.

Every civilization that's ever been built has had an idea of what the perfect life would be, what happiness is—always an inadequate idea. The civilization's members arrange their lives—or their lives fall into a half-accidental pattern—in pursuit of that goal. And insofar as they've forgotten something, insofar as they've gotten the idea of happiness wrong (for instance, if they think it's happiness for me but not for my neighbor, or if they think it's a static condition rather than a mode of action), then that mistake destroys them. The member of the self-centered civilization can't keep his happiness because his neighbor is trying to keep happiness too, and pretty soon he comes out with a machete because the first citizen is in the way of the second's happiness. The mistakes are always of the same kind: a failure to define happiness wisely. Definitions of happiness are always pretty largely unconscious, unfortunately. Philosophy comes along when it's needed to justify what everybody is doing already or else to figure out what's wrong. Existentialism was around for a long time, but it was only when the French underground was living an impossible life in which the odds were overwhelmingly against it that suddenly existentialism came in as a persuasive philosophy. Because existentialism tells you a wonderful lie—which is that you can do something today that violates all history; that you can reverse your own momentum; that your own past has nothing to do with what you decide to do today or tomorrow; you can change it all. Or the history of the world has nothing to do with what tomorrow will give the world. That's a wonderful theory—if you are a French existentialist in the underground, where because of history's momentum—the odds—you haven't got a chance. If you believe, you die happy. But it's a lousy theory except in that situation. Well, all the philosophies that we have developed have developed out of real-life situations. Plato comes after the events which bring him about; he's a necessary response.

I think what really happens in a civilization—since civilizations do go a long time and do make a lot of adjustments and do narrowly escape a lot of dooms—I think what happens is that all civilizations have a pretty good idea of what they want—what will bring happiness. They almost make it; and philosophy helps. Americans, for instance—I don't know if they're right, I think it's a kind of silly idea, but, basically, when Americans speak of happiness they generally mean the freedom to have material comforts. They go after that happiness and gradually things begin to go wrong. They don't see that they are going wrong; they're too busy looking at the grindstone and its benefits. But they feel an increasing vague distress. The philosopher thinks it over and at last he says, 'Wait! The thing that is wrong is this: we've got to stop throwing away styrofoam', or whatever. When things get bad enough, the commoners grab his idea and maybe it helps them; maybe not. Perhaps I shouldn't say philosophers make the discovery. Maybe it's the crazies. People push toward happiness and they begin to make errors, and the errors become fairly radical before they notice them; then a few people, usually the crazies on the fringe of society, say, 'Look, this is what is wrong,' and they try to lay out, in public demonstrations, in philosophy books or in bills which at first fail to become law, what ought to be done. When the situation gets really horrible, people grab those ideas. They're the only ones at hand. Reason is not very reasonable, as a rule. It arises out of the same roar lions are born of.

HZ: I'd like to change direction somewhat by asking about your concept of parody in *The King's Indian*. It seems to me that your use of parody is specific. Normally, I think, parody is understood as a literary device oscillating between imitation, regarding form, and play, regarding content. Now, you seem to substitute exaggeration for imitation (John Hunter, for example, in 'The Ravages of Spring,' is resurrected in *three* little children; or Captain Dirge in 'The King's Indian,' who is modelled after Captain Ahab, is literally propelled by coils and springs); and you seem to substitute seriousness for play (for example, when you say at the end of the book that it is not 'one more bad joke of exhausted art' but that 'you are real, reader, and so am I, John Gardner'). Thus what you seem to do is shift the play element in parody towards form, the imitation element towards content. Do you thereby mean to signify that we are supposed to take the content of your literary model seriously?

JG: Yes, I do. But first I should say that the American idea of parody is in general very different from the European. Most of the great American writers were conscious parodists in the same way I am. Edgar Allan Poe in 'The Devil in the Belfry' writes a parody of 'The Legend of Sleepy Hollow' by Washington Irving. Washington Irving tells the story about this intellectual, gangly guy, Ichabod Crane, who comes to this Dutch town and, since Washington Irving was fundamentally a philistine—maybe that's too strong, but he was a trifle anti-intellectual, loved the common people, didn't trust intellectuals, and so on—Irving makes Ichabod a comic, grotesque figure who is chased out, scared to death, driven away from the community by an apple-cheeked, beefy Dutchman. Poe brings back Ichabod Crane; he doesn't give his name but he has the same red-cheeked Dutch characters, smoking their pipes, listening to rigidly timed martial music, and so on, and Poe's Ichabod, sawing away *rubato* on his violin, goes up in the belfry and beats up the bell-ringer. Poe uses the style of Washington Irving because he wants the reader to be thinking about what Irving said—notice how wrong it was. If Poe's imitation of Ichabod Crane is clear enough, then the reader who's been reading Washington Irving will catch all the connections, and Poe doesn't have to spell them out; so Poe cannot only flat-out disagree with Irving, he can make a fool of him, in the beloved style of nineteenth-century American politicians. Poe imitated all the time, he loved parody. He even parodied painting in 'Landor's Cottage,' this time for a serious and noble effect. Melville used parody again and again. The most obvious example—kind of horrifying, in a way—is in *The Confidence-Man* where he has this terrible action, you know, where the devil is personally perverting the world towards his murderous doctrine of materialistic capitalism. Awful things are happening, in Melville's tale, and the characters are for the most part missing it because they're responding in a sweet, mindless, so-to-speak Dickensian way. And so Melville uses the style of Dickens to give you the horror of what's happening. The effect is striking—chilling. It makes him seem a quite nasty man if you happen to love Dickens—but that's the point! Melville knows Dickens's virtures as well as anyone does. In the opening of *Pierre,* Melville parodies Byron among others, because he's attacking self-regarding romantic ideals, and the whole book is a bitter, horrible sort of excoriation of the romantic—especially the Byronic way of thinking. Stephan Crane—his first works were literally parodies, and then he became a parodist in the higher sense . . . The critic Eric Solomon has a wonderful book on the subject. So! I'm in an American tradition in doing what I do.

What I was doing in *The King's Indian,* sort of, or at least what I was consciously doing, was setting up—well, I started out, in the first of the book's three parts, with a set of notions which are common among contemporary writers, basically gloomy notions that the world is a terrible place, doomed. Then I used one after another of the styles of well-known English and American writers, finally bringing them all together, in the book's third part, into a sort of fancy orchestration of several major American styles plus the main person behind the American tradition, or so it seems to me, Samuel Taylor Coleridge, one of the main inspirations of Emerson and others, a poet whose vision, for better or worse, is still set deep in the American psyche. I think 'The Ancient Mariner' really influenced an awful lot of the work of Poe and Melville: *Arthur Gordon Pym, Benito Cereno, Moby Dick* . . . What I wanted to do was set up a group of stories in which you take the blackest view you can—the typical contemporary American writer's, intellectual writer's, dark view of things—and then analyse it, taking the style and basic premises of some great writer—a technique which gives you a kind of triangulation. I'm saying, in effect, 'This is how it used to seem in the nineteenth century on these issues; and this is how it seems now.' I didn't stick only to American writers—obviously I used Browning, Kafka, and other Europeans—but basically, especially in the novella, I focus on American writers and American positions. And then I wanted to move toward the second section, from the notion that things are really terrible and that we can only make the best we can of them as forlorn individuals—which is what happens in the early stories—to the pivotal story, 'John Napper Sailing Through the Universe,' where John Napper, a real painter who spent some time in this country, says, 'Yes, it's awful, we will just have to make up a different world and make it a possibility, a model for the future.' Then I offer, in the book's second part, a set of stories which are fantasy, a better world made up by fiat, in a kind of existentialist way—the Queen Louisa stories—in which you simply make a better world by denying the world that exists. That's what Queen Louisa does essentially. Her daughter has died. She can't face it, so in fact she doesn't face it, she changes the world for the better by a mad program, a fantasy she happens to have the power to enforce. But that's not really enough, of course. That's the second movement of the collection. It's a bad option, but it's better, you know, than staring at the abyss and groaning. And then the final section is the novella, in which all of these things get a positive restatement, a positive program which is not existential fantasy—oh, I obviously play a lot with fantasy, and I imitate and echo just about everybody I've ever read. It's a book about literature and life, sort of.

A novel—any work of literature—can be just about life, can be just about literature, as Donald Barthelme's things are, or can be about both, can be about the interplay of literature and life. I was fascinated with the whole metafictionist business at the time I wrote this collection. All the things that I was working on then, *The King's*

Indian, the beginnings of *October Light,* and the beginnings of the
new *Suicide Mountains,* in all of those I was constantly playing
literature against life, looking for the answers literature gives, or so
we're told. Contemporary writers are over-concerned about the
whole business, but the questions are interesting . . . The Heisenberg
principle as it applies to literature: if you're trying to tell the truth and
if the way you tell the story changes the truth, does literature ever get
to the truth at all? What I obviously think is that every element in a
piece of fiction, that is to say, every element of plot, every element of
character—fatness, thinness, meanness, stinginess, whatever—every
single element, discrete as a tree or a mountain in a painting or
whatever, is a word, the complex language of literary art. You put the
elements together in a way that expresses yourself, your intuition of
truth, and I don't think you're talking nonsense, you know. If it's true
that you can write a description of how to make a bomb and
somebody else can read your description and make a bomb that will
explode, then language has some relation to reality and those who
deny the relation are wrong. And if literature or the arts are a very,
very sophisticated language; if the kidnap plot, you know, the
archetypal kidnap plot, already means something inherently, well,
then writer after writer will understand what it means, however
unconscious the understanding may be. Take *ordinary* language.
Most Americans don't know what *matrix* means, right? They know
what it does, how to use it in a sentence, but they don't know that it
has anything to do with the womb. Nevertheless they use the word.
In the same way, I think, a writer who doesn't know *exactly* what
kidnapping means, inherently or fundamentally, as a piece of artistic
language, an element—that writer nonetheless, when he writes a
kidnapping story, feels out the essential meaning and works out what
he believes to be the truth; that is, he makes the characters do what
they really would do and doesn't force them, bully them. He ends up
saying something, something very complicated about the treatment of
people as objects, the theft of personality, the general idea of
psychological tyranny. The more unconscious he is the better, in a
way—the better he uses his literary language. Anyway, given that
premise that *every* element in fiction, including literary style, has a
meaning, it becomes interesting to play one against the other. In the
'King's Indian' novella, the two root styles are those of Edgar Allan

Poe and Herman Melville; and then, of course, Twain and Coleridge play through it; and then minor writers, other people down to, say, William Dean Howells.

Poe and Melville offer an interesting contrast on basic American values. Poe was a Southerner and a very self-conscious Southerner, thought of himself as a Southerner, wanted to be a southern gentleman. He believed in slavery, or so he says, because he thought the alternative to human slavery was slavery to the machine, which had, he thought, more terrible implications. He thought that with human slavery, you would eventually get civilization evolved properly: humane treatment of slaves, eventually a situation where the people who were slaves would be the least intelligent, least sensitive, least hurt. The Man with the Hoe kept from harming us, that sort of thing. Melville, on the other hand, was a Yankee through and through and believed very much in big industry. He had his criticisms, God knows; nevertheless, he thinks slavery to that super machine, the whaler, is preferable to human slavery. He introduces speeches against slavery—all kinds of human slavery—again and again. The opposition of the two views is one of the deep oppositions in the American spirit, and so I copy the way Poe writes and the way Melville writes in my attempt to get at the basic ideas, the American 'problem.' By using parody, by using Poe against Melville and then commenting on the two of them with the help of Mark Twain, the great literary exponent of the flim-flam man—Jonathan Upchurch as trickster—you get the whole spectrum of American opinion on freedom and responsibility. So the answer is: Yes, I certainly am using parody very seriously and I definitely want the voices to be heard.

It's important that one knows, as one reads, apropos the sense of the novel or whatever it is, who is talking, what style it's in, because, particularly in parody, the style is part of the meaning. I think that is probably more true of American than it is of European forms of parody because Americans started out as thieves, that is, the American literary tradition begins as a pirating tradition. The great books in America in the nineteenth century are mostly the ones they stole from England and elsewhere, lots of translations, all kinds of things. Americans imitated those pirated books. That was the easiest way to sell a book for one thing, because American literature itself had no prestige. It wasn't until Poe and Hawthorne that people really began to take American literature seriously, and even that came mainly in France and Germany and England—not in this country. You almost had to be a parodist. It was the same with the Romans, of course, who imitated the Greeks.

HZ: So parody establishes, if I understand you correctly, a connection between aesthetics and morals, literature and life—by constantly playing one against the other. And as you imply, you again dramatize this connection in your latest book, *In the Suicide Mountains*. Here you seem to twist the Aristotelian notion that art imitates life by maintaining that after a while life will begin to imitate art. 'The mimic is doomed to become what he mimics.' The abbot who expounds this theory and who is a masked incorporation of evil therefore becomes his own 'victim': by imitating the saintly abbot whom he has killed, he himself has to become saintly. This notion that life imitates art certainly attributes a great importance, even power to the artist. But doesn't the ensuing responsibility weigh him down too much?

JG: I don't think so, because I think it is what serious artists have always assumed, whether or not the society around them assumed it; I think that when Homer wrote, he very consciously attempted to build a certain kind of society. The reason he puts all the different dialects in, the reason he uses all the gods even when he knows perfectly well that some of them are doubles—different pronunciations of the same goddess's name and so on—was that he believed that, by powerfully presenting a model for life, he could make it happen. He wanted the world to be a better place in specific ways. I think that every great artist does this. Wilde's image of the artist as indifferent to morality is merely a reaction—disingenuous, I think—to pretentiously moralistic Victorian art. I think that Shakespeare talks about the things he talks about because they were the most important questions in Elizabethan England. He names them and he offers you ways of living, gives you possibilities of a future, sometimes in a tragic way—'Don't do this,' as in *Macbeth,* and sometimes in a direct, almost preacherly way, as in *The Tempest.* I wouldn't really want to call that a sermon but he does tell you: 'This is how to live, this is what to do.' I think artists have always taken the position— particularly literary artists—that they are telling the world how it should behave. It's also true of musicians, obviously people like Beethoven very clearly saying, in emotional terms, 'This is what I am for, this is what I am against.' It's also true of certain kinds of painters, though perhaps not of all painters; painters are much more mystical and private in dealing with individual sensation. But I think every artist starts out wanting to tell the world how to be, how to feel, how to avoid insincerity and falsehood. I think there really is a basic relationship between the priest and the poet. The difference between the two is that the priest gives you fables and insists that they are true, and if you don't believe they are true, he kills you—at least the old-fashioned priest did that. He slaughters you, sacrifices you to the hungry gods because you're wicked. But the artist gives you metaphors and says, 'Yes, I know they're metaphors but never-theless, listen to this; it's true.' And I think that's what he wants.

Bad artists do the same thing; Harold Robbins—well, not a bad artist—a slick entertainer. To take better examples, John Hersey or James Michener are very much preachers—good ones, understand. They wouldn't sacrifice anybody. Michener wrote *Tales of the South Pacific* because he was horrified by the treatment of Hawaiians in America at the time, and he had enormous effect. After *South Pacific*, the musical, came out (it was much more popular than the book, I think), people just couldn't look at Hawaiians the same way they had before. I mean, they really had looked at them as animals. Every time a James Baldwin comes along, he changes the world. I think it has always been true that art leads life, not the other way around. That whole notion of the self-transcendent, you know: you cast ahead into a future what you want and then you try to create it; that is the fundamental process of real art. Real artists make up a world that would be worth living in, recognizing the faults in our world, the faults that in theirs will no longer exist. Every generation of artists talks about, I think, the same old values but applies them each time to a new group. In Homer's day it seemed perfectly obvious that the individual should have dignity, that if he doesn't get his due, he should yell. But Homer didn't stop to notice that that should apply not just to kings but to the woman or to the slave or to the barbarian. Generation after generation we have applied the ancient universals more broadly. In every generation, there is always somebody who is getting screwed. The person whose business it is to notice that is the artist. I think there are artists now who don't do that. I mean serious artists do a lot of things. One of the things that legitimate artists do is to describe the way the world is right now; just getting a good image of it, a good photograph, is sufficient for them—and that's fine; that's realism. But the kind of art I particularly value doesn't do that. The kind I like sets up visions of what is possible and helps to move humanity toward them.

HZ: *In the Suicide Mountains* is subtitled: *A Tale,* and the tale—the fairy tale, the gothic tale, the epic tale—tends to reappear in your fiction. It is almost as though the tale had a certain redeeming quality for you. It seems to be able to transcend the nature of evil, as expressed by the old priest in *Grendel:* the two facts that 'Things fade' and that 'Alternatives exclude.' Regarding the first issue, the tale has a timelessness which is not inhuman as is the timelessness of the dragon in *Grendel,* who knows past, present, and future; it is, rather, a timelessness which rests upon the possibility of repetition. Regarding the second issue, in the tale nothing is lost, that is, every part retains its meaning throughout the tale; not in the way that nothing is lost for the dragon in *In the Suicide Mountains,* who 'embraces good, evil, and indifference,' but in the way that, within a tale, evil can turn into good or vice versa and yet coexist with the good or the evil respectively.

JG: Yes. That's true. I love the form of the tale. When I was starting to write, I wrote nonrealistic fiction and it was at a time when realistic fiction was very popular in this country. The most published writer in America was John O'Hara, a realist, a sort of bitter realist—I guess, that is rather common in that tradition. But everything New York was publishing was realistic. All the books on understanding fiction included only realistic short stories. And I was writing these things about dragons and so on, and everybody said, 'No, you can't write that for grown-ups, this is ridiculous, John.' It took me a long time to get stuff published because I kept insisting on doing these non-realistic things. In fact, one of the reasons that I wrote *Nickel Mountain* was that I wanted to write a pseudo-realistic piece. It feels like solid realism and yet there are ghosts in it and talking windows and all kinds of things like that. It seems to me that what is wonderful about the tale is that it goes right straight for the moral universe, which is what I am interested in—a universe in which you are responsible for what you do. If the universe is orderly, then your behavior has to be orderly, and if it isn't—trouble.

There are all kinds of things about tales that are wonderful though. The fact that tales are always in their pure form set in some remote place, old buildings, characters larger than life—the whole remoteness and oldness of the tale implies values which hold on and which curse you if you go against them. The problem in the tale is to find out what are true values and what are false values; what works and what doesn't. In an ordinary piece of fiction, in a realistic piece of fiction, what happens is whatever is causally likely—plausible. In a tale, what happens is what morally has to happen. And so without any pussyfooting, without lots and lots of pages proving that this story takes place in St. Louis, you know, where you fill in all the kinds of ethnics and you name the streets—instead of that, you go right to the heart of what you're talking about. Even in my seemingly realistic stuff I do that. In *Sunlight Dialogues*, I have a veneer of realism all the time but underneath that realism, things are bubbling to the surface. Quite literally in one case. An old car in which two people have been murdered comes bubbling up to the surface of a creek. Nobody knows who they are or were, but what you know when you read that scene is that these policemen, Clumly and his friend, who are trying to make a just world, are doing it in a world where there are old evils, crimes which aren't understood and will never be explained, and they have to make some sense of a moral universe in spite of the mysteries that come from the past. So that I have always inclined in that direction rather than in the direction of realism—merely because I want to talk about what I want to talk about: responsibility. What goes wrong when you get the rules wrong, through selfishness or through a notion that you are right and everybody else is wrong or whatever, is that you begin to do things which destroy yourself and other people. The tale is an efficient way of getting at that.

HZ: Is that why the dragons of your tales are the real horror? Because for them there is no distinction between good and evil, no boundaries between past, present, and future; because the dragon is a metaphor for entropy?

JG: Yes, the thing about dragons—and I think it's traditionally true—the reason they are the way they are is that they're practically invulnerable; there's hardly anything you can do to a dragon. If you're not vulnerable, and if nothing you love is vulnerable, there's no reason to be good, no reason to be orderly. It's mortality that makes morality. The dragon is a classic symbol of all that's beyond that rule. But it's nice to have dragons around, to keep us honest.

John Gardner: The Art of Fiction LXXIII

Paul F. Ferguson, John R. Maier, Frank McConnell,
and Sara Matthiessen/1973, 1977, and 1978

In *John Gardner: A Bibliographical Profile,* John M.
Howell reports that this interview incorporates three interviews over a period of about five years: Frank McConnell
interviewed Gardner during the winter quarter of 1973 at
Northwestern University; Paul Ferguson and John Maier
conducted a video-taped interview at the State University
of New York College at Brockport, in October 1977; at the
Bread Loaf Writers' Colony in the spring of 1978, Sara
Matthiessen interviewed the writer. Gardner read and annotated the synthesis.

After interviewing him in 1973, Frank McConnell wrote
of the thirty-nine-year-old author as one of the most original and promising younger American novelists. His first
four novels—*The Resurrection* (1966), *The Wreckage of
Agathon* (1970), *Grendel* (1971) and *The Sunlight Dialogues* (1972)—represented, in the eyes of many critics
and reviewers, a new and exhilarating phase in the enter-
prise of modern writing, a consolidation of the resources of
the contemporary novel and a leap forward—or backward—into a reestablished humanism. "One finds in his
books elements of the three major strains of current fiction:
the elegant narrative gamesmanship of Barth or Pynchon,
the hyperrealistic Gothicism of Joyce Carol Oates and
Stanley Elkin, and the cultural, intellectual history of Saul
Bellow. Like so many characters in current fiction,
Gardner's are men on the fringe, men shocked into the
consciousness that they are living lives which seem to be
determined, not by their own will, but by massive myths,
cosmic fictions over which they have no control (e.g.,
Ebeneezer Cooke in Barth's *Sot-Weed Factor,* Tyrone
Slothrop in Pynchon's *Gravity's Rainbow*); but Gardner's

characters are philosophers on the fringe, heirs, all of them, to the great debates over authenticity and bad faith which characterize our era. In *Grendel,* for example, the hero-monster is initiated into the Sartrean vision of Nothingness by an ancient, obviously well-read Dragon: a myth speaking of the emptiness of all myths: 'Theory-makers. . . . They'd map out roads through Hell with their crackpot theories, their here-to-the-moon-and-back lists of paltry facts. Insanity—the simplest insanity ever devised!' His heroes—like all men—are philosophers who are going to die; and their characteristic discovery—the central creative energy of Gardner's fiction—is that the death of consciousness finally justifies consciousness itself. The myths, whose artificiality contemporary writers have been at such pains to point out, become in Gardner's work real and life-giving once again, without ever losing their modern character of fictiveness.

"Gardner's work may well represent, then, the new 'conservatism' which some observers have noted in the current scene. But it is a conservatism of high originality, and, at least in Gardner's case, of deep authority in his life. When he guest-taught a course in 'Narrative Forms' at Northwestern University, a number of his students were surprised to find a modern writer—and a hot property— enthusiastic, not only about Homer, Virgil, Appolonius Rhodius, and Dante, but deeply concerned with the critical controversies surrounding those writers, and with mistakes in their English translations. As the interview following makes clear, Gardner's job in and affection for ancient writing and the tradition of metaphysics is, if anything, greater than for the explosions and involutions of modern fiction. He is, in the full sense of the word, a *literary* man.

" 'It's as if God put me on earth to write,' Gardner observed once. And writing, or thinking about writing, takes up much of his day. He works, he says, usually on three or four books at the same time, allowing the plots to cross-pollinate, shape and qualify each other."

Sara Matthiessen describes Gardner in the spring of 1978 (additional works published by then included *October Light; On Moral Fiction* was about to be published). Matthiessen arrived with a friend to interview him at the Bread Loaf Writers' Colony in Vermont: "After we'd knocked a couple of times, he opened the door looking haggard and just-wakened. Dressed in a purple sateen, bell-sleeved, turtle-neck shirt and jeans, he was an exotic figure: unnaturally white hair to below his shoulders, of medium height, he seemed an incarnation from the medieval era central to his study. 'Come in!' he said, as though there were no two people he'd rather have seen than Sally and me, and he led us into a cold, bright room sparsely equipped with wooden furniture. We were offered extra socks against the chill. John lit his pipe, and we sat down to talk."

Interviewer: You've worked in several different areas: prose, fiction, verse, criticism, book reviews, scholarly books, children's books, radio plays; you wrote the libretto for a recently produced opera. Could you discuss the different genres? Which one have you most enjoyed doing?

Gardner: The one that feels the most important is the novel. You create a whole world in a novel and you deal with values in a way that you can't possibly in a short story. The trouble is that since novels represent a whole world, you can't write them all the time. After you finish a novel, it takes a couple of years to get in enough life and enough thinking about things to have anything to say, any clear questions to work through. You have to keep busy, so it's fun to do the other things. I do book reviews when I'm hard up for money, which I am all the time. They don't pay much, but they keep you going. Book reviews are interesting because it's necessary to keep an eye on what's good and what's bad in the books of a society worked so heavily by advertising, public relations, and so on. Writing reviews isn't really analytical, it's for the most part quick reactions—joys and rages. I certainly never write a review about a book I don't think worth reviewing, a flat-out bad book, unless it's an enormously fashionable bad book. As for writing children's books, I've done them because when my kids were growing up I would now and then write them a story as a Christmas present, and then after I became sort of successful, people saw the stories and said they should be published. I like them, of course. I wouldn't give junk to my kids. I've also done scholarly books and articles. The reason I've done those is that I've been teaching things like *Beowulf* and Chaucer for a long time. As you teach a poem year after year, you realize, or anyway convince yourself, that you understand the poem and that most people have got it slightly wrong. That's natural with any poem, but during the years I taught lit courses, it was especially true of medieval and classical poetry. When the general critical view has a major poem or poet *badly* wrong, you feel like you ought to straighten it out. The studies of Chaucer since the fifties are very strange stuff: like the theory that Chaucer is a frosty Oxford-donnish guy shunning carnality and cupidity. Not true. So close analysis is useful. But writing novels—and maybe opera libretti—is the kind of writing that gives me greatest satisfaction; the rest is more like entertainment.

Interviewer: You have been called a "philosophical novelist." What do you think of the label?

Gardner: I'm not sure that being a philosophical novelist is better than being some other kind, but I guess that there's not much doubt that, in a way at least, that's what I am. A writer's material is what he cares about, and I like philosophy the way some people like politics, or football games, or unidentified flying objects. I read a man like Collingwood, or even Brand Blanchard or C. D. Broad, and I get excited—even anxious—filled with suspense. I read a man like Swinburne on Time and Space and it becomes a matter of deep concern to me whether the structure of space changes near large masses. It's as if I actually think philosophy will solve life's great questions—which sometimes, come to think of it, it does, at least for me. Probably not often, but I like the illusion. Blanchard's attempt at a logical demonstration that there really *is* a universal human morality, or the recent flurry of theories by various majestical cranks that the universe is stabilizing itself instead of flying apart—those are lovely things to run into. Interesting and arresting, I mean, like talking frogs. I get a good deal more out of the philosophy section of a college bookstore than out of the fiction section, and I more often read philosophical books than I read novels. So sure, I'm "philosoph-ical," though what I write is by no means straight philosophy. I make up stories. Meaning creeps in of necessity, to keep things clear, like paragraph breaks and punctuation. And, I might add, my friends are all artists and critics, not philosophers. Philosophers—except for the few who are my friends—drink beer and watch football games and defeat their wives and children by the fraudulent tyranny of logic.

Interviewer: But insofar as you *are* a "philosophical novelist," what is it that you do?

Gardner: I write novels, books about people, and what I write is philosophical only in a limited way. The human dramas that interest me—stir me to excitement and, loosely, vision—are always rooted in serious philosophical questions. That is, I'm bored by plots that depend on the psychological or sociological quirks of the main characters—mere melodramas of healthy against sick—stories which, subtly or otherwise, merely preach. Art as the wisdom of Marcus Welby, M.D. Granted, most of fiction's great heroes are at least slightly crazy, from Achilles to Captain Ahab, but the problems that make great heroes act are the problems no sane man could have gotten around either. Achilles, in his nobler, saner moments, lays down the whole moral code of *The Iliad.* But the violence and anger triggered by war, the human passions that overwhelm Achilles' reason and make him the greatest criminal in all fiction—they're just as much a problem for lesser, more ordinary people. The same with Ahab's desire to pierce the Mask, smash through to absolute knowledge. Ahab's crazy, so he actually tries it; but the same Mask leers at all of us. So, when I write a piece of fiction I select my characters and settings and so on because they have a bearing, at least to me, on the old unanswerable philosophical questions. And as I spin out the action, I'm always very concerned with springing discoveries—actual philosophical discoveries. But at the same time I'm concerned—and finally *more* concerned—with what the discoveries do to the character who makes them, and to the people around him. It's that that makes me not really a philosopher, but a novelist.

Interviewer: The novel *Grendel* is a retelling of the *Beowulf* story from the monster's point of view. Why does an American writer living in the twentieth century abandon the realistic approach and borrow such legendary material as the basis for a novel?

Gardner: I've never been terribly fond of realism because of certain things that realism seems to commit me to. With realism you have to spend two hundred pages proving that somebody lives in Detroit so that something can happen and be absolutely convincing. But the value system of the people involved is the important thing, not the fact that they live on Nine Mile Road. In my earlier fiction I went as far as I could from realism because the easy way to get to the heart of what you want to say is to take somebody else's story, particularly a nonrealistic story. When you tell the story of Grendel, or Jason and Medeia, you've got to end it the way the story ends—traditionally, but you can get to do it in your own way. The result is that the writer comes to understand things about the modern world in light of the history of human consciousness; he understands it a little more deeply, and has a lot more fun writing it.

Interviewer: But why specifically *Beowulf?*

Gardner: Some stories are more interesting than others. *Beowulf* is a terribly interesting story. It gives you some really wonderful visual images, such as the dragon. It's got Swedes looking over the hills and scaring everybody. It's got mead halls. It's got Grendel, and Grendel's mother. I really do believe that a novel has to be a feast of the senses, a delightful thing. One of the better things that has happened to the novel in recent years is that it has become rich. Think of a book like *Chimera* or *The Sot-Weed Factor*—they may not be very good books, but they are at least rich experiences. For me, writers like John O'Hara are interesting only in the way that movies and TV plays are interesting; there is almost nothing in a John O'Hara novel that couldn't be in the movies just as easily. On the other hand, there is no way an animator, or anyone else, can create an image from *Grendel* as exciting as the image in the reader's mind: Grendel is a monster, and living in the first person, because we're all in some sense monsters, trapped in our own language and habits of emotion. Grendel expresses feelings we all feel—enormous hostility, frustration, disbelief, and so on, so that the reader, projecting his own monster, projects a monster which is, for him, the perfect horror show. There is no way you can do that in television or the movies, where you are always seeing the kind of realistic novel O'Hara wrote . . . Gregory Peck walking down the street. It's just the same old thing to me. There are other things that are interesting in O'Hara, and I don't mean to put him down excessively, but I go for another kind of fiction: I want the effect that a radio play gives you or that novels are always giving you at their best.

Interviewer: You do something very interesting in *Grendel.* You never name Beowulf, and in the concluding scene you describe him in such a way as to give the impression that Grendel is really confronting, not Beowulf or another human being, but the dragon. That seems a significant change from the poem.

Gardner: I didn't mean it to be a change. As a medievalist, one knows there are two great dragons in medieval art. There's Christ the dragon, and there's Satan the dragon. There's always a war between those two great dragons. In modern Christian symbolism a sweeter image of Jesus with the sheep in his arms has evolved, but I like the old image of the warring dragon. That's not to say Beowulf really is Christ, but that he's Christ-like. Actually, he is many things. When Grendel first sees Beowulf coming, Grendel thinks of him as a sort of machine, and what comes to the reader's mind is a kind of computer, a spaceman, a complete alien, unknown. The inescapable mechanics of the universe. At other times, Beowulf looks like a fish to Grendel. He comes in the season of Pisces when, among other things, you stab yourself in the back. On other occasions, Grendel sees other things, one after another, and for a brief flash, when he is probably hallucinating—he's fighting, losing blood very badly because he has his arm torn off—Grendel thinks he's fighting the dragon instead of Beowulf. At the end of the story, Grendel doesn't know *who* he's fighting. He's just fighting something big and horrible and sure to kill him, something that he could never have predicted in the universe as he understood it, because from the beginning of the novel, Grendel feels himself hopelessly determined, hopelessly struggling against—in the profoundest sense—the way things are. He feels there's no way out, that there's no hope for living consciousness, particularly *his* consciousness, since, for reasons inexplicable to him, he's on the wrong side, Cain's side instead of mankind's.

Interviewer: It seems to me that determinism is affliction imposed on him by the *scop.*

Gardner: It's true, but only partly. In the novel, he's undeniably pushed around by the universe, but also not to believe, not to have faith in life. What happens is, in the story, the shaper, the *scop,* the court poet comes to this horrible court that's made itself what it is by killing everybody, beating people, chopping them to death, and the poet looks at this havoc around him and makes up a story about what a wonderful court it is, what noble ideals it has. The courtiers are just dumb enough to believe it, just as Americans have believed the stories about Sam Adams and Ethan Allen and all those half-mythical heroes. George Washington once stood for thirty minutes stuttering in a rage before executing a private for a minor misdeed. Sam Adams was like a well-meaning Marxist agitator. Constantly lied. He told Boston that New York had fallen when it hadn't fallen. Or anyway so one of my characters claims. I no longer remember what the truth is.

Interviewer: But that's an important moment in Grendel's development, isn't it, when he hears this story?

Gardner: He hears the story and is tempted to believe it. And for certain reasons, partly because he is kicked out of the mead hall, he decides to reject the myth. That's Grendel's hard luck, because when he goes to the mead hall and wants to be a good monster and doesn't want to kill people anymore, Hrothgar's warriors don't know that, and they throw spears at him and hurt him.

Interviewer: You don't see yourself, as a novelist, analogous to the *scop* in the telling of a story?

Gardner: Oh, sure. Absolutely. I absolutely believe every artist is in the position of the *scop*. As I tried to make plain in *On Moral Fiction,* I think that the difference right now between good art and bad art is that the good artists are the people who are, in one way or another, creating, out of deep and honest concern, a vision of life-in-the-twentieth-century that is worth pursuing. And the bad artists, of whom there are many, are whining or moaning or staring, because it's fashionable, into the dark abyss. If you believe that life is fundamentally a volcano full of baby skulls, you've got two main choices as an artist: You can either stare into the volcano and count the skulls for the thousandth time and tell everybody, "There are the skulls; that's your baby, Mrs. Miller." Or you can try to build walls so that fewer baby skulls go in. It seems to me that the artist ought to hunt for positive ways of surviving, of living. You shouldn't lie. If there aren't any, so far as you can see, you should say so, like the *Merdistes.* But I don't think the *Merdistes* are right—except for Céline himself, by accident, because Céline (as character, not as author) is comic; a villain so outrageous, miserable, and inept that we laugh at him and at all he so earnestly stands for. I think the world is not all merde. I think it's possible to make walls around at least some of the smoking holes.

Interviewer: Won't this have the effect of transforming the modern writer into a didactic writer?

Gardner: Not didactic. The didactic writer is anything but moral because he is always simplifying the argument, always narrowing away, getting rid of legitimate objections. *Mein Kampf* is a moralistic book—a stupid, ugly one. A truly moral book is one which is radically open to persuasion, but looks hard at a problem, and keeps looking for answers. It gives you an absolutely clear vision, as if the poet, the writer, had nothing to do with it, had just done everything in his power to imagine how things are. It's the situation of Dostoevsky and Nietzsche—an illusion I use in *On Moral Fiction*. Nietzsche sets up this abstract theory of the Superman according to which a person can kill or do anything he wants because there is no basis of law except the herd. God doesn't speak; dead. So the people get together and vote to have a red light on Highway 61 where there's no traffic. It's three o'clock in the morning. You're travelling, and there's a red light, and you decide to jump the light. A car pulls out of the weeds, a policeman and he comes after you. If you're a superman, you politely and gently kill him, put him back in the weeds, and drive on. The theory of the superman is kind of interesting, abstractly. The question is, is it right? Will it work? Can human beings live with it? So Dostoevsky sets up the experiment imaginatively. Obviously he doesn't want to go out and actually kill somebody to see if it works, so he imagines a perfectly convincing St. Petersburg, and a perfectly convincing person who would do this. (What student in all St. Petersburg would commit a murder? What relatives would he have? What friends? What would his pattern be? What would he eat?) Dostoevsky follows the experiment out and finds out what does happen.

I think all great art does this, and you don't have to do it realistically. Obviously Raskolnikov could have been a giant saurian, as long as his character is consistent and convincing, tuned to what we know about actual feeling. The point is realism of imagination, convincingness of imagination. The novelist pursues questions, and pursues them thoroughly. Not only when does it rain and when doesn't it rain, but can we tolerate rain? What can we be made to tolerate? What should we not allow ourselves to be made to tolerate?

And so on. So that finally, what's moral in fiction is chiefly its way of looking. The premise of moral art is that life is better than death; art hunts for avenues to life. The book succeeds if we're powerfully persuaded that the focal characters, in their fight for life, have won honestly or, if they lose, are tragic in their loss, not just tiresome or pitiful.

Interviewer: So you have a strong sense of mission, or of a goal, in modern fiction.

Gardner: Yes, I do. In my own way, anyway. I want to push the novel in a new direction, or back to an old one—Homer's or the *Beowulf*-Poet's. Of course, a lot of other writers are trying to do something rather different—Barth and Pynchon, I grant them their right—grudgingly. But to paraphrase the Imagists, I want "no ideas but in *energeia*"—Aristotle's made-up word for (excuse the jazz), "the actualization of the potential which exists in character and situation." Philosophy as plot. I think no novel can please for very long without plot as the center of its argument. We get too many books full of meaning by innuendo—the ingenious symbol, the allegorical overlay, stories in which *events* are of only the most trivial importance, just the thread on which the writer strings hints of his "real" meaning. This has been partly a fault of the way we've been studying and teaching literature, of course. Our talk of levels and all that. For instance, take John Updike's *Couples*. It's a fairly good book, it seems to me, but there's a good reason no one reads anymore: contrived phrases bear all the burden. Symbolically constructed names; descriptions of a living room which slyly hint at the expansion of the universe; or Updike's whole cunning trick with Christian iconography, circles and straight lines—circles traditionally associated with reason, straight lines with faith. You work the whole symbolic structure out and you're impressed by Updike's intelligence—maybe, in this book, even wisdom—but you have difficulty telling the fornicators apart. Reading *Couples* is like studying science while watching pornographic movies put together from random scraps on the cutting-room floor.

Interviewer: You want novels to be whole entertainments, then.

Gardner: Sure! Look: it's impossible for us to read Dostoevsky as a writer of thrillers anymore, because of this whole weight of explanation and analysis we've loaded on the books. And yet *The Brothers Karamazov* is obviously, among other things, a thriller novel.

(It also contains, to my mind, some pretentious philosophizing.) What I've wanted to do, in *The Sunlight Dialogues,* for example, is write a book—maybe not a novel—that you could read as entertainment. Where there's straight philosophizing, here as in *The Resurrection,* it's present because that's what the character would say (or so I thought at the time), present because that's what makes him behave as he does. No meaning but emotion-charged action and emotional reaction.

Interviewer: The classical forms, like *Grendel,* are not your only models, nor do you always adhere to the superficial nature of the form you've chosen—for instance, there are parts in the *Sunlight Dialogues* that parody Faulkner.

Gardner: Sure. In fact, the whole conception of the book is in a way parodic of Faulkner, among others—the whole idea of family and locale. A lot of times I've consciously taken a writer on. In the first novel I did, I used the title *The Resurrection* to give the reader a clue as to what's wrong with Tolstoy in his *Resurrection.* I don't think many readers notice, and of course it doesn't matter. In fact, a friend of mine who's a very good critic asked me one time if I were aware that I'd used a title that Tolstoy had used. That's all right. If I sounded too much like Tolstoy, then my novel would be a critical footnote.

Interviewer: How about your contemporaries? Has any of their work influenced your writing?

Gardner: Of course I'm aware of modern writers . . . and some writers have changed my way of thinking. I don't always like what Bill Gass does—though I do immensely like much of his fiction—but I certainly have changed my writing style because of his emphasis on language, that is, his brilliant use of it in books. It has always seemed to me that the main thing you ought to be doing when you write a story is, as Robert Louis Stevenson said, to set a "dream" going in the reader's mind . . . so that he opens the page, reads about three words, and drops into a sort of trance. He's seeing Russia instead of his living room. Not that he's *passive.* The reader hopes and judges. I used to think that words and style should be transparent, that no word should call attention to itself in any way; that you could say the plainest thing possible to get the dream going. After I read some early Gass—"The Pedersen Kid," I think—I realized that you don't really interfere with the dream by saying things in an interesting way.

Performance is an important part of the show. But I don't, like Gass, think language is of value when it's opaque, more decorative than communicative. Gass loves those formalist arguments. He's said, for instance, that it's naïve to think of characters as real—that it's absurd to cry for little Nell. It may be absurd to cry at that particular death, because in that case the writing is lousy. But what happens in real fiction is identical to what happens in a dream—as long as we have the right to wake up screaming from a nightmare, we have the right to worry about a character. Gass has a funny theory. But I have borrowed a great many elements from it—I'm sure I owe more to him than to any other living writer. And I have learned a few things from slightly contemporary writers. About symbols, for instance. If you stop with James Joyce, you may write a slightly goofy kind of symbolic novel. Joyce's fondness for the "mannered" is the least of it. At the time Joyce was writing, people were less attuned than they are now to symbolic writing, so he sometimes let himself get away with bald, obvious symbols. Now, thanks largely to the New Criticism, any smart college freshman can catch every symbol that comes rolling along. The trouble is that if a reader starts watching the play of symbolism and missing what's happening to the characters, he get an intellectual apprehension of the book, and that's pretty awful. He might as well read philosophy or meditations on the wounds of Christ. But you still need resonance, deep effect. You have to build into the novel the movement from particular to general. The question is, how do you get a symbolic structure without tipping your hand? A number of modern writers have shown ways of doing it. The red herring symbols of Pynchon, the structural distractions of Barth, the machine-gun energy of Gaddis. Above all, Gass's verbal glory.

Interviewer: Do you, like Joyce, play to the reader subliminally through symbolism, or do you make fairly overt statements by demonstrating what certain values can lead to?

Gardner: I try to be as overt as possible. Plot, character, and action first. I try to say everything with absolute directness so that the reader sees the characters moving around, sees the house they're moving through, the landscape, the weather, and so on. I try to be absolutely direct about moral values and dilemmas. Read it to the charwoman, Richardson said. I say, make it plain to her dog. But when you write fiction such as mine, fantastic or quasi-realistic fiction, it happens inevitably that as you're going over it, thinking about it, you recognize unconscious symbols bubbling up to the surface, and you begin to revise to give them room, sort of nudge them into sight. Though ideally the reader should never catch you shaking a symbol at him. (Intellect is the chief distractor of the mind.) The process of writing becomes more and more mysterious as you go over the draft more and more times; finally everything is symbolic. Even then you keep pushing it, making sure that it's as coherent and self-contained as a grapefruit. Frequently, when you write a novel you start out feeling pretty clear about your position, what side you're on; as you revise, you find your unconscious pushing up associations that modify that position, force you to reconsider.

Interviewer: You began *October Light,* you've said, with the idea that "the traditional New England values are the values we should live by: good workmanship, independence, unswerving honesty—" but these proved oversimple. Is the process of fiction always the process of discovery for you? In other words, do you often find that the idea that prompted the fiction turns out to be too simple, or even wrong?

Gardner: I always start out with a position I later discover to be too simple. That's the nature of things—what physicists call complementarity. What's interesting is that my ideas prove too simple in ways I could never have anticipated. In everything I've written I've come to the realization that I was missing something, telling myself lies. That's one of the main pleasures of writing. What I do is follow the drama where it goes; the potential of the characters in their given situation. I let them go where they have to go, and analyze as I'm going along what's involved, what the implications are. When I don't like the implications, I think hard about it. Chasing implications to the wall is my one real skill. I think of ways of dramatically setting up contrasts so that my position on a thing is clear to me, and then I hound the thing till it rolls over. I certainly wouldn't ever fake the actions, or the characters, or make people say what they wouldn't say. I never use sleight-of-wits like Stanley Elkin—though no one can fail to admire a really good sophist's skill.

Interviewer: How important is setting?

Gardner: Setting is one of the powerful symbols you have, but mainly it serves characterization. The first thing that makes a reader read a book is the characters. Say you're standing in a train station, or an airport, and you're leafing through books; what you're hoping for is a book where you'll like the characters, where the characters are interesting. To establish powerful characters, a writer needs a landscape to help define them; so setting becomes important. Setting is also a powerful vehicle of thematic concerns; in fact, it's one of the most powerful. If you're going to talk about the decline of Western civilization or at least the possibility of that decline, you take an old place that's sort of worn out and run-down. For instance, Batavia, New York, where the Holland Land Office was . . . the beginning of a civilization . . . selling the land in this country. It was, in the beginning, a wonderful, beautiful place with the smartest Indians in America around. Now it's this old, rundown town which has been urban-renewalized just about out of existence. The factories have stopped and the people are poor and sometimes crabby; the elm trees are all dead, and so are the oaks and maples. So it's a good symbol. If you're writing the kind of book I was writing in *Sunlight Dialogues* or *The Resurrection,* both of them books about death, both spiritual death and the death of civilization, you choose a place like that. I couldn't have found, in my experience, a better setting. It's just not a feeling you have in San Francisco. If I was going to write a book about southern Illinois, which in fact I did in *King's Indian,* that's another, completely different feeling. There it's as if human beings had never landed; the human beings—the natives, anyway— seem more like gnomes. You choose the setting that suits and illuminates your material.

Interviewer: *The Resurrection, Sunlight Dialogues, Nickel Mountain, October Light,* all take place in your native surroundings, more or less; do you find that you need distance on a place before you can write about it? Would you have been able to get a proper perspective on these places in the East, and the type of people who live there, if you'd not spent a good deal of your time in the West and Midwest?

Gardner: I don't really think so. It's true that *The Resurrection* and *Sunlight Dialogues* take place in Batavia. I wrote one of them in California, the other partly in California, and partly in southern Illinois. So I was using memories from my childhood. Every once in a while, I'd go back and see my parents and go over and see the Brumsteds and the characters who show up in the story, and I'd look the streets over and think, that'd be funny to put in a novel, or whatever. But *Nickel Mountain* is set in the Catskills, which I'd only passed through once or twice, and when I did *October Light,* which came out of a very direct and immediate experience in the East, I'd just moved back to the East after years away. I'd never been in Vermont, and the landscape and the feeling of the people is not at all like western New York. I had never seen anything like it; I certainly didn't have any distance on it. It may be that ten years from now when I look the book over I'll see that I didn't do it very well, but now it feels just as authentic to me as the other books I've written. So I don't think you necessarily do need distance. It is certainly true though that memory selects well. What you keep in your memory is psychologically symbolic, hence powerful, so that when you write about things that you knew a long time ago, you're going to get a fairly powerful evocation of place. I think one sees that in Bernard Malamud's work. When he writes about his childhood, his early memories of New York, you get a very powerful sense of the place. But I think in *A New Life,* written out of immediate experience, you get a more superficial sense of place.

It's different; nobody could deny that the landscapes in *A New Life* are vivid, it's just that they don't have that *lived* feeling that the earlier cityscapes have. You have to write about what's useful and that's the problem; you can't just write about the place that's the most digested for you. In a really good writer's work you'll see that a writer doesn't have to have to have been around a place very long at all. John Fowles' novel *Daniel Martin* has got some long sections on Los Angeles which seem to be absolutely incredible. You'd swear he grew up there. Most people writing about Los Angeles can only see the phoniness, the greenery, and the gilt. Fowles sees everything, and he gets in it.

Interviewer: Your *belief* in literature, your affection for it as a living force, goes back pretty far in your childhood. Did you read mostly the classics when you were a boy?

Gardner: Not mostly—we had a lot of books. My mother was a schoolteacher, and my father was a farmer who loved to read: classics, Shakespeare, and of course, the Bible. They were great reciters of literature, too. I've had visitors—sophisticated people— who've heard my father recite things, and have been amazed at how powerfully he does it. It's an old country tradition, but my father was and is the best. We'd be put to bed with a recital of poetry, things like that. At Grange meetings, for instance, my mother and father would do recitations as part of the evening's entertainment. Or while my father was milking the cows my mother would come out and read something to him—*Lear*, say—leaving out the part of whomever my father felt like being that day, and he'd answer his lines from the cow.

Interviewer: He actually had the whole thing memorized?

Gardner: Oh, sure. Lots of plays. And he'd write things—lay sermons, stories—while he was driving his tractor: compose them in his head, rather like Ben Hodge in *Sunlight*. Not that Ben Hodge is exactly like my father. My father isn't weak-willed. My father knows hundreds of poems, including some very long ones. Beautiful to listen to. A lot of people that we dismiss as terrible poets, like Longfellow, are changed entirely when you say their poems out loud—as they were intended to be. It's like singing; a song can't be very complex; the tune takes up part of the energy so that the words are kind of silly on the page, but when you sing it, it may be wonderful. The same thing happens with oral poetry—lots of stuff that's thin, even goofy on the page can be recited beautifully. That's one of the reasons I write the way I do. Oral stuff written. I hope that comes through.

Interviewer: Did you do any writing as a child?

Gardner: I started writing stories when I was five or so—making these books I'd send to relatives every Christmas. And around eight, I was writing longer things . . . I wrote in ledger books given to me by my grandmother the lawyer. I really enjoyed writing on ledger paper: there's something nice about a page with a red line down the middle.

Interviewer: Do you still use them?

Gardner: No, I own my own typewriter now. Very professional.

Interviewer: Is there an advantage to growing up on a farm?

Gardner: Farm boys have some advantages; it depends on the family. I learned to love the land at least partly because my parents did—working it, watching things grow. Farm boys spend a lot of time with animals of all kinds. I liked it. Some don't. Also, sometimes on the happiest farms, the hunger comes to get away from all that work, and so they may see New York with more excited eyes than some New Yorkers do; or Chicago, or Los Angeles. I love all those places, even the ones that everybody else hates. I have a little trouble with

Cleveland, but parts of it are nice. But except for short stints in San Francisco, Chicago, and Detroit, my whole life has been spent in the country, working with plants and animals, reading and writing. It's nice to live in the country when you grew up there and worked yourself to death in the old days and now you don't have to; you just have a few horses and you play.

Interviewer: What did you study at college?

Gardner: The usual things—wanted to major in chemistry for a while. In graduate school I studied creative writing and medieval literature mostly. It was useful. I learned a lot of things about an older kind of literature that I thought would be handy in writing my own works, if only because I wouldn't be doing the same thing as everybody else.

Interviewer: Is your fiction at all autobiographical? Do you write about people you know specifically, do you write about yourself?

Gardner: Sometimes. My fiction is usually autobiographical, but in a distant, almost unrecognizable way. Once in a while, as in the story "Redemption," I write pretty close to what happened. But I fictionalized that too—which worries me, in fact. When you get to an event that close to real life and you change the characters, you run the risk of your sister, or your mother or father, thinking: "You don't understand me. That wasn't what I was thinking." I *know* that's not what they were thinking, but I need searchlights on a piece, so I have to change characters, make them more appropriate to the fictional idea, the *real* subject, which isn't just history. Usually, though, I'm not interested—as Updike and Malamud are—in celebrating my own life. I use feelings that I have myself—the only feelings I know, directly— and I deal them out to a group of characters, and let the characters fight out the problems that I've been fighting out. Characteristically there's a battle in my fiction between the hunger for roots, stability, law, and another element in my character which is anarchic. I hate to obey speed laws. I hate to park where it says you have to park. I hate to have to be someplace on time. And in fact I often don't do those things I know I should do, which of course fills me with uneasiness and guilt. Every time you break the law you pay, and every time you obey the law you pay. That compulsion not to do what people tell me, to avoid tic repetitions, makes me constantly keep pushing the edges. It makes me change places of living, or change my life in one way or another, which often makes me very unhappy. I wish I could just settle down. I keep promising myself that really soon now I'm going to get this little farm or maybe house and take care of it, never move again. But I'll probably never do it. Anyway, the autobiographical element is more emotional than anything else.

Interviewer: How do you name your characters?

Gardner: Sometimes I use characters from real life, and sometimes I use their real names—when I do, it's always in celebration of people that I like. Once or twice, as in *October Light,* I've borrowed other people's fictional characters. Naming is only a problem, of course, when you make the character up. It seems to me that every character—every person—is an embodiment of a very complicated, philosophical way of looking at the world, whether conscious or not. Names can be strong clues to the character's system. Names are magic. If you name a kid John, he'll grow up a different kid than if you named him Rudolph. I've used real characters in every single novel, except in *Grendel,* where it's impossible—they didn't have our kinds of names in those days—but even in *Grendel* I used jokes and puns that give you clues to who I'm talking about. For instance, there's a guy named Red Horse, which is really a sorrel, which is really George Sorel. And so on. Sometimes I put real, live characters into books under fictional names—to protect the real person from what the fiction makes of him—and thus I get the pleasure of thinking, for example, what my cousin Bill would do if he were confronted with a particular problem. I get to understand my cousin Bill, whom I love, in a way I never understood him before. I get to see him in a situation perhaps more grave, certainly more compromising, than any he's ever been in. Besides using real people, as I've said, I get great pleasure out of stealing other people's writings. Actually, I do that at least partly because of a peculiar and unfortunate quality of my mind: I remember things. Word for word. I'm not always aware of it. Once in college, I wrote a paragraph of a novel which was word for word out of Joyce's "The Dead," and I wasn't aware of it at all. I absolutely wasn't. My teacher at the time said, Why did you do this? He wasn't accusing me of plagiarism, he was just saying it was a very odd thing to do. I realized then that I had a problem. Of course, it was a big help when I was a teacher, because I could quote long passages of Beowulf and things like that. Once I realized that I also accidentally quote, that I'm constantly alluding to things I'm not consciously aware of, I began to develop this allusive technique—at least when it's fiction—so that nobody could accuse me of plagiarism, since it's so obvious that I'm alluding. In fact, sometimes I have great fun with it. Particularly in *Jason and Medeia,* where I took long sections of writing by Bill Gass, whom I'm enormously fond of, and with whom I completely disagree on almost everything unimportant, and altered a few words to mess up his argument. And in *The Wreckage of Agathon* I took long sections out of Jean-Paul Sartre, changed all the images, but kept the rest directly translated. So I use everything.

Interviewer: How do your victims react? Is Sartre aware? Or Gass?

Gardner: I'm sure Sartre has never heard of me. I hope he'd be amused. As for Gass, he knows why I do it: partly from impishness, partly for a comically noble reason which has to do with Gass's present and future fame.

Interviewer: How do you react to Peter Prescott's insinuation in *Newsweek* that you plagiarized in your *Life and Times of Chaucer?*

Gardner: With a sigh.

Interviewer: How about the charge that you're, excuse the expression, a male chauvinist?

Gardner: Consciously, I'm a feminist; but neither the best things we do or the worst are fully conscious. That's why the effect of art is so important. One does not consciously make oneself more bestial by reading pornographic books, and I think only the worst sort of people become consciously "better" people by reading the Bible. When I'm accused of male chauvinism, as I was in one review of *Nickel Mountain,* I'm indignant and hurt; but I watch myself more closely to see if it's true. I've also been accused of being antihomosexual. I'm glad I was accused, because although I wasn't aware of that bigotry, the accusation was just. I don't want to hurt people.

Interviewer: What about the influences of being a teacher?

Gardner: My academic career has, of course, had considerable influence on my writing of fiction and poetry, though I hope my writing has had no effect on my scholarship and teaching—except to boost my university salary, attract students I might otherwise not meet, and get me invited to visit now and then at other universities.

When I first began teaching my main job was in creative writing, and I discovered very quickly that it's fairly easy to transform an eager, intelligent student to a publishing creative writer. Silly as it sounds, that discovery was a shock to my ego and changed my whole approach to writing fiction. (I was twenty-four, twenty-five at the time.) Since I found out that anyone has stories he can tell, and, once you've shown him a little technique, can tell them relatively well, I was determined to set myself apart from the herd (I was reading that devil Nietzsche then) by writing as other people couldn't. I became a mildly fanatic stylist, and experimenter with form, and so on. Also, I quit teaching creative writing, maybe partly from annoyance that my students were as good as I was, but mainly in hopes of learning the things I had to know to become a good writer. I began teaching history of criticism courses, which turned out to be one of the most valuable experiences in my life.

Interviewer: I don't mean to dwell on this, but it's obviously a subject you've thought about a lot. Any more specific effects of your teaching on your writing?

Gardner: Two more, at least. One is, it's given me material—a lot of it—with which to give a modern story-line resonance. For instance, though I don't mention it in the novel, Chief Fred Clumly in *Sunlight* once read Dante on a ship, though he no longer remembers it. It sank deep into the swamp of his mind and now throws strange light of his modern-seeming problems. The narrator of the novel has obviously read and pondered hard on Malory's *Morte D'Arthur,* which presents a medieval world view totally opposed to Dante's. I mention this not because I care how readers read the novel but because it shows, more clearly than anything else I can say, the usefulness of my scholarly work in my writing. Nobody but Blake—except possibly Stanley Elkin—can churn up ideas and images with the genius of Blake. But stealing the ideas and images of brilliant men like Dante and Malory (and of course many others), forcing them into confrontation, trying to find some sane resolution to the opposition of such minds and values, a writer can not only get new insights but get, far more important, rich texture and an energy of language beyond the energy of mere conflict in plot. Which is to say, my subject really is (as one critic once mentioned), human history—the conflict of ideas and emotions through the ages.

The other important effect of my teaching on my writing is that, working with intelligent undergraduate and graduate students—and working alongside intelligent teachers—I have a clear idea of my audience, or anyway of a hypothetical audience. I don't think a writer can write well without some such notions. One may claim one writes for oneself, but it's a paltry claim. One more word on all this, I'm obviously convinced that my scholarly career has made me a better writer than I would have been without it, but I'm no longer concerned—as I was in my tempestuous, ego-maddened youth— with proving myself the greatest writer of all time. What I notice now is that all around me there are first-rate writers, and in nearly every case it seems to me that what makes them first-rate is their similar involvement in teaching and scholarship. There are exceptions— maybe William Gaddis, I'm not sure. (A brilliant writer, though I disapprove of him.) Perhaps the most important exception is John Updike, who, unlike John Hawkes, Bill Gass, Stanley Elkin and Saul Bellow and so on, is not a teacher. But the exception means nothing, because, teacher or not, he's the most academic of all.

Interviewer: What about the teaching of creative writing?

Gardner: When you teach creative writing, you discover a great deal. For instance, if a student's story is really wonderful, but thin, you have to analyze to figure out why it's thin; how you could beef it up. Every discovery of that kind is important. When you're reading only classical and medieval literature, all the bad stuff has been filtered out. There are no bad works in either Greek or Anglo-Saxon. Even the ones that are minor are the very best of the minor, because everything else has been lost or burned or thrown away. When you read this kind of literature, you never really learn how a piece can go wrong, but when you teach creative writing, you see a thousand ways that a piece can go wrong. So it's helpful to me. The other thing that's helpful when you're teaching creative writing is that there are an awful lot of people who at the age of seventeen or eighteen can write as well as you do. That's a frightening discovery. So you ask yourself, What am I doing? Here I've decided that what I'm going to be in life is to be this literary artist, at best; I'm going to stand with Tolstoy, Melville, and all the boys. And there's this kid, nineteen, who's writing just as well. The characters are vividly perceived, the rhythm in the story is wonderful. What have I got that he hasn't got?

You begin to think harder and harder about what makes great fiction. That can lead you to straining and overblowing your own fiction, which I've done sometimes, but it's useful to think about.

Interviewer: What are some specific things you can teach in creative writing?

Gardner: When you teach creative writing, you teach people, among other things, how to plot. You explain the principles, how it is that fiction *thinks*. And to give the kids a sense of how a plot works, you just spin out plot after plot after plot. In an hour session, you may spin out forty possible plots, one adhering to the real laws of *energeia,* each one a balance of the particular and general—and not one of them a story that you'd really want to write. Then one time, you hit one that *catches* you for some reason—you hit on the story that expresses your unrest. When I was teaching creative writing at Chico State, for instance, one of many plots I spun out was *The Resurrection.*

Interviewer: How does this work?

Gardner: One plot will just sort of rise above all the others for reasons that you don't fully understand. All of them are interesting, all of them have interesting characters, all of them talk about things that you could talk about; but one of them catches you like a nightmare. Then you have no choice but to write it; you can't forget it. It's a weird thing. If it's the kind of plot you really don't want to do because it involves your mother too closely, or whatever, you can try to do something else. But the typewriter keeps hissing at you and shooting sparks, and the paper keeps wrinkling and the lamp goes off and nothing else works, so finally you do the one that God said you've got to do. And once you do it, you're grounded. It's an amazing thing. For instance, before I wrote the story about the kid who runs over his younger brother ("Redemption"), always, regularly, every day I used to have four or five flashes of that accident. I'd be driving down the highway and I couldn't see what was coming because I'd have a memory flash. I haven't had it once since I wrote the story. You really do ground your nightmares, you *name* them. When you write a story, you have to play that image, no matter how painful, over and over until you've got all the sharp details so you know exactly how to put it down on paper. By the time you've run your mind through it a hundred times, relentlessly worked every tic of your

terror, it's lost its power over you. That's what bibliotherapy is all
about, I guess. You take crazy people and have them write their story,
better and better, and soon it's just a story on a page, or, more
precisely, everybody's story on a page. It's a wonderful thing. Which
isn't to say that I think writing is done for the health of the writer,
though it certainly does incidentally have that effect.

Interviewer: Do you feel that literary techniques can really be
taught? Some people feel that technique is an artifice or even a
hindrance to "true expression."

Gardner: Certainly it can be taught. But a teacher has to *know*
technique to teach it. I've seen a lot of writing teachers because I go
around visiting colleges, visiting creative writing classes. A terrible
number of awful ones, grotesquely bad. That doesn't mean that one
should throw writing out of the curriculum; because when you get a
good creative writing class it's magisterial. Most of the writers I know
in the world don't know how they do what they do. Most of them *feel*
it out. Bernard Malamud and I had a conversation one time in which
he said that he doesn't know how he does those magnificent things
he sometimes does. He just keeps writing until it comes out right. If
that's the way a writer works, then that's the way he had to work, and
that's fine. But I like to be in control as much of the time as possible.
One of the first things you have to understand when you are writing
fiction—or teaching writing—is that there are different ways of doing
things, and each one has a slightly different effect. A misunderstanding of this leads you to the Bill Gass position: that fiction can't tell the
truth, because every way you say the thing changes it. I don't think
that's to the point. I think that what fiction does is sneak up on the
truth by telling it six different ways and finally releasing it. That's what
Dante said, that you can't really get at the poetic, inexpressible truths,
that the way things are leaps up like steam between them. So you
have to determine very accurately the potential of a particular writer's
style and help that potential develop at the same time, ignoring what
you think of his moral stands.

I hate nihilistic, cynical writing. I hate it. It bothers me, and worse
yet, bores me. But if I have a student who writes with morbid delight
about murder, what I'll have to do (though of course I'll tell him I
don't like this kind of writing, that it's immoral, stupid and bad for
civilization), is say what is successful about the work and what is not. I

have to swallow every bit of my moral feelings to help the writer write his way, his truth. It may be that the most moral writing of all is writing which shows us how a murderer feels, how it happens. It may be it will protect us from murderers someday.

Interviewer: You've recently had essays appear on the subject of what you call "moral fiction" and "moral criticism." Some readers might have trouble with the word "moral." Could you explain what you mean by "moral"? The word, as you've acknowledged, has pejorative implications these days.

Gardner: I know. It shouldn't. I certainly don't mean fiction that preaches. I'm talking mainly—though not exclusively—about works of fiction that are moral in their process. That is to say, the way they *work* is moral. Good works of fiction study values by testing them in imagined/real situations, testing them hard, being absolutely fair to both sides. The real moral writer is the opposite of the minister, the preacher, the rabbi. Insofar as he can, the preacher tries to keep religion as it always was, outlawing contraceptives or whatever; his job is conservative. The writer's job, on the other hand, is to be radically open to persuasion. He should, if possible, not be committed to one side more than to the other—which is simply to say that he wants to affirm life, not sneer at it—but he has to be absolutely fair, understand the moral limits of his partisanship. His affirmation has to be earned. If he favors the cop, he must understand the arguments for life on the side of the robber.

Interviewer: What would be "immoral" literature?

Gardner: Mainly, fiction goes immoral when it stops being fair, when it stops trusting the laboratory experiment. You lie about characters, you make people do what you want them to do. This is characteristic of most hot-shot writers around now. I would agree with people who get nervous around the word "morality," because usually the people who shout "immoral" are those who want to censor things, or think that all bathroom scenes or bedroom scenes or whatever are wicked. That kind of morality is life-denying, evil. But I *do* think morality is a real thing that's worth talking about. I thought of using some other word so that people wouldn't be mad at me for talking like a minister, but I decided that's the right word. It means what it means, and the fact that it's out of style doesn't matter very much. It's like patriotism, which has got a very bad name because devils keep yelling for it. Ultimately patriotism ought not to mean that you hate all other countries. It ought to mean that you love certain things about your country; you don't want them to change. Unfortunately, when you say "patriotism," everybody goes "aargh." Same thing with morality.

Interviewer: Do you see the risk of dogmatism in your thesis on what fiction and criticism ought to be?

Gardner: No, only a risk of dogmatism in stubborn or witless misinterpretations of my thesis, of which there have been, alas, many. I'm sure that no matter how carefully I write about true morality, some self-righteous ignoramus will read it too fast and say, "Aha, he's on our side." He will use me to support awful ideas, and I'm sorry about that. I don't think real morality can ever be codified. You can't say "Thou shalt not," and you can't say "Thou shalt." What you *can* say is that this is how people feel and why they feel the way they do. My argument in *Moral Fiction* is this: that immoral fiction is indifferent to the real issues. I'm saying that there's good and evil. And in particular situations, maybe the only healthy situation is universal destruction. I would never set up a morality that's goody-goody. Sometimes morality is awful. Fiction can never pronounce ultimate solutions, but it can lead to understanding. It leads, and that's all. It gives visions of what's possible. If I were going to write a book which told people how to live, I would write an incredibly meticulous book about Indian gurus, Jewish heroes, Christian saints. I would present every right argument and show clearly and logically what the wrong sides are. It would be simple, except that logic is never to be trusted. And everybody who read my book would say, if I did my job brilliantly, that's the way to live. The trouble is they wouldn't read the book because it would be boring, and even if they did read and understand, they wouldn't be moved to action. The book wouldn't be interesting because it wouldn't show people we care about growing toward the truth. If you show characters struggling to know what's right, and in the process of the novel you work out their issues more and more clearly, whether the character heroically wins or tragically loses, *then* you move the reader, having first moved yourself. I think morality has to be persuasive. And you can only be persuasive if you start with imperfect human beings. Of course, if you wind up with *perfect* human beings, that's a bore too. I guess the morality of the fiction is the seriousness of the question and the seriousness of the concern with imaginary people's lives and feelings—a reflection of real people's lives and feelings—not the seriousness or logicality of the answer.

Interviewer: Should the writer examine the morality of a piece before, say, the quality of its prose, its interest and saleability?

Gardner: Certainly morality should come first—for writers, critics, and everybody else. People who change tires. People in factories. They should always ask, Is this moral? Not, Will it sell? If you're in construction and building houses out of shingles and you realize that you're wiping out ten thousand acres of Canadian pine every year, you should ask yourself, Can I make it cheaper or as cheaply out of clay? Because clay is inexhaustible. Every place there's dirt. A construction owner should say, I don't have to be committed to this particular product: I can go for the one which will make me money, *and* make a better civilization. Occasionally businessmen actually do that. The best will even settle for a profit cut. The same thing is true of writers—ultimately it comes down to, are you making or are you destroying? If you try very hard to create ways of living, create dreams of what is possible, then you win. If you don't, you may make a fortune in ten years, but you're not going to be read in twenty years, and that's that. Why do something cheap? I can't understand people who go for the moment of the book. In the long run, Melville's estate is worth vastly more than the estate of Octave Thanet. Octave Thanet was, I think, the best-selling novelist of the nineteenth century. Melville told the truth, Thanet told high-minded lies. All liars are soon dead, forgotten. Dickens' novels didn't sell half as well as a novel of Octave Thanet's called *A Slave to Duty.* But you haven't heard of her right? I know of her only because I know obscure facts.

Interviewer: And that is why certain works of fiction have lasted, and others have disappeared?

Gardner: Of course. So I believe. The ones that last are the ones that are true. You look at Faulkner and John O'Hara. John O'Hara outsold Faulkner, he circled Faulkner at the time they were writing. Ten years after his death, O'Hara's books are out of print. We all read Faulkner, nobody reads O'Hara. Dreiser in some ways, some of the time, is one of the worst writers who ever lived. *An American*

Tragedy, for instance, is an endless book with terrible sentences like "He found her extremely intellectually interesting." But by the time you finish the book, you've sopped your vest. He's a great writer, though he wrote badly. But what he does morally, that is to say, what he does in terms of analysis of character and honest statement about the way the world is, is very good. Of course, some writers last a long time because of their brilliance, their style; Fitzgerald is a good example—a fine stylist. But he never quite got to the heart of things. *That's* what should concern the critics. If a critic is concerned with only how well the sentences go, or how neat the symbolic structure is, or how new the devices are, he's going to exaggerate the importance of mediocre books. Samuel Beckett—surely one of the great writers of our time, despite my objections—is loved by critics, but except for John Fowles, I hear no one pointing out that the tendency of all he says is wrong. He says it powerfully, with comitragic brilliance, and he believes it, but what he says is not quite sound. Every night Samuel Beckett goes home to his wife, whom he's lived with all these years; he lies down in bed with her, puts his arms around her, and says, "No meaning again today . . ." Critics can say, and do say, Well, it doesn't matter what he says, it's how well he says it. But I think in the long run Beckett is in for it. Because great writers tell the truth exactly—and get it right. A man can be a brilliant writer who writes wonderful lines, and still say what is just not so; like Sartre, Beckett—and in his lapses, Faulkner. Faulkner's sentimentality in the bad moments—every reader knows he's missing a little. I like Dilsey. I believe Dilsey really exists, but I just don't believe that Faulkner understands her or really cares. He's more interested in Dilsey as a symbol than as a person. Everything that Faulkner says about Dilsey is no doubt true . . . it's just all those things he didn't say, the things that make her fully human, not just a symbol. Mythologizing her—or accepting the standard mythology of his age— he slightly skews the inevitability of his story. He does the same thing every time he turns on his mannered rhetoric—distorts the inherent emotion of the story and thus gets diverted from the real and inevitable progress of events.

Interviewer: You've said there are exceptions to your thesis on moral fiction. Could you mention a few?

Gardner: First, there's fiction that's neither moral nor immoral—

minor fiction, pure entertainment. I'm accused of not valuing it, but actually all I say is that it's trivial: I'm not at all against it except when some critic takes it seriously. I favor it as on a hot day I favor ice cream. Second, there's fiction I'd call moral only in the earnestness of its concern. This kind of fiction I would *not* call trivial. There's one man whose name is Ernest Finney. He's a wonderful writer. He sent me his fiction, he's been writing for years, unpublished. He writes grim, frightening stories. But I would certainly publish them if I had a magazine. Absolutely no question. One is about a lower-class guy, tough; he's got a good car, a T-Bird, third-hand. He marries this beautiful girl who's kind of a whore. She finally gets his money and disappears. He's making his money stealing. He goes to prison. All the time he's in prison, he plans on killing her. That's all he cares about, that's all he thinks about. His idea is to put a shotgun up her and blow her to smithereens. You understand exactly why he feels the way he does. It's a very powerful, terrifying story. Because you become the character. You would do it too.

Interviewer: How does this fit any standard we've talked about?

Gardner: Well, I think it's moral fiction, but in a tricky way. Finney does honestly describe a situation. He's not looking for ways that we could live better—the highest way—but he's describing exactly, and with original genius, how it feels to want to kill your wife. Terribly difficult. It's moral fiction of the third degree. Moral fiction can exist in only three forms. The highest form is moral fiction in which you see absolutely accurate description of the best people; fiction that gives you an idea how to live. It's uplifting: you want to be like the hero. You want to be like Jesus, or Buddha, or Moses, whatever. Tolstoy does it. Everybody wants to be like Pierre in *War and Peace*. Everybody wants to be like Levin in *Anna Karenina*. In the next form of moral fiction you see an evil person and you realize you don't want to be like that. Like Macbeth. You see there's an alternative. You don't have to be like Macbeth. It's kind of negative moral fiction, or moral fiction in the tragic mode, where you want to be different than the protagonist—you want to be better. Then there's the third form, wherein alternatives don't exist. Not for fashion's sake or for the cheap love of gruesomeness, but from anger and concern, you stare into the smoking volcano. That's the world of Ernest Finney's fiction, or Constance Urdang's. You understand exactly why a wife would want to kill her husband, saw up the body, and put it in a suitcase. We've all read the newspaper stories about this kind of thing. It happens. But only a great artist can show it happen so that you feel that you saw it, and saw it from inside the murderer's mind: you understand. That doesn't tell you what you should do. It doesn't tell you, I don't want to be like that. But it makes you understand and, understanding, hunger for a world not like this. It's obviously the least uplifting of the three kinds of moral fiction, but it's morally useful. Mostly what we get, it seems to me, is "serious" fiction not in any of those three categories. People kill people, we don't understand why they did it, we don't care why they did it, we read it because it's cheaply thrilling, an escape from the common decency we sometimes feel trapped in. Blood drips, people piss on people or live their boring "lives of quiet desperation." It's at worst a kind of sick daydream, at best useless actuality, not morally worth reading.

Interviewer: What effect do you think your writing has had?

Gardner: I think it has given a few readers pleasure. And I suppose it may have depressed a few. I hope it does more good than harm.

William Gass and John Gardner:
A Debate on Fiction

Thomas LeClair/1978

From *The New Republic*, 180 (10 March 1979), 25, 28-33.
Reprinted by permission of *The New Republic*.

This discussion between William Gass and John Gardner
took place on October 24, 1978, during a Fiction Festival
sponsored by the University of Cincinnati and the National
Endowment for the Arts. The discussion was moderated
by Thomas LeClair, who teaches at Cincinnati. John
Gardner is the author of *On Moral Fiction* and many
novels. William Gass, novelist and teacher of philosophy, is
the author most recently of *The World Within the Word*, a
volume of literary criticism.

Moderator: *Is there a use of language in fiction which is inherently
moral?*

John Gardner: When I wrote *On Moral Fiction*, I was talking
about a particular kind of fiction which I think is consciously moral,
fiction which tries to understand important matters by means of the
best tool human beings have. Many of the most academically popular
writers of our time are completely uninterested in understanding
these matters. They are more interested in understanding juxtaposi-
tions than in understanding how we should live. They are concerned
with making beautiful or interesting or ornate or curious objects. As
for language—when I talk to you, I speak English and try to choose
words, from all the possible words in the world, which seem most
likely to say what I mean. If I am writing and find that one of the
words that I choose is wrong, I put in a better word for my precise
meaning. While English is just noises that we make with our mouths,
teeth, throat, lungs and so on, fiction is an enormously complicated
language. It has much more discreet, much more delicate ways of
communicating. When I create a character, I want to make a lifelike
human being, a virtual human being. Maybe by using the right kind

172

of weather, I can give you a hint of what this person is. By comparing him to a bear or a rhinoceros or a spider, I can give you another hint. In other words, everything I choose in writing a piece of fiction is aimed at communication. I think that beauty in fiction is finally elegant communication, where the very form of the work helps to say what I'm trying to say. If I'm writing about an ordered universe, I write an ordered novel. If I'm talking about a tension between order and disorder, I write a novel in which the form expresses that tension. But always I'm using the tool of language to dig a hole. Other people sometimes use the tool of language to chew on.

William Gass: John's saying that a number of contemporary writers are really not interested in solving problems is a little misleading. I think the difference lies in whether they believe one can understand important human issues by writing novels; they might be so concerned with these problems that they would rather not trust the solution of them to novelists. My own feelings are, of course, that moral issues surround us everywhere, that they are deeply important, and that the survival of the human race is necessary so that parasites like myself can diddle away in corners. The question that lies between John and me here is whether or not writing fiction, rather than, for instance, doing philosophy, is a good method for such an exploration. Philosophy has its own disciplines, its own methods of coming to clarity about these issues, so the way one talks about them won't twist the conclusions. Because fiction is a method which, by its very nature and demands, deforms, I am suspicious of it.

John goes on to say that in writing he faces the problem of revision and getting his best words by constantly asking "Is this really what I believe?" I think that's fine. I don't care how the right words get on the page as long as they're the right words. But my condition is much bleaker. I don't know, most of the time, what I believe. Indeed, as a fiction writer I find it convenient not to believe things. Not to disbelieve things either, just to move into a realm where everything is held in suspension. You hope that the amount of meaning that you can pack into the book will always be more than you are capable of consciously understanding. Otherwise, the book is likely to be as thin as you are. You have to trick your medium into doing far better than you, as a conscious and clearheaded person, might manage. So one of the problems that I face is exactly the opposite of John's. John's concern is to communicate; I have very little to communicate. I'm not sure I understand what little I do have. I think it would be thin and uninteresting and hardly useful. If I did want to communicate, I would move over to philosophy and submit to the rigors that are concerned with the production of clarity, of logical order, truth and so on. In fiction, I am interested in transforming language, in disarming the almost insistent communicability of language. When you are not asserting, you are not confusing, and I would be happy to avoid that.

Does this kind of purity of creation have a moral value in the world as well as an aesthetic one?

W.G.: Sure, John wants a message, some kind of communication to the world. I want to plant some object in the world. Now it happens to be made of signs, which may lead people to think, because it's made of signs, that it's pointing somewhere, But actually I've gone down the road and collected all sorts of highway signs and made a piece of sculpture out of these things that says Chicago, 35,000 miles. What I hope, of course, is that people will come along, gather in front of the sculpture, and just look at it—consequently forgetting Chicago. I want to add something to the world which the world can then ponder the same way it ponders the world. Now, what kind of object? Old romantic that I am, I would like to add objects to the world worthy of love. I think that the things one loves most, particularly in other people, are quite beyond anything they communicate or merely "mean." Planting those objects is a moral activity, I suppose. You certainly don't want to add objects to the world that everybody will detest: "Another slug made by Bill Gass." That's likely to be their attitude, but you don't hope for it. The next question is, why is it that one wants this thing loved? My particular aim is that it be loved because it is so beautiful in itself, something that exists simply to be experienced. So the beauty has to come first.

J.G.: There's no question that an object made simply to be beautiful is an affirmation of a kind, and any affirmation of that which is good for human beings is moral. But Bill and I, in our writing, are concerned with different kinds of affirmation. When I write, I try to find out, by honest thought, moment by moment, psychological response by psychological response, what it is that I can affirm as true and good. I think, for example, it's better to be an American democratic person than a headhunter. I think I think that. When I work it out in a novel, I might change my mind a little. But in the process of discovering what I really believe, what I can say yes to: "yes, I affirm that, that's good, that's helpful to people, that makes it possible for individuals to live in society," in the process I create an effect.

By telling a moving story, I've led the reader to an affirmation of the value I have come to find that I can affirm. The difference between what I am doing and what a philosopher is doing is that my activity leads to a feeling state, whereas the philosopher has only cold clarity. I'm after an affirmation of how to live, but it's a difficult affirmation. Again and again people read my books and misunderstand the endings; they think the end of *Grendel* is a curse. It's such a marginal affirmation that maybe it might as well be a curse. There isn't an awful lot one can affirm, but I try to get to the affirmation that I can really believe and that will move people. I'm trying for an affirmation that has something to do with how to live; Bill and other writers like him are trying for an affirmation of just living. A guy walks along the street and sees this magnificent sculpture made out of signs and his day is better for it. But what I want the guy to do is continue past the signs and go do his job.

W.G.: One of the problems that I find with John's view is that it might lead you to say harsh things about great writers, a terrible thought. Suppose you have a writer who clearly inspects what he believes and ends his great long work by saying "You must go on, I can't go on, I'll go on." That's about as affirmative as Beckett gets, and there are other writers who, in following a process of being honest about what they can affirm, find only "going on" left and are not even sure of that without writing another book to make sure they're still going on. Gaddis hasn't made a habit of hooray. Since I think, quite independently of any theory, that Beckett is one of the greatest writers of this period, I'm wondering, John, if your view allows you to regard him in that way?

J.G.: I don't think that's a problem because one is terribly moved by Beckett and one does go on, and one even feels he has a reason for going on, although the reason may be in the technical sense absurd. There are other writers who would persuade you not to go on, that everything is nonsense, that you should kill yourself. They, of course, go on to write another book while you have killed yourself. If we look back through the history of literature, those writers have not been the ones who have been loved and who have survived. Again and again we're moved by Achilles, we're moved by the best of Shakespeare, Chaucer and the others we keep going back to. Writers who give us visions to which we say, with all our unconscious minds as well as our conscious minds, "That's just not so," we don't read.

I'm not saying that other people shouldn't make wonderful sculptures; I'm saying they shouldn't be mistaken for the big tent, the most important kind of work. The theory that I'm proposing says, fundamentally, that you create in the reader's mind a vivid and continuous dream. The reader sits down with his book just after breakfast, and immediately someone says, "Hermione, aren't you coming to lunch?" One instant has passed although 200 pages have passed because the reader has been in a vivid and continuous dream, living a virtual life, making moral judgments in a virtual state.

. . . The real problem with this argument is that Bill Gass is a sneaky moralist. His books end in magnificent affirmation. I'm arguing against his theory, but his books don't follow it.

Bill, what about this vivid and continuous dream?

W.G.: It's rather imaginary. In music, let's say, the motion of the work comes from the performance. That's true also in the theater. So if there's an interruption, or your mind goes blank, or someone rattles a bag, you miss something and that's too bad, it's lost. In reading fiction, however, the motion that moves the text comes from the reader. Now the writer can indicate or try to indicate how that motion should go and at what rate. But I don't think that anyone writes a book now supposing that the reader will sit down and read 200 pages through in a continuous dream. He's going to, in fact, stop, brush a fly off his nose, go back to the first page, read it over, skip, look around for the juicy parts. The book is more like a building which you're trying to get someone to go through the way you want him to. The experience of a novel can occasionally be what John describes. I remember it happening when I was 12 or so reading *Boy Scout Boys on the Columbia River.*

J.G.: You're right if you're talking about the concert hall, but with a record you can go back. And when you go back, you remember what came before, you know where you are, and you know where you're going. If a novel is plotted, if you have the actualization of the potential that exists in a character in a certain situation, then the argument of the novel—the movement of the plot, the development of the characters in their response to problems—leads you through the novel. What argument is to philosophy, plot is to fiction. Most philosophers set up a syllogism and move steadily through it. You have a feeling of profluence, of forward flowingness. When a novel has a plot, it doesn't matter if the reader goes to chapter eight, then ducks back to chapter five, and then goes forward again. Finally, the ultimate apparition, the ultimate dream of the novel, is a continuous one. When you decide as a writer that the novel is just a house you're trying to get somebody to go through in various ways, you have broken faith with the reader because you are now a manipulator, as opposed to an empathizer. If the novelist follows his plot, which is the characters and the action, if he honestly and continuously proceeds from here to here because he wants to understand some particular question, the reader is going to go with him because he wants to know the same answers. On the other hand, if the writer makes the reader do things, then I think he puts the reader in a subservient position which I don't like.

Let me elaborate with the plot of a story someone told me once. A woman has had a perfect marriage. After her husband dies, she finds a walnut box of perfectly labeled feathers in the garage. She finds out that all his life he has had a secret hobby, and at that moment she begins to wonder how come he didn't tell her? The next time she hears a conversation about her husband, she's going to listen in a different way. The next time her kids talk about him, she's going to listen in a different way. The next time she meets his 30-year-old secretary, she'll look at her a different way. We're on to a real problem, which is human doubt, human faith, and as long as we're on that, we don't want the author pushing us around. We want someone honestly, gently taking us through an exploration of this situation. There is an act of faith, whereas when the author manipulates the reader he is solipsistic in the worst sense: he's not in a love relationship with the reader.

W.G.: I didn't mean the manipulation of the reader when I compared reading to going through a building. The kind of response to novels that John is talking about certainly was appropriate 200 years ago, when there were lots of novels written in that form. There

are just not many of them being written that way anymore. When
Fielding comes to the end of *Tom Jones*, for example, I suspect that
he expects us to remember about as much of the first chapter as we
would of that early part of our life, if we were thinking back. Not
every detail, not every adjective attached to a noun in a certain way.
In someone like Joyce, quite the contrary is true. He wants an
experience that can happen only when the reader moves constantly
about the book. The notion of the space in which this kind of book is
constructed is quite different from the notion of the time through
which the Fielding work moves. While I don't mind Fielding's having
written the way he wrote, John begrudges some people writing in this
newer or different way, in which the kind of attention the reader is
expected to pay to the page transforms the way the work exists.

J.G.: I think we both agree that we're trying to create something
that the reader will love. Is it possibly the case that the fiction you're
advocating, Bill, is simply not lovable, that it simply doesn't hook
readers? You can quickly say, "But the most sophisticated reader
. . ." I'm not sure that's true. In the academy we teach Pynchon
instead of Trollope. About Trollope there's nothing to say because it's
all clear. On the other hand, every line of Pynchon you can explain
because nothing is clear. So the academy ends up accidentally
selecting books the student may need help with. They may be a
couple of the greatest books in all history and 20 of the worst, but
there's something to say about them. You get an artificial taste in the
academy. The sophisticated reader may not remember how to read;
he may not understand why it's nice that Jack in the Beanstalk steals
those things from the giant.

W.G.: I suspect, John, that you want not things that will be loved
but things that will be promiscuous. If you had a daughter to send
into the world, would you want everybody to love her? I might be at
my winery turning out bottles of Thunderbird which everybody loves.
It wouldn't give me much satisfaction. It's not just that books are
loved, but why they're loved. If you've given them the properties that
make them worthwhile, then it doesn't matter if no one does love
them. Frequently very few people do, or a work will go unobserved
for years.

*Do the two of you write from different motives? We've heard love
mentioned several times. I know that Bill Gass has used the word*

anger. Do the motives for your writing produce the differences in the kind of fiction that you write?

W.G.: I have a view I'm sure John wouldn't agree with. Very frequently the writer's aim is to take apart the world where you have very little control, and replace it with language over which you can have some control. Destroy and then repair. I once wrote a passage in which I had the narrator say "I want to rise so high that when I shit I won't miss anybody." But there are many motives for writing. Writing a book is such a complicated, long-term difficult process that all of the possible motives that can funnel in will, and a great many of those motives will be base. If you can transform your particular baseness into something beautiful, that's about the best you can make of your own obnoxious nature.

J.G.: I agree with almost everything Bill says except the nonsense about human nature. I think human beings are a little lower than angels and a hell of a lot more important. One does take the world apart and put it back together, but I would express it differently. You write the book to understand and get control of in yourself things that you haven't been able to control and understand in the world. When you have the kind of problem that will come to you in repeated dreams, you work it out on the page. Maybe it's an illusory understanding, but I think it helps you live. I think with each book you write you become a better person. It's certainly true that a great many famous writers, Marcel Proust for instance, were awful human beings, were much better in their writing. The reason is, I think, that when one is writing a book one gets to think over a nasty crack, and to gentle it and put it in a way that's not quite so cutting. Bill might say it's more elegantly expressed. "I want to rise so high that when I shit I won't miss anybody" is so well said the meanness is partly muted. It becomes a joke, a kind of self-mocking, so it's not saying the same thing that the writer might say if drunk and angry. I believe that we revise our lives in our work and with each revision we find a mistake we don't have to make again. I also think people become gradually slightly better people as they write books. That may not be true, but that's my conviction.

W.G.: Do you think Alexander Pope got better as a person?

J.G.: I think that Bill values a great deal of literature that I don't value. Alexander Pope expresses a mood that we all have—

meanness—and he expresses it very well. But one ultimately says, "I don't feel like reading Pope tonight. *Kojak* is on; I'll get my meanness quick." One always reads through the mean writers with a certain amount of fascination, the same way you watch the female praying mantis eat the male. But that doesn't mean you go home every day and watch the praying mantises.

W.G.: Some of us do.

The concept of character in fiction is one you differ on. Would you talk about your notion of character?

W.G.: It's complex. I'll try to simplify it very quickly. A character for me is any linguistic location in a book toward which a great part of the rest of the text stands as a modifier. Just as the subject of a sentence, say, is modified by the predicate, so frequently some character, Emma Bovary for instance, is regarded as a central character in the book because a lot of the language basically and ultimately goes back to modify, be about, Emma Bovary. Now the ideal book would have only one character; it would be like an absolute, idealist system. What we do have are subordinate locales of linguistic energy—other characters—which the words in a book flow toward and come out of. A white whale is a character; mountains in *Under the Volcano* are characters. Ideas can become characters. Some of the most famous characters in the history of fiction are in that great novel called philosophy. There's free will and determinism. There's substance and accident. They have been characters in the history of philosophy from the beginning, and I find them fascinating. Substance is more interesting than most of my friends.

Now why would one adopt such awkward language—why not just talk about character in the traditional sense? The advantage is that you avoid the tendency as a reader to psychologize and fill the work with things that aren't there. The work is filled with only one thing— words and how they work and how they connect. That, of course, includes the meanings, the sounds, and all the rest. When people ask "How are you building character?" they sometimes think you're going around peering at people to decide how you're going to render something. That isn't a literary activity. It may be interesting, but the literary activity is constructing a linguistic source on the page.

J.G.: I obviously don't agree with Bill on all that. It seems to me a character is an apparition in the writer's mind, a very clear apparition based on an imaginative reconstruction or melting of many people the writer has known. The ideal book has to have more than one character, because we know a character by what he does: what he does to other people, and what they do back to him. Bill wants to avoid the reader's "filling in," but when we read J. D. Salinger, for instance, we understand many things about his characters that aren't in the book because we know what people mean when they make the gestures that Salinger's made-up people make. So we're all the time seeing more of the picture than is given. In the good novel, the reader gets an apparition, a dream, in which he sees people doing things to each other, hurting each other or exploring each other or loving each other or whatever, and a tiny linguistic signal sets off a huge trap of material which gives us a very subtle sense of these imaginary people. It's true that one can analyze them as words on a page, but I have never cried at the fate of free will or determinism in a good philosophy book.

Bill has argued that it's wrong to be frightened by a character in a book or to cry at the death of a character. I say it's not. I say a book is nothing but a written symbol of a dream. If someone jumps at me with an axe in a nightmare, I scream and I have every right to scream because I believe that person is real. In the same way, when the dream is transported to me by words and I see that character leap out at me with an axe, I have every right to believe that my head is going to be knocked in. I think it's very useful to talk about character in the traditional ways. Contemporary philosophy has reconstructed the world into its own words while distrusting the words that we've used over and over and over. Meaning exists in literature because of the way thousands of generations of people have used words. With just the slightest tap, you ring the whole gong of meaning. I'm more interested in the gong than the tap. I think Bill concentrates on the technique of the tap.

. . . First it matters to him that [a novel] is elegant and well-done and that it has other characteristics I think are perhaps secondary. But given two well-done books, one of which strikes him as absolutely truthful while the other is not what he would affirm in his life, Bill would take, he says, the one that he thinks is true.

W.G.: Yes, but that's just wanting thickness to experience. If, for instance, I play golf for my health and to persuade some client and because I'm hooked on the symbolism of getting a ball into a hole, that's better than playing golf just to have a good score. But ultimately, whether you play golf well or not is determined by how well you score—your performance—and that's what ought to be used as the aesthetic measure. If a beautiful book is a source of virtue and a source of truth—fine. That's jolly. The composer of such a work would be a fine philosopher, a noble saint, and an artist. But he's not a good artist because he's a fine philosopher or a noble saint.

. . . There is a fundamental divergence about what literature is. I don't want to subordinate beauty to truth and goodness. John and others have values which they think more important. Beauty, after all, is not very vital for most people. I think it is very important, in the cleanliness of the mind, to know why a particular thing is good. A lot of people judge, to use a crude example, the dinner good because of the amount of calories it has. Well, that is important if you don't want to gain weight, but what has that got to do with the quality of the food? Moral judgments on art constantly confuse the quality of the food. I would also claim that my view is more catholic. It will allow in as good writers more than this other view will; John lets hardly anybody in the door.

J.G.: I love Bill's writing, and I honestly think that Bill is the only writer in America that I would let in the door. For 24 years I have been screaming at him, sometimes literally screaming at him, saying "Bill, you are wasting the greatest genius ever given to America by fiddling around when you could be doing big, important things." What he can do with language is magnificent, but then he turns it against itself. Our definitions of beauty are different. I think language exists to make a beautiful and powerful apparition. He thinks you can make pretty colored walls with it. That's unfair. But what I think is beautiful, he would think is not yet sufficiently ornate. The difference is that my 707 will fly and his is too encrusted with gold to get off the ground.

W.G.: There is always that danger. But what I really want is to have it sit there solid as a rock and have everybody think it is flying.

J.G.: Bill Gass is quoted as saying that his ambition in life is to write a book so good that nobody will publish it. My ambition in life is to outlive Bill Gass and change all of his books.

An Interview with John Gardner
Ed Christian/1978

From *Prairie Schooner*, 54 (Winter 1981), 70-93. Copyright ©
1989 by Ed Christian. Reprinted by permission of Ed Christian.

Gardner looks like a cross between an aging biker and a
gnome. Throughout the three days I spent with him he
wore a motorcycle jacket and never washed his greasy,
blood-stained mechanic's hands. He is short and stocky
with long white hair yellowed in the front by smoke from
his ever-present pipe. Gardner talks in a brash, staccato
voice, his words often tumbling together in their haste to
get out, then slowing suddenly as he *emphasizes* words in
an accent which seems a combination of New England,
New York City, and California. Very few talkers are more
interesting: his top speed conversation is full of allusions,
quotes, burlesques of foreign accents, and snatches of
songs.

This interview took place at Loma Linda University,
Riverside, California, on December 5-7, 1978, a time
when his novel *Freddy's Book* was still a short story called
"King Gustav, Lars Joren, and the Devil."

E.C.: When did you decide to become a writer?

Gardner: I slipped into it. I wrote all the time, starting when I was
eight, and I wrote, wrote, wrote, all through high school and college. I
did other things—I took a chemistry major—but eventually I
discovered that I was spending all my time writing, and I finally
admitted to myself that I was writing from inferiority.

E.C.: Did you have a lot of childhood stress or mental pain? Do
you agree with the theory that great literature, especially poetry, rises
out of pain?

Gardner: I don't think that's true, but I don't know.

E.C.: Is the contribution of literature as important as the
contribution of chemistry?

Gardner: A story is the most valuable thing in the world. Nothing
is as precious as a good story, a perfectly told story. It fascinates in a

way nothing else in the world, not even music, can fascinate us. Fiction must be a totally honest, serious thing, even if it's kidding around and playing jokes. The relationship between a writer and a reader ought to be a model love relationship. It ought not to be a rape, which is what happens when the writer's tricking the reader, pushing the reader on, making the reader angry. It ought not to be a cruel and cunning seduction, something very clever at the beginning that will seduce the reader into reading the story. It's a love relationship in which you give the reader the best story you can think of.

E.C.: How did you happen to become a medievalist? Do you see certain characteristics about you which made you lean in that direction?

Gardner: Sure. I liked Walt Disney when I was a kid. I liked tales rather than realistic fiction. Medieval literature is loaded with wonderful tales of knights and dragons and that kind of stuff, and that's my thing.

E.C.: Do you see medieval influences on your novels and on your way of thinking?

Gardner: Absolutely. If you teach it for twenty years, you can't help but slip it into your own novels. The advantage is that you *sound* like you're a completely different writer from anyone else. You work from a different base. It's nice to sound different.

E.C.: Do you find it difficult to be both a scholar and a novelist?

Gardner: No, although I don't do much scholarship anymore, just novels.

E.C.: Doesn't scholarly writing demand a different way of thinking?

Gardner: Sure it does, but scholarship is easy. It's a very simple kind of thought, just logic, just research, just hunting it down. Novels are *much*, much harder.

E.C.: You've said that modern criticism has become both trivial and more difficult. Isn't much of this triviality due to pressure on students and professors to publish and the difficulty in having articles accepted for publication if they are on so subjective a topic as the morality of a novel?

Gardner: I think it's probably true that a lot of people who are *asked* to publish and pressured to publish don't want to, so they write bad books. I think that the people who *love* to write criticism are the people who ought to write criticism and ought to be teaching. When I taught *Gawain*, I had to figure it out because there's no good book explaining the symbolism, and I wanted to tell not just my students but *everybody*, "Wow, look, what a wonderful poem!" You want to sell the poem to people who aren't reading it. I think that when criticism works like that, it's doing the right thing. But, of course, I think that what has happened is that editors and scholars have become, like novelists, a little embarrassed by emotion, so they resist the very best kind of criticism, which is a celebration of a book just figured out.

E.C.: You've been writing for a long time now, and you've matured a great deal since you published your first novel. Looking back, how do you feel about your books?

Gardner: I love them. I think they're just marvelous.

E.C.: Good. When I read your first novel, *The Resurrection*, it seemed evident from the first page that you were retelling a vegetation myth, and I expected that the meaning would deal with new life springing from death, those around James Chandler as he died of leukemia gaining a new involvement in life. This actually seemed to be happening; there were foreshadowings, and the characters were evolving, then suddenly in the last ten pages or so, the theme seemed forgotten, and everything went dead. What happened?

Gardner: I think you're missing something. I don't think the novel dies. There really is a resurrection of sorts. What you have just outlined is what the ordinary person would write about, the unthoughtful book, the cliché thing, life rises out of death. Life rises out of death in a very complicated way. For one thing, Viola is pretty badly neurotic, and she warms up to James Chandler, but he's not functioning very well; he's got aleukemic leukemia and his brain's not working very well, and he's missing important things. He's also got important defects in his character; he loves but in a philosopher's kind of way. I *like* James Chandler, but he has some real problems, for instance he never mentions a student. He's a teacher, but yet he has no student friends. He doesn't understand his wife, he doesn't understand his children, he theorizes about things. He gets involved with Viola because he thinks he can help her, but as a matter of fact

he's misunderstanding *that* situation. He's misplacing his own kind of
pain, even though he tries to help her. In the end he *doesn't* help her.
What happens is he dies in some other woman's house, which is
gonna hurt his wife's feelings, to say the least. Everything's gone
horrible; the old lady has wandered off into the night, and so his
attempt to turn death into life misfires horribly. And yet, all the
people who are left, sort of clinging to each other, sitting together, the
wife and the daughter, and the old, mad piano teacher, society is
kind of closing up the wound. The old woman has gone deaf, and
plays loudly, horribly, and it's like a kind of crazy cancer, the music
itself has become a sort of cancer. And you would think from that,
"Ah ha, everything's awful, death leads to death," except that there is
that closing of the circle, people clinging to each other and nourishing
each other. And then the last line of the book which explains,
ironically, what *nobody*, no god, no outer-space spirit, could
understand except the people who lived it. It's saying that *one* of the
real sacral things about life is its tragedy, that out of death comes, in a
mysterious way, a way you'd never expect life going on and
improving with wisdom.

   E.C.: That was part of the problem; I couldn't see any real,
permanent growth of wisdom in the last few pages.

   Gardner: Well, you see *love* between the wife and the daughter.

   E.C.: To some extent.

   Gardner: The thing is, the daughter has been desperately trying to
get at least one parent to love her, and she goes to her father, but her
father misunderstands, she goes to Viola, but Viola is sick. Finally, the
two people who *need* love, the mother and the daughter, can talk.

   E.C.: When Marie and Viola meet in the graveyard in the
prologue, they don't recognize each other.

   Gardner: The daughter and Viola are opposites, the true daughter
and the false daughter, kind of, and Viola was not saved by
Chandler's death, but the daughter was. I really think of it as a double
plot thing, Adam and Satan in *Paradise Lost*; one wins, one loses.

   E.C.: Were you thinking of Tolstoy's *Resurrection* at the time you
wrote the book?

   Gardner: Sure. I have allusions to it here and there. I disagree
with Tolstoy, of course, and I wanted to answer him. Sort of an

arrogant, foolish thing to do, but that was part of what I thought I was doing.

E.C.: In *The Wreckage of Agathon* you give us an old "prophet" who is physically despicable and morally dangerous.

Gardner: That's right.

E.C.: He has no faith in what he says, so it isn't surprising that he continually presents various lies as truths. To what extent did Agathon reflect your own beliefs at the time you wrote the book and the political situation around you?

Gardner: It certainly *is* about Vietnam and the American division between East and West. Agathon does not reflect my views, except in one sense; Agathon is essentially a mocker. He sees the absurdity in everything and is unable to leap this hurdle into acceptance, love, and affirmation because he is always seeing the truth. He gets angry, but he has no positive program to offer. He doesn't *love* anybody, except maybe to some extent Peeker. He hurts everybody he's around, yet he wants to teach Peeker to be like him, to be a seer.

E.C.: Why?

Gardner: Ego. He thinks seers are important. He thinks every-one's stupid, and that the most important thing is not to be deluded. But the thing is that what Peeker learns from him is something very different. Peeker never does become a clairvoyant. Agathon is literally a clairvoyant.

E.C.: Seeing clearly doesn't seem to help him very much.

Gardner: Agathon sees the future, but it doesn't do any good because he has no love of the future, he just knows these things are happening.

E.C.: Would you consider *Agathon* a moral book, in the light of your new book *On Moral Fiction*?

Gardner: Sure I would. The hero of the book is Peeker, not Agathon. The last word Agathon says in his life is "Ox," which is the name of a blind man. Agathon is the great seer, and his last vision is of a blind man. Peeker, on the other hand, goes back to see Agathon's family and is delighted by Agathon's kind, sentimental, sweet, silly daughter and in effect falls in love with Agathon's wife.

E.C.: Do you find it more difficult to write about characters a couple thousand years in the past?

Gardner: No, I just make them up, like anybody else. Of course I use Plutarch, who gave me a lot of help. He tells such wonderful stories.

E.C.: Despite their popularity, *Grendel* and *Agathon* embody many of the faults you've pointed out in other people's books. They seem disorganized nearly to the point of incoherence, you don't seem sure of what you want to say, little love for the characters shows, and, although there are frequent instances of well handled rhythms and poetic language in *Grendel*, both books suffer from distracting attempts at cleverness, especially the scatology, which comes across like a freshman comp. student's discovery that the teacher doesn't mark off for expressiveness. Were these books chiefly ways of honing your technique?

Gardner: No, they were serious books. I think they're great works of art. I think you're mistaken; you missed the meaning. I think it may be that you're reading them with a critical eye and thereby missing the books. I think *Grendel* is *very* highly organized, *intensely* organized. There are some faults in all of my books, but I don't think they're the faults you're pointing out. At the climax *Grendel* falters a little bit, fools around. That's okay, but I could have done it better, especially the ninth chapter. In *Agathon* you really are in two different fictional modes, and I didn't really give the bridge between the tight realism and the mythic cartoon simplicity. But nobody I know of writes books *quite* so carefully organized. It may not show.

E.C.: One of the problems with *Grendel* is the frequently false foreshadowings. You give us hints that both the queen and the king's nephew are planning to murder the king, then let it dangle. Grendel is untouchable until, without warning, some big stranger comes and rips off Grendel's arm. Is this fair?

Gardner: Grendel is untouchable exactly as in the poem; he's untouchable by metal, you can't touch him with a sword. It's all in the myth, all in the legend of *Beowulf*.

E.C.: Were you attempting to copy some of the rhythms and alliterations found in the Old English *Beowulf*?

Gardner: Not copy. Do a modern equivalent, yes. I did want to get the rich, gilded texture of *Beowulf*, but it's a whole different kind of language.

E.C.: I've noticed that your book *Nickel Mountain* has four copyright dates listed, beginning in 1963. How did the book develop?

Gardner: I published several of the chapters separately. It falls into episodes which can be published as short stories.

E.C.: Why did you decide to write an epic poem?

Gardner: Well, I'd been teaching epics, and I had a theory about what all the epics had in common. I was working on a translation of Apollonius Rhodius and I was working on a book about epics. And then I decided that instead of writing about what the epics do, I'd do my own epic in which I'd use materials from all the others, do it as art instead of criticism. Besides, I love to write that sort of thing. It's kind of a mock epic poem, but so is *Argonautica.*

E.C.: How long did it take to write?

Gardner: Oh, I don't know. Several years. I spent one whole year in London, just polishing it up.

E.C.: How much were you able to write in a day? Did it come as fast as prose?

Gardner: Oh yeah, sure, in the rough draft. You get so you think in verse.

E.C.: *October Light* is a really wonderful book, quite possibly the best novel written in the past decade. It seems to be the embodiment of your theories in *On Moral Fiction.* The characters of the exterior book are true and complex, and it is obvious throughout that you care deeply for them. By contrast, the interior novel is, as it's meant to be, trash. From the style and subject matter, one suspects that it was written in the late sixties, rather than as a part of *October Light.* Is this true?

Gardner: I was probably working on it then, yeah. I had the whole plan of the novel, but I probably was working on that first. I'm not really sure.

E.C.: You didn't write it to be published by itself?

Gardner: No . . . Although I did think of publishing it by itself at some point. That really would have been terrible!

E.C.: Bears are mentioned many times in *October Light,* in many settings, and in many emotional contexts. The result is the brilliant ending which ties together the whole book and illuminates its meaning: the bear about to be blasted away saying "Oh James,

James." Did you consciously develop the symbol of the bear from the beginning of the book, stumble upon it halfway through, or did it pop into your mind only at the end? Perhaps you discovered it afterward?

Gardner: I developed the symbol of the bear from the beginning, but then I added the other animals to make the bear more at home; chickens and ducks and things.

E.C.: So you had the ending planned before you started the book?

Gardner: No. I didn't know what the last paragraph was going to be, the last page, the last chapter. I knew how the plot went, and I knew that bears, of course, were going to be important, but I didn't realize that I was going to use an actual, live bear.

E.C.: It was a perfect ending.

Gardner: I like it.

E.C.: The ending of *October Light* is very positive. There has been progress made, the characters understand themselves and each other better. The old brother and sister find that even though they are suffering the final frosts leading to the "locking up," they can still experience life fully, much as James Chandler in *The Resurrection* has his final insight that he should be experiencing *all* of life, not just the beautiful parts.

Gardner: But it's just an insight, he doesn't make it.

E.C.: It was rather ambiguous.

Gardner: A pretty dark ending, but I meant it to be positive. Certainly the ending of *Grendel* is positive.

E.C.: Are you a strong believer in people understanding better as they get close to death? So many of your characters seem to wake up just before they die.

Gardner: I think I use that for dramatic purposes. That is to say death is a backdrop that *really* makes the characters stand out. I think people should desperately try to understand each other, sympathize with each other. When you're dramatizing that, what do you choose: a love story, which is always coming toward understanding, or an approach of death story? I normally use an approach of death story. *Grendel, The Resurrection*, they all work that way. Even *Nickel Mountain* is an approach of death.

E.C.: In most of your novels a major character is in a prison of some type. James Chandler in *The Resurrection* is in the hospital, Grendel is imprisoned in his body and in society's hatred for him. The grotesquely fat Henry Soames in *Nickel Mountain* is also imprisoned in his body. Agathon is in a real prison, and Sally Abbott in *October Light* is locked in her room. Do you consider many of those around you to be imprisoned?

Gardner: No, but it's a metaphor; we all *can* be. The real prison is the prison of the intellect. We're locked into logical systems, unwilling to have faith in the things that count, like love.

E.C.: Many of your novels deal with grotesques, abnormal people unlikely to be thought of as heroes. Why?

Gardner: Well, I always want to do the best show I can, and a circus needs some very funny characters, as well as straight men and ringmasters. I like to deal with characters who create an extremely vivid image. When you read about them, you *notice*, because they're so freaky looking and funny looking. There are a great number of characters in my books who *aren't* funny looking, but there are always the clowns. It's a Walt Disney effect.

E.C.: You do seem able to avoid caricature with these people.

Gardner: Right. You start with caricature, and then you fill it in.

E.C.: You've mentioned that the form of your writing sometimes changes the ideas you try to express. You find yourself learning from your own characters. Have you *ever* had to alter a book radically because of this?

Gardner: Sure. I did considerably in *October Light*. A *lot* of changes, because I started out much more on James Page's side than I ended up. You know, I *do* have a tendency to just *hate* television. On the other hand, "Ed's Song," in that book, is, among other things, a celebration of television because television does wonderful things. In any book what I try to do is to be fair, honest, and try in a dramatic way to take back anything that's too one-sided, so the book ends up with a balanced vision. I always start out with a simpler vision than what I end up with. *Grendel* started out *really* simple. I wanted twelve chapters for the twelve zodiac houses. I wanted Grendel to be a creature trapped in determinism by his own nature because he refuses fate, he says no. He sees the image of the hero and he says, "No, it's a knee-jerk," and he sees the image of love and all that. I *wanted* to present him just as a monster, dark, wrong. I started out thinking I was going to do a sort of tirade against the intellectual stuff you get in the universities—this locked in, systematic thought. But, then, in order to make him an interesting character, I had to become more and more sympathetic, so the trap becomes very complicated. Partly he's locked in by other things, by situations, and partly by his own stupidity. Not until I get to the ninth chapter, where he begins to *dance* on his lack of faith and play games, did I begin to get Grendel as a real monster. But, of course, at the same time he began to play games, he also, and I didn't anticipate this, he begins to be bored by the games, which is what I think happens. A "cheerful nihilist" like John Barth (that's his phrase) starts out cheerful, but as he gets older and keeps insisting on this nihilistic view of the universe, he gets meaner, and pretty soon there's no smiling left. What, to my surprise, happened in *Grendel* is that Grendel at the moment he becomes most ferocious also longs most for death. He wants to punish himself for what he feels to be an inadequate state of being. He became much more human and goes through his conversion.

E.C.: Paragraph and sentence structure and length can be arranged to emphasize meaning. For example, a short paragraph with a major idea following a long paragraph gets the point across better than putting the idea at the beginning of a long paragraph. Do you consciously make use of these techniques?

Gardner: Any serious writer uses all the techniques available, and paragraphing is one of them.

E.C.: How much of this is conscious and deliberate?

Gardner: It doesn't have to be conscious any more than riding a bicycle is conscious. You're better off if you don't think about it. But every bit of it is deliberate. I read and reread my stuff, making sure that everything feels right. If you set up a paragraph with an idea *too* clearly, you can sometimes make the idea sentimental. That's what's called "the fractured paragraph," and I avoid that, except when I'm making fun of somebody, as I am of Vonnegut in *Grendel* when I write, "So it goes."

E.C.: Many of your books seem to be sparked by characters in an interesting situation; *Beowulf* from Grendel's point of view, a disgusting philosopher. . . . How does your first idea for a novel usually develop?

Gardner: *Grendel* came about because I was teaching an Anglo-Saxon class, and I told the kids that the three monsters in *Beowulf* are very symbolic, and Grendel is symbolic of the rational soul gone perverse. Somebody asked me in class if that was just old-fashioned Christian talk, or was it possible in the modern world for the rational soul to go perverse. And I said, "Sure, Sartre's Existentialism is perverse rationality." As soon as I said it, I realized what I was going to do, and I began planning *Grendel*.

E.C.: Once you have your first idea do you usually develop it systematically, or let it sit awhile, push it back under?

Gardner: I start right away. You've got to figure out what are the hot issues in the conflict you've set up. They may not be the first ones you think of, but they are the ones that are always going to lead to fulfillment or nonfulfillment. You must raise a serious issue, which is serious for every human being. Nothing in the world is a more serious issue than prejudice, for the simple reason that as human beings we are vulnerable, that is to say put a sword inside my chest and I don't go so good. Therefore, we see people who are different from us, immediately we're a little afraid of them. We see cultural habits different from ours, and we're afraid. In a nice Anglo-Saxon, Welsh community like Batavia, New York, where I was born, everything's fine until the Italians come. The Italians start singing and drinking wine. The Anglo-Saxons and the Welsh of Batavia don't drink wine and they don't sing. Maybe a little beer. There's a problem, right? They're afraid. Inevitably, the story is unfulfilled unless the problem's fulfilled. Finding the focus of the story is, in a way, finding the hottest issue.

E.C.: Do you start writing before you have an ending?

Gardner: Sure. I never know *exactly* what an ending's going to be. That's something that grows out of a book. Like when you play chess, you set up favorable conditions for a mate, where you have *this* power, and *this* power, and this ambush possible, and so on. How the game ends depends on how the other player plays. In the novel, you set up favorable conditions, but then what the characters want to do, and what ideas come to you in the process all shape the ending. I *can't* know the ending in advance. Some novelists do.

E.C.: When do your best ideas come to you?

Gardner: Anytime.

E.C.: Are there certain conditions which spark ideas for you?

Gardner: Sure. Reading books. When I *happen* to read some book that comes along, just any old thing, I get ideas. Just recently I was reading a book on aesthetics which I had heard about for a long time, and I found it very exciting and got three short stories out of it. It *spurred* ideas and drama. I just finished a book called *The Ordeal of Civility*, which is about the assimilation of the Jews, and it's an interesting, weird, wonderful book, with a curious point of view on Freud and Marx and others. And I just wrote one thing after another. I hardly finished the book because *every* page was so full of wonderful ideas, ways of seeing things that I had never thought of, so I wrote a play about Helen of Sparta and Troy and part of an opera and a long story and a book-length tale, ideas just *pouring* out of that book. It's often the case, particularly if I'm reading philosophy, or theology, or something like that, that I'm sparked by dramatic situations, dramatic thoughts that I haven't had before. It doesn't usually happen when I'm reading novels; I get a different kind of pleasure out of reading novels. I *sometimes* get ideas when reading Tolstoy and Dostoyevsky, Thomas Mann a couple of times. Several times I've stopped reading the book and written something because I've disagreed with him.

E.C.: Do you write a great deal of material which isn't published?

Gardner: Yeah.

E.C.: From your conversation, one gets the idea that you read voluminously.

Gardner: I used to. I don't read so much anymore; I've been pretty busy. I just can't get any reading done if I'm teaching Creative Writing, which takes all day three days a week, and trying to write. But there was a *long* period in my life when I read all the time. Well, read and wrote. And I still read a fair amount. I love to read; if I had more time I would read all the time.

E.C.: Do you have to be in a particular frame of mind to write?

Gardner: No, I don't think so. I think terrible depression can lead to poetry: *bad* poetry, but I've often written poetry when depressed. But fiction I write out of joy. I love storytelling, and I love to dicker with it and work with techniques and so on. I wake up in the morning, and I think about the story I'm going to write today, and I jump out of bed, and I write it.

E.C.: Do you have set ways of writing? Longhand? Typewriter?

Gardner: Usually on a typewriter, sometimes with a pencil. I compose anywhere, anytime. If I'm on an airplane going to a lecture or workshop someplace, I compose with a pencil and a pad of paper. If I'm at home I use a typewriter. If I'm in my office, I use the clunky old office typewriter. The same page will have pencil on it and two different typewriters.

E.C.: Do you drag everything around with you?

Gardner: I drag my manuscripts around with me. Whatever the big thing is I'm working on, I carry around everywhere. In fact it's right here . . . I think.

E.C.: What are you working on now?

Gardner: I've just finished a thing called "King Gustav, Lars Joren, and the Devil." It's about Gustav I of Sweden and how he, with a little help from his friends, murdered the devil.

E.C.: Is it scholarly or a short story?

Gardner: It's a long tale, two hundred pages maybe.

E.C.: When you begin a book, do you already have everything about your characters at hand, or do you find observations you'd forgotten popping into your mind as you write?

Gardner: Sometimes I have it all, sometimes it comes to me as I write.

E.C.: Although most of your novels are experimental to some extent in that you often use a novel idea or situation, their greatness seems to be in ratio with the depth of their characterization and the solid quality of their prose. What place is there today for the experimental novelist struggling with new forms? Can he ever write "great literature"?

Gardner: He *could*. I think that in any age that favors experiment, and ours is one, you're going to get a lot of failed experiments and a few successful ones. Shakespeare, of course, lived in an experimental age, and most of the people around him are of importance only because he existed. Marlowe and Ben Jonson are exceptions.

It's fun to do tour de force stuff, and I've always done it. *Sunlight Dialogues* is a tour de force, a goofy thing to do, a silly way to write a book. *Grendel* was, in its time, a goofy way to write a book. Now everybody does it, but at that time it was a little strange.

Now there's a high priority on experimental fiction for bad reasons, the main one being that Americans in this moment of history are a *little* embarrassed by emotion and by affirmation because for years we were so optimistic and cocksure that we had the right answers and were wonderful. I think with Vietnam and other things, even the aftermath of World War II, when we realized about the bombing of Dresden and Osaka and so on, we weren't so sure of ourselves. Now it's embarrassing for a great many people to take any strong stand because they're afraid that maybe it's foolish. I suspect it's mostly unconscious, and they would resent my even *saying* it about them.

E.C.: What about experimentation with punctuation and that sort of thing.

Gardner: I think it's alright. Other people can always learn from the experiments. In itself it doesn't mean much.

E.C.: What should the budding novelist read?

Gardner: Anything he likes, but a lot of it. The Hardy Boys is fine if that's what you love. It's silly to read things that are good for you, but you don't like, because then you just won't get the habit of reading.

E.C.: How much should one practice before publishing?

Gardner: Publish as fast as you can. If you've got a good story, publish it. If you've got a bad story, call that practice.

E.C.: Very few really good books are written by authors under thirty-five. Should the young writer publish his books even though he realizes they are lacking?

Gardner: It depends on how lacking they are. If they're really awful he shouldn't do it. If they're pretty good he should.

E.C.: What can young writers write today? Are there subjects they should avoid?

Gardner: They can write anything they want to so long as they care about it. A good writer will stay away from sentimentality because the whole purpose of writing is getting the emotion down correctly.

You think of all the characters in the world you could write about. You could write about some ordinary mailman in Southern California, or you could write about a griffin. If you're the type of person who really likes griffins and isn't too interested in mailmen, you should write about the griffin. You should *always* write the best thing you can think of. In my experience, young writers almost never ask themselves, "What is the kind of story I would *most* like to write about?" They're ashamed to, maybe. In writing, as in anything in the world, if you think it's worth doing, you just have to do it wonderfully, with total self-abnegation. It's probably true that writing doesn't change much, that lives aren't wildly altered by novels, although lives are sometimes *saved* by novels, but generally fiction doesn't have that much effect. Nevertheless, when you're a writer you have to pretend, believe that writing has an enormous effect. You have to convince yourself that every story you write is something wonderful.

E.C.: Your later books seem to go through a lot of revisions. Is this so, or do you take particular care in your first draft?

Gardner: I always revise a lot, early books and late books. Every book I've published has been through hundreds of drafts. I work all the time, and most of the time I spend on revision.

When I write I have to listen, I have to read what I write aloud, even if everyone looks at me funny. I have to hear it because sometimes there will be terrible assonance and alliteration, edgy junctures and so on. If you get so you can read it out loud, you can fool editors half the time. If you write like a poet, which is what every prose writer has to do, you'll be all right. A prose writer has to be an absolute *master* poet in terms of rhythmic juxtaposition, lightning fast lines, getting a slow, solemn statement. If you write with beautiful rhythms, editors won't notice that a story's no good. They'll believe the characters because they're listening to the singing.

E.C.: How long does it usually take you to write a book?

Gardner: Ten years, twenty years.

E.C.: But you publish one nearly every year.

Gardner: Well, I've been working for a long time. There were also fifteen years when I was working constantly and nobody was publishing what I wrote. I'm just about out of my backlog, right now. This year I'm publishing the plays that I wrote and the radio plays and libretti, which are older. Everything's new from then on. It may go slower now, and it may not.

E.C.: How long did you write before you began making money from it?

Gardner: I started making money with *The Sunlight Dialogues.*

E.C.: Wasn't *Grendel* rather popular?

Gardner: It was popular, but only in paperback and with college kids, so I didn't make very much money with it. But *Sunlight Dialogues* took off. It was a bestseller.

E.C.: Joyce Cary wrote that "when we recognize beauty in any ordered form of art, we are actually discovering new formal relations in a reality which is permanent and objective to ourselves . . . we are recognizing aesthetic meaning in the character of the universe . . . [and it gives us a] sense of belonging to a rational and spiritual whole. . . ." Is this something like what you mean by "moral fiction"?

Gardner: Yeah, a little. I would maybe have one kind of reservation, which is that Joyce Cary has, in all of his work, a pretty clear point of view that the rational order is there all the time, and we can rise to it and glimpse it. I would say that we create it, that history is progressive, that things aren't as bad as they were sixty years ago. The Indians were incarcerated in Fort Sumter, or massacred, and vice versa; they did their massacres too. A hundred years ago the world was rougher and less just. In the war in Angola, of all places, a country which has forever been filled with genocide, they took prisoners, which means some progress has been made. I think that what happens is that artists, philosophers, theologians, all kinds of people create a dream of a world better than this one, that this one can struggle toward. Once the dream is there, we all struggle toward it. If writers create a dream of an ugly world, then what you get is an ugly world. Whatever is held up as a goal is what humanity has a tendency to run toward.

E.C.: In your book *On Moral Fiction* you write that the great writer must have a settled system of moral belief from which to write and must feel a love for his characters, must empathize with them, whether they are good or bad. When did you become a great writer?

Gardner: *I* didn't say I was a great writer. I think I'm a better writer than several.

E.C.: Your later books radiate much more care for and involvement with your characters than your early books do.

Gardner: I think you underestimate the early books. I think the early books are deeply moral. They're always on the same moral subject. Faith versus rationality is what I always talk about. Grendel is, from beginning to end, a character distrusting faith.

E.C.: When one reads a book one can tell, just by the way the author writes about his characters, whether he really cares for them or not.

Gardner: It's obvious in *Grendel. Anybody* can see *that.* Everybody falls in love with the monster.

E.C.: You write that the great writer will know the truth and write it. What of the writer who firmly believes, and reflects in his books, ideas which you consider false? Can he write great books, so long as he is true to his own beliefs?

Gardner: No. He *has* to be true to his own beliefs—no writer can fake his beliefs—but history, the majority of mankind, will say, "No, that's not right." We've again and again had writers who just *died.* They were wonderful in their time, highly respected in their time, but they are forgotton now. The nihilists are *wrong*, but they're *there* so I argue with them, disliking what they do, disapproving of much of what John Barth does, although he's a genius in his way, of course. I read John Barth and I'm disgusted.

E.C.: "Moral action," you've written, "is action which affirms life." This seems to be a kind of situation ethics, implying that morality is relative to the situation. Is this correct?

Gardner: No. I don't have a whole lot of love for situation ethics; it's no ethics. I think you have to have principled ethics which are based on a deep understanding of human nature and human need. It's intuitive like a Christian code, sort of "Be like Jesus." I accept that, but I have a little trouble with some of the definitions of Jesus, so I just say "Be like the hero."

E.C.: And so on what principle do you base your decisions?

Gardner: Love. Whatever is the most loving thing to do.

E.C.: You've written that the novel should explore openmindedly, searching for what it should teach. At what point should it begin teaching?

Gardner: Probably the last line. Probably the process of discovering what can honestly be said *is* the novel, and the reader who reads the novel goes through the same process the writer went through. He doesn't go through the dead ends and blind alleys, but he discovers, as the writer does, what it is that *can* be said, without exaggeration and without oversimplification.

E.C.: Is there any place in great literature for the novel without hope?

Gardner: No.

E.C.: Hardy?

Gardner: No. I don't think Hardy is utterly without hope, but in so far as he is it's sentimental. I think Hardy does border on sentimentality most of the time. There are some wonderful moments in all of his things, but ultimately you just say, "That's not the way it is." It's not acceptable to feel tricked into tragedy.

E.C.: What about *Waiting for Godot*?

Gardner: I don't think that's without hope. As long as they're still waiting there's hope. Also, Beckett is so profound, and there's so much love, love of the author for the characters, and love of the characters for each other. Crazy, goofy people, but there's always that human contact. And there's the humor, which is a kind of affirmation.

E.C.: Is there any place for cynicism in great literature?

Gardner: Some characters can be cynical. But cynicism is a character flaw. If the novelist himself is a cynic, it goes beyond character flaw to flawed novel.

E.C.: If the author is a cynic he can't properly care for his characters?

Gardner: He can't rightly *understand* his characters. A cynic is a person who assumes the worst about people's motivation. And that assumption is sometimes going to be false.

E.C.: What about satire?

Gardner: Satire's fine. There's no place in *great* literature for satire, but satire's a very valuable sideshow. It's a necessary kind of thing. Sometimes it can rise slightly above its usual height, as it does in Jonathan Swift, but it's still satire. It's a secondary mode.

E.C.: My biggest problem with *On Moral Fiction* was figuring out that you are distinguishing between good literature and great literature.

Gardner: Yeah, probably I got confused, too. There's a lot of literature that one is glad to have around, but it's just not *great*. Moral art is like an experiment. The artist takes ideas and puts them under stress in order to determine their validity. Bad art uses tricks to convince the reader that what *isn't* true *is* true. Not only must the ideas be true, but the emotions must be true.

E.C.: What place is there for the comic in moral fiction?

Gardner: Lots of room for the comic and lots of room for the tragic. Some things are authentically funny.

E.C.: You've said that the writer should give joy, but you come down hard on many writers who have a great love for words. Many readers gain a great deal of joy from words, even if the writer has nothing in particular to say. For example, Christopher Fry, Virginia Woolf, and Dylan Thomas are enjoyable for their wordplay, even if their meanings are not always immediately clear.

Gardner: Right. They love words, but the words *do* in most of those cases support, and in Virginia Woolf's case, *totally* support the vision of the characters. Dylan Thomas is not a great prose writer, he's a great poet, and his language is less in control in the prose than in the poetry.

E.C.: Fry is easily carried away with words, but it doesn't matter because he's so much fun to read.

Gardner: Yeah, it's delightful. I don't mind it with Fry because I don't think he's got too much to say. I *do* mind it with William Gass because he has a great deal to say, and rather than say what's most important, he gets lost in language. I think he's wonderful anyway, but I'd like to see him go more for the material and less for the effect.

E.C.: You've mentioned the despair many contemporary authors have which keeps them from writing really great books. How much of this do you think is heartfelt and how much simply fashionable?

Gardner: I think a lot of it is simply fashionable. Sure. I don't think Jack Barth *seriously* feels despair. He just parades it. I think Jack Hawkes really does feel a touch of it, it sounds more authentic from him.

The three big sins of contemporary writing are frigidity, sentimentality, and mannerism. Frigidity comes about when the writer takes his characters less seriously than does the reader. We see in a great deal of modern fiction authors choosing characters they don't like and then failing to watch them closely. We know why they don't watch the characters closely: they don't love them. They don't really care. The result is a boring book which is inaccurate and clumsy.

Sentimentality is a pursuit of effect without giving due cause. Every form of sentimentality, as opposed to sentiment which is noble and honorable, is an attempt to make the reader cry without giving him a good clear reason for crying. Very often it turns out to be a use of language instead of drama.

Mannered writing is writing where you're constantly reminding the reader that you're a really good storyteller. When language is used properly, as it is in the best of William Gass, every word goes to

further the progress of the vivid and continuous dream, vivid because
of sharp, concrete detail rather than abstraction, continuous because
it avoids such distractions as bad grammar, cleverness, and mannered
language. If language is wonderful but doesn't destroy the dream,
then it's okay. When it's used improperly, it's calling attention to the
pyrotechnic abilities of the writer. What happens is that the more
energy the writer grabs, the less comes out in the scene.

E.C.: Your later work shows that you now have moral beliefs
which you want to communicate, while this was not so obvious in
your earlier novels. Do you see this as part of the growth toward
maturity?

Gardner: I don't want to communicate moral beliefs, I want to
explore moral questions and *come* to moral beliefs. I wouldn't just
preach.

E.C.: But you aren't just exploring. It's obvious that there are
things which you *do* firmly believe, and it comes out in your writing.

Gardner: Sure. That's true. I've worked my beliefs out in other
novels, and now I can stand on them and explore farther. But I don't
want to just communicate my morals. I'd rather just follow character
and understand people and see the relationships between others.

E.C.: To what extent should the teacher assign books to high
school and general college students which deal extensively with sex,
violence, or the seamy side of life students are used to seeing on
T.V.? Such books can be moral or true, but where can the teacher
draw the line between evil which should be understood in order to be
avoided and evil which causes students to copy it?

Gardner: I think that teachers should give the best books they can
find to kids, books which will encourage kids to become lovers of
books. If *Catcher in the Rye* is a book which high school students
adore, which it is, I say give it to them, let them read it. If they don't
like it that much, then don't give it to them. I don't care if Salinger
uses a few naughty words in the book; the moral effect is *obvious*.
Holden Caulfield is a kid who thinks you can hate everybody, and he
learns something very important to teenagers, which is that you
mustn't hate everybody, you just *can't* hate everybody, you finally
have to give in to love. It's a very important and moral book. If a
book's got some sex and violence, but it's *that* kind of book, a totally
helpful book, terrific. On the other hand, an awful lot of books kids

have to read in high school are no good. The attitude that "we *have* to give kids these modern books because that's what people are writing and thinking" is false. They think that the kids are going to like a book because it has sex and violence in it, but that's not true. You assign a kid fifty pages of reading, and he won't care if it has sex and violence in it; he has fifty pages to read when he wanted to play basketball. So, the teacher might as well choose things that don't have sex and violence. Let the kid get it from *Kojak*.

Interview with John Gardner

Gregory L. Morris/1979

Reprinted by permission of Gregory L. Morris.

This previously unpublished interview occurred in Lanesboro, Pennsylvania on 22 February 1979.

GM: You seem a writer who juggles two types of fiction: the realistic and the fabulous. I've heard you talk to writers, telling them to get character and dialogues "down right." Yet you also frequently tend to write a very non-realistic kind of fiction. What distinction do you draw between realistic and fantastic?

JG: Well, the problem of realistic and fabulous fiction is no problem because any fabulous character that you make up is going to be based on human character as we know it. So that if you introduce a talking bat, that bat is going to have to have concerns and language like some person you know. So you make the bat talk like your mean old grandmother or your kind old Uncle Fred. If you have a coffeepot that talks to a lady in the kitchen, the coffeepot is going to have to talk like a real person; maybe it talks Yiddish, or maybe it's an old German baron, but somehow it has a real character. So whether the thing is real or fabulous is irrelevant, you're still following the laws of realism. Fabulism allows you to go places faster and to do more interesting things in certain respects, but always creatures in a story have to talk sense. The thing is, if characters stop talking consistently, if they are inconsistent with the character set up for them, then the reader doesn't believe the scene, and some of the energy of the scene leaks out. It's never a powerful scene unless we believe every step of it; even if you're following real speech accurately and you forget to get the pauses in, it sounds phony. So that it's all the same—you've just got to keep your eye on reality, no matter what type of fiction you write.

GM: You like to put your characters in tragic situations, having them face that reality of death. That's a confrontation that has been very close and very real in your own life. Has your own illness intensified your desire to place your characters in that situation?

JG: No. It's just an artistic matter. I'm not interested in death except as a wonderful backdrop to life. Death is the only thing that makes life serious. You want to make what the characters do important, and the ultimate importance is that whatever we do is going to blow away like the dust. Personally, I'm not scared of death—I haven't been since my illness. When you're close to death, you can examine it critically.

GM: Do you think perhaps that more cynical writers, more ironic writers tend to find death more fearful? I'm thinking of Stanley Elkin and *The Franchiser*, where his main character is very close to death.

JG: It's hard to talk about a specific writer without carefully thinking about it. I think that ironic writers, not Stanley, but a great many ironic writers, are a little afraid of emotion. Death is only one of the many emotions that they're afraid to face, so they keep taking everything back with little sneers and winces and twitches, kind of winking at the reader all the time. I think that if you really love life, then you face emotions boldly. Stanley Elkin faces images boldly, and can do anything with his imagination. His particular concerns as a writer of fiction don't lead him to my kind of concern with death as a background, because he's not as confident as I am that people are generally good and that life is a wonderful thing and that love is a sort of basic emotion in human beings.

GM: Do you see as one of your concerns, as an artist, the political nature of human beings?

JG: Politics is necessary to keep the world going. Politicians have to tell lies—it's necessary. Art doesn't lead to anything—or if it does, it leads to a kind of moral statement, but not to any kind of political statement. When you settle down with a real book, like *Anna Karenina* or whatever, you see how enormously complicated things are, how in fact you can hardly act; there are certain things that simply have to be (you look outward, like Levin, instead of inward). Then you get up from the chair and close the book and go back to work because you have to fix the roof, even though as a matter of fact there are other things that make a statement. You have to vote, vote for the guy whose lies are closest to the necessary truth.

I couldn't possibly take a political side in a novel. There are political issues that are real. The Second World War was full of real issues, but interestingly none of them were brought up during the War. It's a strange thing, in a way. For example, the American people could have been mobilized faster, but there were very complicated problems. One was that the U.S. had strong pro-German sentiments. The American Bund was a very strong sector. So that to raise that issue fully would have been, perhaps, to let loose a monster in this country.

Art *can* have a political effect, though. It gives the general sense that it's better to reason things out. It's complicated. In *Nickel Mountain* there are Republicans and Democrats; in particular, there are the New York City Democrats who hate the "upstate apple-knockers," as they called them. And I wanted to show those people that the "upstate apple-knockers" are every bit as politically and morally astute as they are.

I got a letter from a Jewish girl who lived a couple of years in rural New Hampshire, and she wrote me that the people there were bigoted and narrow-minded and cruel. It's just not true. It may be that because of the way they were raised, that they were prejudiced and other things, but I know what they're like. I grew up with farmers. I learned more from farmers than from professors.

GM: You speak of *Nickel Mountain* as being a political book. Certainly, *The Wreckage of Agathon* must also be considered political in nature, don't you think?

JG: In *The Wreckage of Agathon* I set up different kinds of contrasts. The contrast between Sparta and Athens parallels the American West (with its Goldwater attitude), and the New York, megalopolis, whatever—the East Coast. They're both wrong, obviously wrong. The book asks: What would a seer do? The real problem, of course, is that the person who sees that they're both wrong, and therefore who merely mocks both, but who refuses to act significantly, is as wrong as everybody else. Agathon is no better than the leaders of the Spartans or the Athenians. Peeker is the true oracle.

GM: *The Wreckage of Agathon* is also a particularly historical book, one that seems to depend extensively upon Plutarch's *Lives* for much of its history

JG: I used Plutarch heavily. I love Plutarch. The nice thing about

Plutarch, of course, is that he was already revising history. If you go back straight through history, you find it's so hopelessly confused. But Plutarch was already writing pseudo-history, which was not the naked truth. That is to say, he had people living at the same time who, in fact, had died hundreds of years apart, and that's handy. Fiction is like that: it follows with what *ought* to have happened after what happened *did* happen. I have a new book, as a matter of fact, about a historian who writes "pseudo-history."

GM: One of the things that *does* happen in your universe is accident, random catastrophe. Your characters discover themselves acting with and against chance. What sort of system do you see operating within this fictional universe of yours?

JG: I've thought a lot about it, about how we are shocked into reality. It's a major theme in my work. It's a chance universe; so life becomes a question of how you adjust to change, a question of the survival of the fittest. "The wrath of God" sort of thing. The question is, how do you get to a benevolent universe, to a view of the world which makes you feel safe and secure? With a system that includes a god, it's easy enough to feel safe. People can't work well, can't function without guidelines, without feeling completely safe. A God is necessary, but you must question God. If you don't question, it's *too* easy to feel secure. Questioning is necessary for "maximum health." You have to feel afraid that you will die.

GM: And existence becomes a matter not only of knowing *how* to act but *when* to act?

JG: Right. What happens is that people develop models, accidental models. People make people what they are. This is what happens in *October Light*, for instance. People become more conscious of the models they are following and of the models they are providing, which to some extent is a good thing, this consciousness. What happens, however, is that ultimately people become paralyzed by these models; they become incapable of acting, or act in the wrong way or at the wrong time. The moment you start looking over your shoulder and suspecting your friends, you die.

Insofar as my characters are detectives, they get ahold of what they *really* are. Each of the characters is driven by forces that control their novel, and they come to recognize those forces; they learn to act, to jump, or they somehow die for not learning. For example, Peeker, at

the end of *The Wreckage of Agathon*, knows what he is. In *The
Sunlight Dialogues*, Clumly finally recognizes the Sunlight Man's true
nature, he sees the images of the Sunlight Man; the Sunlight Man is
always seeing fire, and Clumly, in that final scene, sees fire—he
becomes one with the Sunlight Man, and so recognizes the forces
that have been driving him throughout the book. He no longer sees
the fire as nightmare, but as part of a vision.

Sure, you can jump at the wrong time. Clumly sometimes jumps
wrong. But the important thing is to jump. Sometimes you get off the
track, and the only thing that can bring you back is a kind of
community ritual. For example, in *Nickel Mountain*, Judkins, who is
an atheist, gives George the opportunity to confess, to come back to
the community—and George is afraid to do it. Maybe the suffering is
congenital and inalienable. You have to get past the suffering, and
act. George values the past, is concerned with the past, but is lost in
the past. You have to act in the present, in the *now*.

GM: And if one doesn't act, or doesn't act "morally," one
becomes another of the world's monsters?

JG: Yes, basically. It's like this: we are born imperfect. Nobody is
capable of taking care of all the troubles in the world, and you
inevitably feel unwhole. But there's something more. When you're a
child, you think of yourself as perfect, as total. And then you check
yourself inside and you find that when you tell a lie, you're called a
liar. So what you have is this image of yourself, and then as you live
you betray that image over and over and over, until you develop a
second image of yourself. And this image is with you all your life.
There are two shadows: one is the shadow of perfection, that keeps
haunting you, and the other is the shadow of the tempter, telling you:
if I'm not perfect, I'm a monster. In your daily life what you try to do
is keep a balance, but what happens is that the possibility that you
are flawed keeps upsetting that balance, keeps nagging you into an
unforgiveable sort of guilt.

Obviously, everything that I write, everything that I think, is a
secular version of traditional Christian morality: the idea of devils and
angels, the Platonic dream, and the devil who comes as a nightmare
image of yourself. In your daily life you talk about the bad things, but
in your dreams they become real. What every novelist and artist does
is work out the conflict between the conscious and the unconscious.

GM: As an artist, you also seem indebted to nineteenth-century American writers like Poe and Melville, artists who share a similar view of our universe. I'm thinking, in particular, of your use of these writers in *The King's Indian.*

JG: I'm probably the only novelist who's read *Clarel*! Sure, I used those two in that book. Poe hated the idea of slavery to machines. Melville hated human slavery. Melville's the artful dodger, you can't get him. He's the con-man. His main characters are all con-men. Ultimately, Melville says, you've got to con God himself. You can't win. The universe is indifferent. The thing about Melville is that if you reach the conclusion that the universe lacks a God, if you decide that the world's a shadow, then you become a pure utilitarian, a pure materialist. If you refuse to play games, you don't say there is a God or there isn't a God—you leave it all open. And you can't function as a human being without other human beings—this is the only security we can reach.

Nowadays, we have science, we have physics to help define our universe. Nowadays, we see the universe as being either Einsteinian and expansive, or entropic; and while neither system is particularly any improvement upon what's come before it, I do think the Einsteinian view is a bit more hopeful, because as the planets get further and further apart, there's less chance of us hurting each other. You can't have interstellar wars because of the immense lapses of time. You can send messages of hate and it will take forever for them to reach other galaxies.

GM: Turning away from your fiction for the moment, I'd like to ask you about your critical work, for which you've taken a certain amount of heat. I'm thinking both of your medieval scholarship, and of *On Moral Fiction*, which has made many enemies for you. What was your purpose in writing that book, and do you feel comfortable as a critic, as a scholar? Do you take that part of your creative life seriously, or as seriously as you take your fiction writing?

JG: When I was a young writer, trying to understand what I was trying to do, I had an intuition of where I was headed, of what I wanted to make in my fiction. And in *On Moral Fiction*, I wanted to express that intuition. Sometimes you write criticism just to write criticism. Sometimes criticism annoys you so much that you want to tell the other writers—who are your friends—you want to try to tell them what it is you think they're doing wrong, so they'll think about it. That's another of the things I was trying to do in *On Moral Fiction*.

The other thing is that you can't write fiction all the time. It takes a certain kind of concentration and involvement that you can't keep up. Whereas mere logic, mere specificity, is not that hard. So you come to a point where you're exhausted—emotionally, intellectually, physically—and you can't write. You can always read *Beowulf* and knock out a theory on *Beowulf*. I don't mean to slight my work. My critical work is enormously serious. It's not exactly orthodox, in that like any artist I have a tendency to be impatient with proofs. An artist is different from a scientific person. He imitates the way a person walks, and the only way he knows that it's right is that he feels that it's absolutely right. He explains how poetry works, and the proof that he's right is that, of course, that *is* how it works. Whereas the traditional orthodox scholar isn't happy with that; he wants a lot more evidence. I think the reason for that is that there are so many *bad* critics, critics who don't understand human emotion, human nature. That girl loves that boy—*that's* why she said that.

GM: Yet you've been known to misunderstand human emotion, to be an unnecessarily harsh critic. I'm thinking specifically of your letter in the *Kansas Quarterly*, explaining your reactions, as a contest judge, to a piece of fiction submitted for that contest.

JG: That letter was really bad. That's the meanest thing I ever wrote. I wrote that after getting out of the hospital. I was really sick, and I had to get it off. Then I read the stories, and they weren't very good. I was, in effect, asked to judge a contest for $50 that wasn't worth judging. I wrote the letter very, very fast. I never had a chance to read it over. And I got one letter from a guy who was furious at me for something I'd said about homosexuals. He was absolutely right. I wrote back to him in a very nice way, but he came back with another nasty letter, though later he wrote a nice letter. Anyway, that was a bad moment in my life.

That's a case where I didn't have the chance to revise. Normally, when I'm writing fiction, I don't worry about being wrong because I sit down and revise and revise and revise. For example, I still think *Nickel Mountain* is my most rounded and complete novel, and I spent twenty years revising it. Sometimes, other people revise for you, even when you don't want them to; Gordon Lish rewrote

"Grendel's Song" for *Esquire*, changing some of the "dirty words" for the sensitive ears of his readers—I was never consulted about the changes. But once my work is done, I don't re-read my stuff. I'd love to—I'm my favorite writer. Everybody's their own favorite writer.

GM: As a writer, you've also worked extensively in opera. In fact, you once remarked that you wanted to be remembered as "the greatest librettist of the twentieth century." Does that sentiment still hold true?

JG: Sure, and I think it'd be pretty easy, the more I look at other librettos, particularly of twentieth-century opera—things like Berg's *Lulu*, or *Peter Grimes, Oedipus*. The glory of an opera is that a really fine drama, one that expresses character, can be matched by a perfectly accentuated score. In too many operas, they nail a character to one place on the stage, literally. They abandon the possibilities of language. And, in many cases, the translations are just wrong-headed.

Only one of my own operas has been performed; the Philadelphia Opera did a horrible production of *Rumpelstiltskin. Frankenstein* has never been performed, and I think never will be, because of the expense. *Pied Piper of Hamlin* has never been performed. And none has been recorded, though *Rumpelstiltskin* was presented on National Public Radio. I've been lucky to work with good composers, guys like Joe Baber (whom I worked with on *Rumpelstiltskin* and *Pied Piper* and *Frankenstein*, and another opera called *Samson and the Witch*; and Lou Calabro, on *William Wilson*)—composers who understand the dynamics of language *and* of drama, and who are patient with my stubbornness.

GM: And as for the immediate future?

JG: Well, my health is good. I've got to go back in March for a check-up, but I feel good. There are limitations, of course—I can't drink wine, for example, and I need a little more sleep than I used to. But I'm writing full-steam. Right now, I'm working on a novel— I've been working on it for a long time—called *Shadows*. It's sort of a metaphysical detective story, and I'd like to see that finished eventually. It's a matter of finding the time to do everything.

John Gardner: Considerations . . .

Marshall L. Harvey/1979

From *The Cresset,* 42 (September 1979), 19-22. Reprinted by permission of *The Cresset.*

John Gardner spends virtually all of his time on literary pursuits. He teaches, he reads, he criticizes, and at any given time he can be found working on at least two fictional projects—presently, a volume of short stories and a novel entitled *Shadows.*

Because he played a major role in helping writers like Bill Gass and Joyce Carol Oates to establish themselves, and because Stanley Elkin is one of his closest friends, there has been a tendency to associate Gardner's fiction with that of other writers who attained prominence in the 1960s, and even to some extent with technical experts such as John Hawkes and Donald Barthelme. However, by his own account—and he has convinced me—Gardner has always written, with the exception of a few short stories and the novel *Grendel,* fiction in which the traditional techniques and traditional values are held very dear. Gardner is innovative in the sense that Melville or Faulkner, or Eliot in poetry, were innovative—never to the elevation of techniques as an end in itself.

During his visit to Valparaiso, Gardner said that he seeks to renew traditional values by discovering, through his fiction, "rules for behavior that will allow people to live in the world harmoniously." He is determined that if a reader finds a message in a Gardner novel, the message will be a good one.

From a technical perspective, Gardner creates new genres from the traditional ones—by synthesis. *Grendel* is partly a philosophical essay; *Sunlight Dialogues* is partly a detective novel, partly an epic; *Jason and Medeia,* an epic poem, shares characteristics with every literary type known to its widely-read author, to whom I now turn.

MH: A few years ago, you said that you were one of the sixties writers, but you also said that it might be time for fiction to "go heroic." Was that a decision you came to gradually? Did you want to create your own identity, apart from the sixties writers, as the moral spokesman?

JG: I really felt always, for most of my writing life, that fiction ought to create heroic figures, or in some limited way, figures nobler than most people, more brave or more honest or more determined. The best fiction is exciting because you see someone is trying something big and trying it with maximum risk. I was a sixties writer in a sense, at one time, but in a very limited sense. That is, at one time I didn't have much of a theory about how fiction should be written, but that was when I was working on my dissertation. The only thing available out of my earliest fiction is *The Old Man,* my dissertation. It's a terrible book, but in that book I was just trying to write. I just wanted to write a good book, a novel that I could read and say, "Yes, that's a novel." It had interesting characters and it was about something and so on. I wasn't asking myself, "Are some kinds of writing better than others?" I was just trying to do anything that would be satisfactory, but it wasn't satisfactory because it ended up saying something I didn't believe and that's why, finally, I got rid of it.

MH: You once talked about a cartoon element in *Sunlight Dialogues,* and I can see it in the "Louisa" stories too. Is your interest in cartoons related to your interest in romance? It's certainly not satirical.

JG: No, it's not satirical. It's just a way of seeing, like the kind of clarity of image that you get in the "Sorcerer's Apprentice" section of *Fantasia* or in any Walt Disney stuff or any other greater, later cartoonist. That's what I go for some of the time.

When I'm describing Clumly in *The Sunlight Dialogues,* I set up everything so that a cartoonist could draw it very easily using a mole as the central character, letting Clumly be a mole, and it would all be there—you'd have that sharp, vivid sense. Obviously, there is a reason that I describe Clumly as being like a mole. He's not really looking at the world. He's kind of burrowing in to a set of rules—although he's ready. He's aware that the world isn't quite what he's letting it be—and so on. By choosing some kind of an animal image, as in the animal in a cartoon, insisting on it, holding to it, and keeping bright colors and simple lines in the description, I get that effect. From that, by what he thinks and by what he says and by what he does, I can complicate it and fill out the image. Consequently, it's not just the straight line, but very dense and comical, whatever—a peculiar image.

MH: Do any of your fictions exist more in a spatial sense—in a pictorial way—than in a temporal one?

JG: Some of my stories are more vivid as "images in the mind" than others. I think I'm pretty much that kind of writer. I don't know. I think that if you say that there are some writers who are mainly melody and some writers who are mainly ideas and some writers who are mainly vision, I think that I am sort of high on all three, and not as high as the most high on any one. But obviously, I am very concerned with ideas and the relationship of ideas in the stories I tell. I am never satisfied with just one version of any particular theme I'm working with. I want to think about how much can be said about it and work it into the fiction so that everything I can say about any given philosophical subject, or dramatic subject, is said. Because of that, the idea-side of my fiction is rich. It's also true that, given my kind of tradition, my kind of special feeling for literature that *sounds,* where *every* word counts, creating sound in a poetic way, is a major part of what I do.

MH: And you are Welsh.

JG: Yes. But I think that I also go for images more than a lot of people. I think that there is a sort of peculiar fondness for images in my work. It's the same kind of thing you see in the poetry of Dylan Thomas who would go any place for an image. I think that that happens in my fiction—it may not be true—but it's my impression that I am always locked up in the physical details: the visually descriptive details, the sounds, smells, colors, and all that. Finally, I think that all my fiction is pretty visual. When I am writing fiction I most consciously think of it as cartoonish, or animated-cartoonish, or Walt Disneyish. A few examples are: *Grendel* and parts of *The Sunlight Dialogues* like "The Ravages of Spring," "The Warden," and the Queen Louisa stories.

MH: The "John Napper" story is a sound story. Isn't it?

JG: It certainly is. Very much a sound story, very calculatedly a sound story. Although I think that the images of the drunken guy, the central character, me, in the black coat, are pretty vivid visual images. Surely, sound is very important.

MH: You've done a lot of work with rhythm, and you've developed your own method of scanning. Is *Jason and Medeia* a six-stress line?

JG: It's what I think of as sprung hexameters. It obviously varies. At certain times I do hypermetrical lines and at certain times I drop into prose—all kinds of things. But most of the poem is cadenced, six-stress verse. That is to say that, sometimes, if you just read prose, you will come down with six major stresses in a line. If you analyze it, you may have trouble figuring out why there are six major stresses. Most of the time you can really see that this is a six-stress line and that some of the stresses are "pushed up" a little bit. Yes, it is hexameter all the way.

MH: You said that you wrote most of the first draft of *Jason and Medeia* while you were asleep. You woke up and copied it down, then revised and revised many times. And there are passages in your other fiction like that?

JG: There are only a few works that I've done that work that way—*Jason and Medeia* the most of any, and parts of *The Wreckage of Agathon,* mainly the Agathon parts, I mean, mainly the cartoonish parts, not the domestic tragedy. A lot of the other stuff is stuff that I thought about a lot, walked around with a lot, eventually would dream and sometimes I would copy down and then revise it. The same thing happened in "Ravages of Spring," which was all a dream. The next morning I sat down and knocked out a first draft of it. It was pretty much dream-language, then I went through and tried to organize it. The first draft was a little irrational. *Grendel* I worked with that way, but *Jason and Medeia* was special because it, of course, consisted of poetic lines. I would go to sleep and dream the stuff and wake up and write it down, then revise and revise until it made some kind of sense.

MH: In your reading, how have your interests developed? Have you had phases in your reading or do you read all kinds of things all the time, whatever interests you, whatever seems to be good?

JG: I have phases, certainly, like anybody else. I read a whole lot of philosophy of a certain period and then I sort of get bored with philosophy and decide that it's all game-playing. I'll read a bunch of novels, then I'll get kind of bored with novels. Suddenly, they become all the same. I'll read a particular novelist and go into a novel-reading binge, reading everything that a certain novelist has written. I pore through Faulkner, or Melville. I've never read Hemingway.

One sort of delves, because usually one has only a half an hour to spend. Just recently I went through a binge of reading Celine, although I dislike him very much. It was a pure accident. I had to spend a couple of hours in the library for some reason so I picked up a bunch of books that were just lying around. I saw a Celine novel, and I started reading it and found it interesting. I had read Celine a long time ago and really hated him, but this time I became fascinated. I thought he was very, very funny and thought I was really wrong the last time. Now I've returned to what I originally thought. Still, I see him in a different way now. He's a great writer in that he's continuously brilliant, but he's extremely wrong-headed morally. Anyway, it was a pure accident that I started reading Celine at that time.

Sometimes I pick up something such as *National Geographic* and that sends me off on something. Often I read about something because a character of mine becomes involved in a particular activity. In the novel I'm doing now, *Shadows*, there is one character who is interested in computers. He fools around with a computer club and he has a great deal of power over people because of that. As a result, I've been reading some computer manuals and speculations which I'm not interested in very much. In fact, I don't even like the character very much, but I'm going to be fair to him even though he's not a good person. I have to know just as much about computers as he knows, or at least know enough about it to suggest knowledge. A lot of times, since I spend so much time writing, and I write about characters in so many different walks of life, what I read is determined by what I happen to be writing about.

For instance, in a novel I'm working on, called *Rude Heads that Staresquint,* the central character is a psycho-historian. I don't like psycho-history particularly. I think that it's amusing and fun, but it's not really worth reading a whole book of it because psycho-history is basically unsound. However, if you've got a nice character who's a psycho-historian, then you have to read some psycho-history and say all the best that can be said about this character.

In the novel *Shadows,* the detective novel, the detective is fascinated by science. I used to love to read science, to read it just for pleasure, but I have gotten out of touch with it. I hadn't read anything scientific for a long time, so for the last year I've sort of gone through a lot of popular science writers, like Asimov, and I started reading articles again. What they say is wonderful. How they say it is terribly boring. My reading is very sporadic, very unsystematic. Whatever I get interested in is what I read, and that, of course, always pours into the novels because one can always assimilate it and fit it into one's system or modify it.

MH: Speaking of psycho-history, do you think that eventually twentieth century psychiatry will be superseded by something entirely different? That Freud's terms may finally prove to be useless?

JG: I don't think they'll prove to be useless. I think that Freud must have known that they would be adapted. I think that modern models of the brain, mechanical models which can cause a machine to feel anguish and various other emotions will have an enormous effect on the whole practice of science and psychiatry. Essentially, the principles that Freud pointed out are going to stand, but they'll be much more complicated. Much more flexibility will have to be introduced into the system, and of course it had begun to happen already in the "Age of Freud," but it's happening much more now.

Certainly, in any case, psychiatry is always going to remain a terribly important concern of human beings. Every child that is born is born with his own peculiar twists in the life-force. The life-force pushes up everywhere. In one case it pushes up a fetus that is inside a mother who smokes and drinks very heavily, and that fetus is going to have certain kinds of problems and limitations, physiological and pyschological. Another fetus falls down the stairs and that one is going to have a different set of problems. As long as there is no way of producing all perfectly normal, perfectly healthy human beings every human being will not feel perfectly normal and healthy. That really means all of us are going to have some problems. Some of them are going to have major problems so that they can't function. Since we, as a species, have a predisposition toward life we don't think people should die needlessly—so eventually, we try to fix them. Psychiatry is certainly always going to be one of the greatest and most important of the sciences.

MH: In the end of *October Light,* is the bear related to Faulkner's bear, or did you have the other ideas in mind?

JG: I was aware that Faulkner had a bear, and I was aware that

Faulkner's bear had to do with wilderness and all that, but he wasn't a primary concern for me. I had a lot of other bear-ideas, ideas about bears, going at the same time, so that Faulkner is a very minor influence. A number of names of Greek gods come from words which, at one time or another, meant "bear"—Artemis, for instance. It's an amazing thing.

Also, there's that whole idea that one separates oneself from nature when one kills a bear, and that that is one of the falls that one can go through. In order to come back to oneness with nature, one has to go through some kind of ritual with the bear. Part of James Page's problem, and part of every human being's problem is that he has separated himself from his own past, his own emotional past. The bear-cults are all based, from ancient Greece to Vermont, on ways of getting back in touch with the bear, ways of getting back in touch with spirit-nature, which is to say, animal nature, ways of escaping one's isolation as a human being.

Also, there are the legends of the bear as the eternal creature; the one who goes through a magic door somewhere and comes back from death, goes in and out, as we can't do, which makes the bear at least a potential Christ-figure.

For me, it ties up with other kinds of things, about Christ and love. The only god that really counts is the God who is represented in life by love between people, which is why the bear talks like James Page's wife. It's probably a whole lot of other things too. I don't mean to nail down the meaning of the symbol because it's a feeling. I have thought it all out very carefully and I know that all the things I have consciously thought about bears have worked their way into the novel. I can't recount all of those thoughts in a few minutes. For example, a friend once told me a story about a guy who rode through Bennington, Vermont, with a bear in the wagon-seat. It was a wonderful story so I told it in the novel. It made the bear prominent once again and it made the bear human-like. I told it in that way simply because it felt right, intuitively, and it felt right to tell it in so many words; no more, no less. Obviously, that bear is related to Ariah, just as the bear at the end of the book is related to Ariah—and so on.

MH: Do you consider yourself a religious writer?

JG: Surely, I do, in a very general way, not writing for any specific sect. I believe in spiritual values and the kinds of things that are important to me in Christianity. As I understand it, they are matters of individual fulfillment and social harmony.

MH: Do you think that it is possible for a writer to be a seer in the true sense, to foresee events?

JG: I think that it is possible for a poet to be psychic and to have a very clear sense of the future, and that may become a part of his poetry. I think that what poetry, or fiction, does, is analyze situations between people. At least that is what it does as far as my own writing is concerned—very carefully and accurately. From a close and right analysis of general conditions in the world, one might make good guesses on what the future is going to be. It's not the main business of poetry to predict the future, but certainly it could.

The Sound and Fury over Fiction

Stephen Singular/1979

From *The New York Times Magazine*, 8 July 1979, pp. 13-15, 34, 36-39. Copyright © 1979 by the New York Times Company. Reprinted by permission.

John Gardner wears a black leather jacket and dirty blue jeans when he rides his Honda 750 onto the campus at the State University of New York in Binghamton, where he teaches creative writing. He is a small, potbellied man and his white hair falls over his shoulders, so he looks something like a pregnant woman trying to pass for a Hell's Angel. As he walks across the campus—he bounces more than walks, often singing aloud to himself—he frequently pauses, draws a small pad out of his back pocket, and begins scribbling: perhaps a new novel, or a screenplay, or a book review, or a poem, or a libretto for one of the three operas he's writing. Gardner, who is 45, wrote fiction for more than 15 years without publishing anything: No one would have him.

Then suddenly, during this decade, he began bringing out what seemed like a book every six months, sometimes every month. The 21 published so far include six novels, a collection of short stories, children's books, fairy tales, criticism, an epic poem and other works harder to classify. (In *Grendel,* he rewrote *Beowulf* from the monster's point of view; in addition to everything else, Gardner is a respected medievalist and has written scholarly works, translations and two books on Chaucer.) "John Gardner," wrote Robert Towers in his review of *October Light*—which the National Book Critics Circle proclaimed the best novel of 1976—"is the dazzling virtuoso among recent novelists: a plausible impersonator, ventriloquist, puppet-master and one-man band."

Gardner has also emerged as the leading warrior in the current battle over the proper substance and form of the contemporary American novel. He has raged against what he sees as the detached, unfeeling direction of modern literature, believing that it undermines many talented writers and even their readers. In a recent book, *On Moral Fiction*, Gardner wrote that "almost all modern art is tinny,

220

commercial and immoral," and concluded with a challenge: "Let a
state of total war be declared not between art and society . . . but
between the age-old enemies, real and fake." He got the literary fight
he wanted—many prominent novelists have struck back—and now
he is on the attack again. In his new book, *The Art of Fiction,* soon to
be published by Knopf, Gardner refines and sharpens his criticisms.
He reveals a near-Messianic complex about the purpose of art, and of
fiction in particular, and his views and novels have clearly touched
raw nerves in both the writers he rails against and the readers he is
trying to convert. Gardner's views reflect a profound and unresolved
debate that has engaged literary minds since James Joyce.

Gardner believes there are no major American writers working
now. In his opinion, John Barth, William Gass, Vladimir Nabokov
(now dead, of course), Donald Barthelme and Stanley Elkin are more
interested in "newfangledness" or in playing games with words or
with literature itself than in concentrating on the moral and emotional
problems of their characters; Norman Mailer, Joseph Heller, John
Updike and Robert Coover, among others, don't even seem to care
about their characters—a fatal flaw in any writer, according to
Gardner—while other novelists are self-indulgent philosophizers (Saul
Bellow) or full of "winking mugging despair" (Thomas Pynchon).

Gardner exhales opinions on his fellow writers. In two minutes he
can say:

"John Updike doesn't revise enough. He feels he's got to publish a
book a year. Again and again he brings out books that don't say what
he means them to say. And you can't tell his women apart."

"Malamud is a great artist, an enormously serious writer, but he
keeps blowing it in his novels."

"*The New Yorker* makes me furious. The magazine has gone
cheap and New York fashionable, like New York painting. *The New
Yorker* likes that cold, ironic stuff, like Barthelme, superrealism. I
think it's just wrapping for their Steuben glass. If you put a real piece
of fiction in *The New Yorker,* you've got to put it awfully far away
from the fur coats and the Steuben glass, or the coats will fly apart
and the glass will shatter. Their nonfiction is wonderful."

"Mailer's just lost. He's got the rage and he's got the idealism, but
he can't find anything to focus on except an individual like
Muhammad Ali or Marilyn Monroe or his mother."

"Joe Heller writes situation comedies. He's smart, so he verges on the serious from time to time, but he doesn't have anything serious to say about good and evil."

"The present scarcity of first-rate fiction," Gardner maintains, "does not follow from a sickness of society but the other way around. . . . Real art creates myths a society can live instead of die by, and clearly our society is in need of such myths. . . . Moral fiction holds up models of decent behavior: Characters whose basic goodness and struggle against confusion, error and evil—in themselves and others—give firm intellectual and emotional support to our own struggles."

Novelist John Barth is one of the most outspoken in his reaction to Gardner's criticisms. "To say that Gass and Barthelme are writing fiction full of literary games is stupid," he said in a recent interview. "Fiction has always done that. *Don Quixote* starts out as a satire of the novel of chivalry, but it is passionately about life. For that matter, Gardner condemns examples of my own writing for these reasons. But I'm very much concerned with real-life contemporary problems and moral problems. There's something very self-serving about his argument. He's making a shrill pitch to the literary right wing that wants to repudiate all of modernism and jump back into the arms of their 19th-century literary grandfathers. Gardner's own later novels do this and are applauded, of course. He's banging his betters over the head with terminology and, when the smoke clears, nobody is left in the room but Mr. Gardner himself."

"His argument in *On Moral Fiction* isn't made well enough," says critic Hugh Kenner. "There's a kind of junk-experimental fiction which is made out of the dictionary and which I would repudiate as heartily as Gardner, but he throws out far too much else."

"I picked up *On Moral Fiction* in the bookstore and looked up myself in the index," says John Updike, "but I didn't read it through. I try not to read things that depress me. Gardner doesn't find me moral or inspiring and that might have been depressing." (He chuckles.) " 'Moral' is such a moot word. Surely, morality in fiction is accuracy and truth. The world has changed, and in a sense we are all heirs to despair. Better to face this and tell the truth, however dismal, than to do whatever life-enhancing thing he was proposing. . . . I thought he was awfully cavalier with Bellow."

"If I'm not Gardner's ideal novelist," says Saul Bellow, "I'm full of regret. I can't suit every taste."

Speaking of Gardner's occasional bits of praise for his contemporaries, Bernard Malamud says, "Whenever Gardner hands you a chocolate cake, it's loaded with worms. I find Gardner lacking in generosity and, sometimes, judgment."

"Gardner is a pretentious young man, talks a lot and has little of intelligence to say," Joseph Heller says. "He writes dull novels and dull carping criticism."

"No comment," says Norman Mailer, and he pauses and smiles. "We'll meet in heaven."

Gardner isn't fazed. "Their criticism is silly," he says. "I am absolutely sure that my ideas will prevail. The only law I'm sure of is the survival of the fittest."

Gardner sees himself as something of a latter-day Tolstoy—the only novelist he seems fully to approve of. Both Tolstoy and Gardner are "philosophical" novelists, influenced by Christianity (Tolstoy's last major novel was *Resurrection,* Gardner's first novel was *The Resurrection*); both men were deeply affected by the death of a brother; and both felt that most contemporary art lacked moral seriousness. "I agree with Tolstoy," Gardner writes, "that the highest purpose of art is to make people good by choice." Yet the man who emerged from the pages of *On Moral Fiction* resembled Tolstoy less than Gardner's re-creation of Grendel, the primeval beast in *Beowulf.* Grendel hides in the forest gnashing his teeth at human stupidity, waiting to swoop down upon the village of Hrothgar, rip it apart, and kill the people there. Gardner himself (like Tolstoy) has an anti–city bias (especially an anti-New York City bias) and one can hear his teeth grinding away through much of his critical writing. He seems fearless and ferocious, and if one had to choose between spending an evening with the author or with the beast you might pause before deciding. It would never occur to you that John Gardner can be gracious and speaks in a quiet tone of voice, that his voice catches whenever he mentions his mother and father, that he is a man who claims to be "absolutely happy."

He was born in Batavia, N.Y., in July 1933. His mother Priscilla was a high school teacher of literature and his father still is a dairy farmer. As a boy, while John Jr. was feeding the cows and his father was milking them by hand, his mother sat in the corner of the dairy barn and read Shakespeare out loud. The father would take the parts of his favorite characters and recite their lines from memory. At night, he would sing his son to sleep with poems. When John was 8, he began writing his own poetry which his mother then copied into small books and sent to friends as Christmas presents. It must have been an idyllic childhood, until he was almost 12. One spring afternoon in 1945, John was driving a tractor and ploughing the fields while Gilbert, his younger brother, was riding along behind him on the cultipacker, a two-ton implement that crushed the newly disked ground. Gilbert fell and John turned around just in time to see the cultipacker's wheels at his brother's pelvis. Both boys knew that Gilbert should never have been riding there, but everyone in the family agreed that John could never have stopped in time to prevent his brother's death.

After that, instead of working on the tractor, John would park it in the field, sit under it and write novels. He made up melodramas, love affairs and murders taking place in the woods. He read the novels to his cousins, who helped on the farm. If they liked the stories, they cheered him and took over his chores so he could write the next chapter. If they didn't like them, they hissed and threw hay in his face. "It teaches you to please the crowd," Gardner says. He invented a city in his head and every afternoon told his bedridden grandmother what the people there were doing. "I made up stories for her. I was a liar as a kid. I lied all the time, but not to get anything. It was just fun to make people believe me. My lying embarrassed me, but I never stopped."

When he was 19, he began writing his first "real" novel—20 years later, it became *Nickel Mountain*—and he married his second cousin, Joan, whom he had known since the age of 2. Joan is a music teacher, composer and "a brilliant pianist," according to Gardner. The couple had two children, Joel, now 19, and Lucy, 17, and the marriage lasted 23 years. Gardner doesn't like to talk about it, but once started he is candid and revealing.

"We had a lot of differences about art, and, since art is *the* most important thing in my life, it was a very serious problem," he says. "She would play her compositions on the piano for me and then say, 'What do you think?' I would say, 'That's wonderful.' She would see that I didn't really think that and then she would say, 'What do you really think?' I would eventually tell her each thing that I didn't feel was exactly right and she would be crushed. I never figured out how to deal with this, at all.

"She liked some of what I wrote a great deal and disliked some of it a great deal. She thinks I rant too much at my fellow writers and go off on hobby-horses in my writing. She liked writers I didn't like and she naturally felt that if I hated *them*, I was passing judgment on her. But I couldn't keep silent because I feel so strongly about what I do. It was ego protection. I have fierce opinions. They're what I live on. Joan did everything in her power to make peace but . . . If she had just been some dumb wench, I could have kept quiet. But she is a terrific artist of a kind very different from me. So we threatened each other a lot—and sometimes we punched."

For years, during his marriage, his teaching career at San Francisco State, Southern Illinois University and Bennington, and his long effort to establish himself as a novelist, Gardner was suicidal. He used to "chug-a-lug martinis"—and tremble in public. "Whenever I thought I was going to leave the house and kill myself," he says, "there was always one thought in front of me: People who commit suicide pretty much doom their kids to commit suicide. There are times when you feel you ought to be dead, but I never feel that anyone else ought to be dead."

He and Joan have been separated for several years and Gardner says he is trying to get a divorce. Gardner now lives in Lanesboro, Pa. (pop. 502), in a century-old home resembling an American Gothic church: 15 huge, high-ceilinged rooms, black marble fire-places, oak floors, wainscoting, the original carved oak cornices over the door frames. (The rent is $250, but in the winter the heating bills run to $400 or $500 a month.) Gardner lives with Liz Rosenberg, a 24-year-old writer who also teaches at SUNY Binghamton. She rides to work on the back of his Honda. He calls her Lizzie and they smile at each other a lot. "If I would have known 10 years ago," he says, "that someday all I would be worried about was that I smoke too much and drink too much coffee and don't exercise, I would have thought that God had come down and kissed me."

Gardner has some reason to worry about his smoking (he claims he can't write without deeply inhaling on his pipe). Two years ago, he was found to have cancer of the colon, and it had to be removed. He is regularly tested for recurrence; thus far the malignancy has not returned. "I feel pressed for time now. My physical situation is threatened just enough, so I don't want distractions or to go to parties or any of that. I only do what I want to do here, and that means reading and writing."

His life is not quite as tranquil as it sounds. During the school year, he teaches on Mondays and Tuesdays and spends his weekends traveling around the country lecturing, reading from his works-in-progress (as far as he can tell there are currently 15 or 16 of them), and throwing barbs at other novelists. The rest of the week, usually late at night, he writes. "It takes most people six months to write a movie script. I can do one in four days. Operas go fast. So do poems and children's books and short stories—a few nights, a few weeks at most. Only the novels go slowly and drain me." He admits that teaching is a financial and time-consuming burden, but he feels he has no choice. "Fiction is the only religion I have. If I don't teach and get my point of view across to younger writers, I will burn in hell for a thousand years." He laughs at the idea. "Eating's a waste of time too, but you gotta do it. A writer is just a center of energy for people. If you're a big enough center of energy, you can write in garbage and it will go down like gold."

When Gardner first wrote *On Moral Fiction* in 1965, no one would publish it; it was too heretical. When he rewrote it in 1975, he toned it down and found a publisher. Several of the essays were excerpted in literary journals, and the title essay won the prestigious Pushcart Prize. Gardner's idea (that much is wrong with modern fiction) was becoming fashionable.

Gardner's best work on the subject appears in the forthcoming *The Art of Fiction*. (The title is borrowed from Henry James; Gardner borrows everywhere and shamelessly. He was accused of plagiarism in *The Life and Times of Chaucer*, but he calls the work derivative. "The critics quote from a previous Chaucer historian and then quote me and then compare the two to show the parallel," he says with a smile. "They don't notice that in the same paragraph I've slipped in sentences from two other historians. I'm more derivative than they think.")

The Art of Fiction is ostensibly a how-to text for beginning novel writers, but it is here that Gardner drops his rhetoric for the most part and spells out what he really means by moral fiction. He says that fiction must create a "vivid and continuous dream" in the reader's mind. "In great fiction," he writes, "the dream engages us heart and soul; we not only respond to fictional problems as though they were real, we sympathize, think and judge. We act out, vicariously, the trials of the characters and learn from the failures and successes particular modes of action, particular attitudes, opinions, assertions and beliefs exactly as we learn from life. Thus the value of great fiction, we begin to suspect, is not just that it entertains us or distracts us from our troubles, not just that it broadens our knowledge of people and places, but also that it helps us to know what we believe, reenforces those qualities that are noblest in us, leads us to feel uneasy about our failures and limitations."

This statement stands at one pole—the conservative pole—in the argument over contemporary fiction. Gardner's good friend and archenemy in literary conventions is William Gass, given this year's "Award of Merit for the Novel" by the American Academy and Institute of Arts and Letters. Last autumn, the two debated literary issues at a Fiction Festival in Cincinnati. The Gardner-Gass debate has been going on for much of the 20th century. In a sense, it began with James Joyce, and the purists on each side judge where they stand by whether they can read, let alone enjoy, *Finnegans Wake*. Someone once said that, more than a decade after his discovery, only 12 people on earth understood Einstein's theory of relativity; one wonders whether even that many really grasp *Finnegans Wake*. Before Joyce, good fiction was thought to evolve around plot, drama, emotion and character. Henry James believed that character was the essence of everything, and took as his dictum: "Character is plot." One read a novel to understand how particular people confronted particular emotional and moral problems. Many artists of the 20th century—Gertrude Stein, John Cage, Jackson Pollock—became more and more preoccupied with other things: new techniques of literary, visual and musical language itself. The results are art forms that are not only less accessible to the nonacademician but may also be less concerned with the age-old human problems. What has been gained in technique has perhaps been lost in feeling.

William Gass describes his concept of character as "any linguistic location in a book toward which a great part of the rest of the text stands as a modifier. Ideas can become characters. There's free will and determinism. There's substance and accident. . . . 'Substance' is more interesting than most of my friends. When people ask, 'How are you building character?' they sometimes think you're going around peering at people to decide how you're going to render something. That isn't a literary activity. It may be interesting, but the literary activity is constructing a linguistic source on the page."

If a work of art is this self-referential and opaque, the response to it may be also. Many people, including the eminent art historian Sir Kenneth Clark, have confessed to being totally baffled by much of modern art. For years, many readers and critics have complained about some of the same things in modern fiction. As far back as the 60's, critic John Aldridge wrote, "There has been no time in recent literary history when so much attention has been paid to the serious novel. Yet never before has the serious novel seemed so remote from the experience most of us recognize as real, so irrelevant to the issues that engage us most intensely, so unchallenging to the imagination, so barren of emotion and ideas, so just plain boring to get through." And Leslie Fiedler echoed him: "To read a group of novels these days is a depressing experience. After the fourth or fifth, I find myself beginning to think about 'The Novel,' and I feel a desperate desire to sneak out to a movie."

John Gardner is one of the first and most outspoken American novelists to articulate this view, and to try and do something about it.

Perhaps the most interesting question surrounding Gardner is not whether he is right but how his own novels measure up to his own pronouncements. In *Grendel,* an early tour de force which the critics called "magical" and "a small masterpiece," Gardner takes the reader so far inside the head and heart of the monster that he finds himself cheering for Grendel even as the beast kills and eats women and men. ("Fiction at its best," wrote critic Richard Locke in an essay that took issue with *On Moral Fiction* but praised *Grendel,* "takes risks beyond morality.")

Gardner followed with *The Sunlight Dialogues,* a 700-page excursion through his hometown of Batavia. There are 81 characters in this best seller and more plots and subplots than one can count. The sheer mass of life he sets in motion (not unlike Dickens) showed for the first time how talented Gardner really is. But the two main

characters engage in a number of endless philosophical dialogues—
intentionally reminiscent of Plato's—that cover everything from the
Mesopotamian dead (circa 2300 B.C.) to the Pepsi generation.
Rereading the book now brings to mind, to Gardner's detriment, one
of his pronouncements: "The chief quality that distinguishes great art
is . . . the good sense and efficient energy with which it goes after
what is really there and feels significant. . . . To say that artistic energy
is 'efficient' is to say that it does not spatter out in irrelevant
directions, needlessly work against itself in futile self-contradiction,
raising more doubts and difficulties than are warranted by the nature
of the thing explored."

October Light, Gardner's latest novel and another best seller, is
about a feud between a constipated old Yankee conservative, James
Page, and his sister, Sally, an 83-year-old budding feminist. James
locks Sally in her bedroom for insubordination and, after she devises
a trap designed to kill him, she finds a "trashy" paperback in her
room and begins reading it to pass the time. Gardner shows us
exactly what Sally reads, and throughout *October Light* we are
forced to jump back and forth between the novel and the novel
within the novel. The reader's "vivid and continuous dream" is
forever discontinuous and frustrated. The "inner novel" is full of dope
smugglers and murderous blacks and orgymongers (all caricatures),
an earthquake and a flying saucer. The characters appear to have
memorized the whole of ancient and modern philosophy. Much of it
sounds like Gardner parodying his earlier work (which is what he
says he was doing). The paperback takes up one-third of the entire
novel.

Even though *October Light* was honored as the best novel of 1976,
many critics would not stand still for it. "Gardner's work," wrote critic
Robert Towers, "gives the impression of having proceeded from a too
well-stocked mind, a mind that cannot resist the temptation, arising
from its own cultivation, that must bring to bear the whole weight of
Greek mythology, Western philosophy, from Plato to the present,
medieval allegory, English literature, and Protestant theology upon
the quotidian lives of farmers, police chiefs and piano teachers."
Diane J. Cole, another literary critic, wrote that "in the odd
economics of fiction, less is often more. Gardner knew once, as
Grendel proves; if only he could learn simplicity again."

William Gass recently speculated on what he thought was wrong with Gardner's later work. "John should revise more, but he doesn't," Gass said. "His greatest weaknesses are his glibness and his preachiness, and his problem is that of almost any writer who has gained some popularity. That popularity is almost invariably based on what is weakest in the writer's work, and then the tendency is for the writer to lean in the direction of that quality which encourages the weakness rather than counteracting it."

Gass was asked why he believed Gardner is so popular. "There is a big public out there squirming for what John gives them," he said. "You read a book like *Sunlight Dialogues* and, in one sense, it's easy reading and yet you can feel you've been reading an important book, one with weight, one full of ideas. It's not one of those damned nervous constructions. Even people of considerable intelligence are not interested in literature per se, but in the good old-fashioned stuff written well. They want things that are fundamentally not upsetting. They want entertainment. . . . John Irving has struck a lode there with *The World According To Garp.*"

When I called Gardner and asked for an interview, he said he was very busy. "I get paid $1,000 an hour for lecturing," he snapped. "I don't make any money talking to you. So this would cost me at least $5000. I don't know if it would be worth my time." He paused, "I'd want to do it fast." His brusqueness seemed to be melting. He talked a little more and then said he'd consider it. Just before hanging up, he said, "Thank you. Thank you for calling. I'll see you on Saturday."

Liz greeted me at the door with a smile and called upstairs to Gardner. A few moments later, I saw a rumpled gnome of a man descending the long winding staircase toward me. His hair swayed with his steps, and he was wearing a crumpled pink shirt—held together with safety pins—paint-spattered blue jeans and broken shoes. His face was red and swollen with sleep—or the lack of it; he had been writing until 6 A.M., five hours before—and his eyes belonged to someone over 70. He smiled, not welcoming me, but resigned to doing his duty. He made coffee, and we went upstairs.

Scattered on the floor of his study and upturned on the window sills were dozens of dead flies. Gardner sat at his desk and began filling his pipe. His fingertips are the color of charcoal from constantly cleaning the pipe bowl. He leaned back, looked out the window and began talking; all pretense of nastiness disappeared. He was open enough, so that after a while I ventured to ask him why he dresses and chooses to look the way he does. (He is handsome, when he pulls the silver locks back from his forehead and eyes.)

"I feel like it," he said, smiling and drawing on the pipe. "It's comfortable. It's more than just comfortable. When Liz tells me, 'You've got to get a haircut and be a normal person,' I feel a moment of panic. You develop certain crutches and you don't even know why they work, but they do. I feel kind of detached from the world, in both a good and bad way. My appearance serves as a wall, so I don't get involved in too many things. If I get to play troll, then I don't have to play quite fair. You're warned," and he smiled again, for a moment. "I don't do it because I think it's attractive."

As he talked, Gardner filled in some of the gaps that critics had pointed out in *On Moral Fiction:* "I don't think my argument is quite sound when I say that great art always leads to life affirmation. I think one of the greatest plays ever written is *Phèdre* by Racine, but I can't get up after I see it. It just kills me."

I asked him why he hadn't mentioned his own work in his literary criticisms.

"I had drafted some stuff about that because I wanted to show that I was talking about general problems and not saying that I was sitting in judgment on everyone else like some smart old rabbi," he said. "It's a problem of the age and, consciously or unconsciously, we slide into it. You try things because you have faith that they can be done. Some periods give you faith and some don't. Everything is against us at the moment. One doesn't feel one has much to say about one's government or one's world. Religion is a funny spot, and so on. There are so many natural discouragers that it's hard to burst out like a broncobuster. But there is no way I could have put any of this in the book without sounding like *Advertisements for Myself.*" He stopped, tilted his head. "You keep violently fighting for life, for what you think is good and wholesome, but you lose a lot. I think all my struggles toward anything worthwhile are pretty much undermined by psychological doubts. But you keep trying."

He went on to say that there was probably room in the world for almost all writers; moments later, he was baring his fangs again and biting into various literary reputations: Updike, Gass, Barth, Bellow. . . .

When he paused, I said, "What about you? Are you a major
American writer?"

"Well," he said, loading his pipe. "I am one of the very serious
pretenders. My books have faults which anybody who thinks about
them can spot, but I'm a serious and careful philosophical novelist.
You can't judge your own work, finally, because you can't judge your
own psychological limitations."

At my request, he went through each of his novels and pointed out
what he felt its flaws were. His criticisms were elaborate and often
similar to the reviews quoted above (although he defended every
word of the "inner novel" in October Light). About the writing style
in Nickel Mountain, he said, "I knew it was a problem when I was
doing the last draft. The style is just slightly whiny and babyish. It
would come to me that that was the problem with the book and I
would think that and then work on something else instead. When it
came out, I realized I'd forgotten to put in the new transmission."

Does he think that working on so many different things at once can
be a problem?

He brushed the question aside. "I do all of these things because
they're fun. I enjoy them."

Why has he written so little about sexual love?

He seemed somewhat taken aback by the question, but he sucked
on the pipe, sighed, and drew himself up. "That's true. That's the
greatest weakness in my fiction—the lack of real sexual love. The
only great artist who ever surmounted an inability to deal with this
was Melville. Shakespeare mastered love. Mozart was great. He
knows about men and women. Chaucer, terrific on it. Dante,
fantastic. Homer, just unbelievable. It's one of the motivating forces—
and I don't have it. It's partly puritanical shyness. Nickel Mountain is
a kind of love story, but it really shies away from it. I couldn't handle
it. But maybe this is changing. Shadows [his latest major novel, in
progress for years now] is the first love story I've ever written flat out.
A real love story requires a woman who is the equal of the man. And
my women . . . this has been a weakness."

Not long ago I had heard Gardner read part of Shadows at a
university. The woman in the book was interesting, and the author
seemed particularly involved with her; it had occurred to me later that
she was based on Liz. When I asked about this, he said it was "pretty
much true."

Is Gardner satisfied with his work?

"No, I haven't been a real writer. I've been learning techniques and making good objects, stories that would get me by, that would lock in my position and make it safe. But what I'm doing in *Shadows* is dredging. It goes down and down and down inside me which I haven't done before. I'm through with the period of becoming a great writer and now I'm just writing. This sounds crazy but I wouldn't even care if my name wasn't on my stories anymore so long as they are wonderful stories."

"When you suddenly begin to feel confident about where you stand, you stop worrying about the platform you're standing on and start looking around for what everything means and feels like. The fiction I'm doing now is assuming life, assuming survival, assuming love. It's more just pure hunting." He took the pipe out of his mouth. "It helps very much to be with somebody who loves you and is not in psychological competition with you. It's nice to be loved."

Gardner has been dredging in places other than *Shadows*. He recently published a story in *The Atlantic* called "Redemption," about a 12-year-old boy named Jack Hawthorne. It begins this way: "One day in April—a clear blue day when there were crocuses in bloom—Jack Hawthorne ran over and killed his brother, David. Even at the last moment he could have prevented his brother's death by slamming on the tractor brakes, easily in reach for all the shortness of his legs; but he was unable to think, or rather, thought unclearly, and so watched it happen as he would again and again watch it happen in his mind, with nearly undiminished clarity, all his life." After the accident, Jack Hawthorne seeks redemption in art—in playing the French horn. One critic wrote in praise of "Redemption" that it "lacks the pyrotechnics, the brittle syntax of a lot of his earlier work. . . . The story is pure power, way beyond the self-consciousness of academics, beyond tour de force." (Tolstoy wrote about his brother's death in *A Confession*.)

Before leaving, I asked Gardner why he has such a Messianic complex about art.

"It's made my life," he said, "and it made my life when I was a kid, when I was incapable of finding any other sustenance, any other thing to lean on, any other comfort during times of great unhappiness. Art has filled my life with joy and I want everybody to know the kind of joy I know—that's what Messianic means."

He began to talk faster, the pipe flapping up and down. "The joy I get from a Tolstoy novel is that you're reading him and he never makes a mistake. He's thinking and he's true to people and true to life and your heart starts to tug. You can't believe he's pulling it off. And you get to the end of the novel and he still hasn't made a mistake and it's just *incredibly* thrilling. Just the fact that he did it! So when the fraudulent stuff comes along, it's outrageous. I yell at what I don't think is the real thing, and I work all the time on my own fiction. I work hard and I work critically because I want to be part of that joy. I want to be a piece of the great conversation."

An Interview with John Gardner

Judson Mitcham and William Richard/1980

From *New Orleans Review*, 8 (Summer 1981), 124-33. Copyright © 1981 by Loyola University, New Orleans. Reprinted by permission of the *New Orleans Review*.

In March 1980 Gardner was interviewed when he came to Fort Valley State College to participate in a symposium on "Christian Values in Modern Literature."

NOR: Is there any merit in a recent *Harper's* article which criticized writers' conferences as having little value and where John Gardner was described as cultivating a "vatic air"?

JG: There's a great deal of justice in describing me as vatic. I have a tendency to behave like the Pope. Other people who go to Bread Loaf and to other writers' conferences wear funny hats and dance funny dances and do all these things that I can't do very well, and so I talk soberly and soundly, as I'm trying to do now, and sound sort of popish. I'm pleased by that description. I'd rather be called that than a pregnant Hell's Angel, as I was in another article. As for the description of what happens at Bread Loaf, I think it was mistaken. The writer takes as certain truth the notion that writing can't be taught. But I don't believe it. In my opinion, nobody would ever say that about painting or about composing. The teaching of musical composition has been going very well since at least Bach and probably centuries earlier. Vienna was what it was because of brilliant teachers like Papa Haydn, Mozart, Beethoven, and so on. In art nobody has ever condemned Cezanne for taking students. But there is a notion, which has to do with the romantic hero image, that writing is pure genius, and you can't teach it. The basic problem with the article attacking Bread Loaf, then, is that it begins with the premise that a writing workshop has to be a fraud, because writing can't be taught. Bread Loaf, in fact, has been going for a very long time and has a very good record of helping extremely talented writers to become solid artists.

Another thing I mind in the article you mention is the notion that
Bread Loaf is run by stars, and that there's a great distance between
the contributors, that is to say, the students, and the stars who teach
the courses. In fact, most of the stars at Bread Loaf came up through
the so-called ranks. Linda Pastan, a famous poet now, began as a
student, became a fellow, that is, an assistant to one of the
instructors, and then became an instructor herself. John Irving and
Tim O'Brien also worked their way up, and I think it's fair to say that
those people who began as contributors and ended up as teachers at
Bread Loaf became the fine writers they became at least partly
because of the superb teaching they got at Bread Loaf. Not
exclusively. Linda Pastan studied with James Dickey at the University
of Virginia. James Dickey, at his best, is probably as good a poetry
teacher, teacher of the writing of poetry, as America has ever seen.
But although I would grant that much of what Linda got she got from
James Dickey in classes, I think she also got help at Bread Loaf.

What happens at Bread Loaf, far more than at any other
conference, I think, is that the selectivity process tends to bring in
young writers at the point when they're almost ready to publish but
have some little problem that needs fixing. Usually the people I teach
. . . and I teach about twenty novelists and short story writers every
year, when I go (I've only taught off and on there) . . . the writers that
I get are either people who used to publish regularly and have lost it
somehow—they fell out of style or went sentimental or lost their old
editors and never found new ones, or something—or else they're first
rate beginning writers who still have a couple of mistakes to get rid of
in their writing. In the two weeks they spend at Bread Loaf those
people are learning the little things they need to become well-
published writers. Then, of course, what happens after that is that
the people they have met at Bread Loaf help them. One of the
comments in the article was that Bread Loafers are always praising
each other, that John Gardner writes a blurb on Irving's book, Irving
writes a blurb on O'Brien's book and so on. That's all true, but it
sounds more like nepotism than in fact it is, because, for instance,
Irving wrote on O'Brien when O'Brien was a Bread Loaf fellow, not a
famous writer yet. That's the usual situation, Bread Loaf teachers
helping Bread Loaf writers just getting started. That's how it
happened that I began promoting and defending Susan Shreve, who

wrote *Children of Power*. She started as a contributor and is now a
teacher at Bread Loaf, a very fine short story writer and novelist.
Susan Shreve showed me work, and we went over it, I told her what
I thought was wrong, and so on. Bread Loaf helps young writers in
other ways, of course. At Bread Loaf we introduce people to agents
and editors who come to visit. It's almost the only workshop where
that's an important part of the program, arranging for young writers
to talk in a social situation with editors and agents. Anyway, once the
novel is accepted I, of course, wave the flag and say "finest novelist
since Tolstoy" or something. From a distance it looks like nepotism,
but in fact I'm not writing blurbs for John Irving now; he no longer
needs me. What we're doing, in giving support to new novelists, is
continuing the teacher-student relationship—the help—after the
Bread Loaf two weeks. I think that's something to be boastful about
rather than ashamed of.

NOR: You wrote for 15 years or so without publishing very much.
You wrote a number of works during that time. Would you say that
their finally being accepted was the result of significant revisions or of
changes in judgments concerning literary merit?

JG: It was more the latter than the former. It's true that I revised all
that time, because you get the novel rejected, and it's sitting around
the house, and eventually you pick it up, and you realize there's a
mistake in it, and you fix it. But I think four of my novels—it's hard
for me to remember at this point—were sitting ready together at the
same time, all rejected. *The Resurrection*, the first one that I
published later, *Grendel, The Wreckage of Agathon*, and *The
Sunlight Dialogues*, maybe a nearly final draft of *Nickel Mountain*,
were all finished before I got any acceptance to speak of. I did get
some acceptance, of course. I published a couple of books of
translation, scholarly articles, one short story in the *Northwest
Review*, eventually stories in *QRL* and the *Southern Review*. But my
fiction wasn't accepted for a long time. I think the climate changed.
At the time, like 1958, 59, 60, 61, I was writing slightly odd, non-
realistic fiction. I was also putting together the magazine *MSS*, which
I'm now starting up again, and found a number of writers who felt as
I did about fiction. There were at that time, of course, various literary
"grand old men" who had published odd fiction, but the non-realistic
movement wasn't strong. The dominant movement at that time was

realism. People like John O'Hara, John Cheever, John Updike. Cheever was a little bit outside the realistic camp, he was a little bit fabulistic at that time but the others, certainly Jerry Salinger, even Kurt Vonnegut in the *Saturday Evening Post* stories, and so on— realistic. So the kind of thing that I was doing—like *Grendel*—those kinds of things seemed odd, maybe childish, as did the idea of publishing novels with illustrations, which I timidly insisted on. And then I think the whole world shifted with the rise of the Beatles and the drug culture and the revival of Disney, and so on. With that fairly sudden change, my work came to be accepted in a way it hadn't been before. It's also true that, as I've said, I had helped to edit a magazine, *MSS*, in which I had published a good deal of very peculiar fiction, like the early work of Joyce Carol Oates, which was already far from realistic. I'd say Joyce was writing then something Liz Rosenberg calls "cartoon realism," the same kind of writing I think I do at my best. But I was publishing various unrealists—Bill Gass, John Hawkes, of course, with his nightmare fiction, William Palme. So in a way I helped make way for my own fiction by publishing those people, and it is true in fact that Bill Gass, after I published *The Pederson Kid*, mentioned me to David Segal, his editor at New American Library, and Segal eventually took *The Resurrection*, and then, shortly after that, *Agathon, Grendel*, and *The Sunlight Dialogues*. So it was both.

NOR: How are your relations with those writers whom you have criticized?

JG: For the most part, good, as far as I can tell. Stanley Elkin once pointed out to me that if you criticize a poet he gets mad, and if you criticize a novelist, he gets hurt, which I think is a wonderful compliment to novelists, and I think it's true. And I think Stanley was a little hurt himself. Stanley is a brilliant writer—he has, I think, the finest imagination since William Blake, an absolutely incredible imagination. But he does things that I don't approve of in his books— small-boyish obscenities, smart-alec stunts unworthy of his genius— which make him, I think, a lesser writer than he ought to be. He knows perfectly well that it's partly for love of him, because I've been a friend of his for a long time, that I yell at him, "Stanley, stop it! Get serious!" But I think it's true that he was hurt when I criticized him. I think Saul Bellow was not hurt, probably. I think Saul Bellow's comment in the *New York Times* was right. "I'm sorry I can't be everybody's model novelist." I think his work has its faults, but I made very clear in *On Moral Fiction* that he's a great writer. Norman Mailer I've been fond of for a long time, and I think he knows it. I don't know whether he was hurt or not, but when he was asked 'what do you think about John Gardner saying . . .' he said "We'll meet in heaven," which seems smart and gentle. I know Jack Barth's feelings were hurt. He's the only writer that I don't think I've been able to make up with, and that's too bad, but, you know, life is long. He'll probably come around, and if he doesn't come around, it's probably good for him to have somebody to hate. Don Barthelme was a little hurt. We got together and talked. However hurt he may have been, at a party we always end up talking together because I'd a lot rather talk to Don Barthelme than anybody else at the party. No writer really likes to be criticized. That's not quite true. Some writers do like to be criticized intelligently. I do, for instance. I think probably Heller ought to be a little mad at me because I think I was wrong; I think I made mistakes in my criticism of him. I think I underestimated *Something Happened*, although on the other hand, I don't feel much chagrin now that he's committed *Good as Gold*. It's written for a particular kind of readership, of course, and I guess he did what he wanted to do. But I think I was unfair about *Something Happened*. Anyway, if you're vatic you're supposed to excommunicate people, right? What I should have said at the start of this is, *On Moral Fiction* was written, published, and debated a long time ago. Why on earth are we talking about all this again?

NOR: What about Updike?

JG: Well, I don't know. John Updike is a magnificent short story writer. I certainly believe that what I said was fair and true. I don't think most of these people have actually read *On Moral Fiction*, nor do I think they should have. I know that in one case one of the writers I criticized didn't even know he was in the book until some friend of his, while he was driving a car, read him the sentences about him. I know that friends of mine have told me that certain writers have never read anything in the book except the very lines I devote to them. I don't see any reason why writers should waste their time reading every piece that mentions them in passing. But Updike's response in the *New York Times* was measured and sensible and accurate. Accurate, that is to say, assuming that he hadn't read the book. He claims that you can't write goody-goody books, and I agree with him. I don't think he has read what I said, but obviously he doesn't need to. We're not friends. I met him once, and I like him. A wonderful man.

NOR: Is John Fowles a friend of yours?

JG: No, I've never met John Fowles. On a couple of occasions there was a chance that we could meet, but it never worked out.

NOR: You've strongly praised Fowles' work. What do you see as the strengths of his fiction?

JG: The most interesting thing about his fiction for me is that he can brilliantly dramatize philosophical questions. He thinks about the human condition in particular terms, in terms of how it relates to people's lives, and he's immensely accurate in describing people, in getting their gestures, getting their patterns of speech, getting their psychological nuances, so that it's convincing. It doesn't feel that at any time he's manipulating the story, forcing the characters to do things. You feel that he's really discovering reality by imitating it carefully. At the same time that he does that he does it in a way that illuminates large questions, philosophical questions. For me, brilliantly dramatized thought is the most exciting kind of writing because I love both big ideas and a well-plotted story, and he's always got that. He's got the mystery woman and the Mystery and all this kind of stuff. And so he manages to do all this, manages to get very close, accurate descriptions of real people, manages to transform them to mythic mysteries, and at the same time manages to talk about big questions that it's fun to think about. As you're reading and after your reading you think, "Is that true, is that the way the world really is?"

A lesser but also valuable quality is that he writes wonderfully. His style is not carefully elegant. There are some writers, the writers in *The New Yorker* tradition—the style that goes back to Joyce's *Dubliners* and comes down through John O'Hara, J. D. Salinger, Cheever, Updike, Ann Beattie, and Laura Furman . . . , a style that's always wonderfully crafted and (in its post Joycean form) icy and cool, carefully leaving a lot of life out, because if it's a choice between elegant style and real life, they'll always take the style . . . , Fowles doesn't do that. A lot of Fowles wouldn't be publishable in *The New Yorker* because of the dirty words. His is a wonderfully crafted style, but it goes for accuracy about the world rather than stylistic ornaments, and that's nice. At the same time he's capable of being very moving.

NOR: Is *Daniel Martin* your favorite work of his?

JG: Well, I think it's the most profound thing he's done so far. In a way I sort of loved *The French Lieutenant's Woman* more because it's such a gorgeous book, but it's a younger book and it's philosophically not up to *Daniel Martin*.

NOR: How do you respond to the use of two endings?

JG: First of all, of course, it was very stylish. At the same time he was writing it everybody was interested in that kind of thing. But secondly, it's pretty profound, that is to say, he's concerned with something that has, since he wrote that book, become extremely popular in critical circles. It's what the deconstructionists are all concerned about, a whole school of criticism which likes to take works of art apart and see if they can get back to life from the scattered members. The deconstructionists are worried about, among other things, the fact that Western literature is always "in search of an ending," and that it comes down to some end that is a great moral affirmation, and in doing so falsifies, from their point of view, reality by coming to an affirmation that's simpler than one could reach in real life. Fowles, in writing a book which is in a way about the Victorian novel—he has, remember, whole essay chapters about Victorians and the Victorian novel—in writing an imitation Victorian novel in twentieth century language and then offering alternative endings, Fowles seemingly violates or abandons the Victorian premises, which are usually considered to be committed to a moral affirmation at the end, and instead he gives us an open, "existential" ending. What he's talking about is a real enough and serious enough thing. The Western tradition of searching for an ending—the Western expectation that at the end of the novel you'll know what's true and true forever—a tendency to set up false expectations in readers, and then life can become a disappointment, and in that way literature can be said to corrupt. What Fowles did in *The French Lieutenant's Woman* is to take that aesthetic-ethical problem on head on, avoiding the traditional kind of ending, giving alternatives, leaving life open. And of course by his arguments on Victorianism throughout the novel, and by his precise choice of characters and alternative-ending situations at the end, he does all this in a way that defends the much-maligned Victorian novel. In *Daniel Martin* he comes to a "real" ending, but the real ending, ironically, is the beginning of the novel, so that everything's open. He's decided to write the novel, and now he knows how to do it, and he admits that he really does come to an end, but it's a very carefully thought out end, and it's not going to mislead anybody: the whole novel we've just read is open, a preliminary position. In other words, he's solved the problem that the deconstructionists are concerned about in a new way. The ending of *Daniel Martin* leaves you as free as does the ending of *The French Lieutenant's Woman* while at the same time satisfying certain kinds of art expectations left unsatisfied in the earlier novel.

NOR: Blacks are absent from most of your fiction. Is this by design?

JG: No, it's not by design. I write about what I know best, and though I have taught a lot of blacks, and known a lot of blacks, black experience is not the thing I know very best. I think there are wonderful writers who can speak authentically for blacks, more and more of them, and I'll leave the subject mostly to them.

NOR: Who are some black writers who do that particularly well?

JG: Well, there are the well known ones like Toni Morrison, Ish Reed, Charles Johnson, not to mention Ellison and the people of his generation, but I'm more comfortable with the newer generation of writers. In fact they are more at the heart of real life experience instead of explaining black experience to other people, as in a sense Ellison did. There are a lot of younger black writers. One of my favorites is John McClusky, an extremely elegant writer. Brilliant, very smooth, very sensitive, very gentle, sweet stories, one of which I'm publishing in *Choice* magazine which I did a guest editing job for. As a matter of fact the Fall 1980 *Choice* magazine is one place to look for good black writers. In that issue I'm publishing Colleen McElroy, a marvelous black poet and short story writer who is about my age, 46 or so, I guess, and she has very little reputation among white readers. She's just terrific, just a magnificent writer. John McClusky has a story there, and Charles Johnson, a number of other people. Another even better place to look for good, young black writers is *Obsidian*, which is a magazine which regularly publishes blacks; *Obsidian* has discovered writer after writer. Wesley Brown is another I'm interested

in. Wesley hasn't published much, one novel, some stories. John
McClusky has published somewhat more—a fine novel, *Look What
They Done To My Song* from Random House, now momentarily out
of print.

NOR: In your review of *Sophie's Choice* you said that Northerners
were not less evil than Southerners, but hid their evil in a different
style. What did you mean by that? In what style?

JG: Well, I think the basic evil in all human beings comes from the
fact that they feel vulnerable—feel their vulnerability as individuals
and the vulnerability of the things they love, their traditions. Rightly
enough, but not always rationally or necessarily, they defend
themselves individually and they defend their traditions. The fundamental Southern style of defense, as far as I can tell—it's always an
oversimplification to talk about any group, but I will anyway—is to act
a very careful role, to play a part they've learned from movies about
the South, or from their fathers or mothers or sisters. So that in the
South there's this one class which is the genteel class, the ladies and
gentlemen, and they play the role. If a girl really loves to read books
and talk intellectually, and if she's never happier than when she's in
New York arguing about Kierkegaard, when she's in Baton Rouge,
she doesn't do it. You just don't do that sort of thing. It would seem
low class. It's not only in the South, of course; that takes place in
parts of England, maybe Indiana. In the parts of the North I know
best that's less likely to occur, that particular kind of closing yourself
in. At least it doesn't occur in the same style.

I would say the easiest way to talk about these styles of defense is
to talk about the kind of novel that's most fashionable with serious
writers in the South. Which I think turns out to be, in one mutation or
another, the Southern Gothic, a novel which looks with a sort of
hothouse intensity at decadence in one form or another—decadent
people, decadent buildings—because Southerners sometimes have a
love, which goes back at least to the Civil War, of what once, they
think, were the glorious grand estates. They like to go back to it
because it reminds them of their fundamental kingship. All of us know
we're really kings, Southerners and Northerners both, and the
Southerners have that proof, the ante-bellum castle. The Southerner,
or at least the Southern Gothic writer, is fascinated by the idiot boy or
the person of mixed blood—the wounded, the fallen, the proof of sad

decline. All these things are, in a way, tangible signs that once the
South was great. Reading of a rich family's idiot child or crazy person,
we're reminded of how things were before the Yankees or maybe
Biblical sin destroyed the economy and culture. Reading of a low-
class idiot we're reminded of how machines and greed destroyed the
pine-forested land and its people, and so on. But in any case, these
are all tangible signs—the idiot, the decadent building, the terrible
violence of the sawmills, things like this—signs to the Southerner that
once his life was noble and aristocratic and good and that it's been
betrayed or demolished by outside and inside forces. The thing is
that this kind of fascination in literature begins to be, after a while,
destructive. It's the neurosis of habitual scab-picking. It prohibits you
from looking at ways of fulfilling yourself. If you're always looking
backward, if you're always lamenting fallen greatness, if you're
always concentrating on how bad things are now, you forget to seize
your potential. The South has some of the finest and fastest-growing
cities in the country, some of the richest and most livable cities, and
some of the finest art works, painters, composers. Southern theaters,
symphonies, even publishers are among the best anywhere. The style
of the South tends to be sentimental and self-pitying, always looking
back, too reluctant to look forward.

The North doesn't have that self-regarding melancholy. It didn't
lose the war, at least not in the ways we count, so that it doesn't have
to go back to the good old days petulantly recalling when we were all
kings. The other thing is, of course, that the North was settled by a
different kind of people. Even when they came from the same town
in England or Wales, they turned out to be different people in the
North and in the South. The New York state group—I sort of exclude
New York City from all this—but the people of Ohio, Indiana, Idaho,
Montana, and so on, were set up much more on an egalitarian basis,
equal farmers. Except for a very few, all of them now long dead, they
were never kings in the first place, so they can't go back to a myth or
half-memory of some grand old house. But they did achieve things in
their individual ways—inventions, railroads, factories, independent
farms, and they look back to that with a degree of pride, possibly
misplaced. The kinds of things that happen in the North that hide
evil, I think, are a different kind. Whereas the South looks with
fascination at decadent people or idiot children or whatever, the

North has tended to deny their existence—burn them as witches or put them away in pantries. Nobody knows if you've got a crazy aunt, not if you can help it. It's a completely different thing. In one way you could say that the Southern fascination with decay is healthier because at least the decaying are allowed to walk the street. The North prides itself on health and good sense. I think the Northern style of evil is repression: pretending everything's all right until someone kills himself or axes his family. The North doesn't have the kind of community the South rightly prides itself on. One of the advantages of a tradition of kingship, which the South has, mythic or not, is that it brings with it the tradition of the obligation of the noble. In a tradition of egalitarian democracy nobody is much obliged to anybody. It's true that if a farmer's arm is cut off, all the other farmers will come and milk his cows for him. But ultimately, where there's no obligation, you're abandoned. The community is a failed option in the North, in many places. Otherwise we wouldn't have so many dead towns. Why stay?

NOR: Do you have any rules or concrete ideas about how to handle time in novels?

JG: No, I do all that intuitively. I think time is what novels are about. I think it's a very essential question in novels, and I think with essential questions it's impossible to have theories.

NOR: You have said that "Good art makes people good by choice." Does good art have the effect of uncovering choices where we thought there were none?

JG: It's certainly true that the very greatest art does precisely that, more than anything else. Put it this way. Say, for the moment, there are two kinds of good art. One is art which talks about the real concerns of people at the moment of the writing. If a writer lives in the seventies and eighties and says and feels nothing about feminism, a major concern of his time, then he's insensitive and by definition can't be a very good writer. So one of the things that good artists do is they express in powerful and moving terms the moral needs of their age. They remind us of the choices we know about and help us make them rightly. But then there's another class of writers who go past that. Melville, for instance, was going far beyond what most people were concerned about at the time he wrote. And of course the things that Melville was concerned about are exactly the things that we're concerned about today. I think the really great artist is the one who says "Yeah, O.K. I see the need for E.R.A., I see the need for Black Liberation, and equal rights in the marketplaces and so on" and goes beyond all that and says "But also" and sees the terrible question where we thought everything was fine. Homer, thousands of years before anybody rose up in arms against slavery, made a moving statement on the evils of slavery. The great writer is the one who always knows what's coming next. Shakespeare went beyond Marlowe. In Marlowe you have the evils of the age very clearly and beautifully represented, but in Shakespeare's *Troilus and Cressida* you confront evils that nobody had dreamed of. Great art, I think, helps you choose wisely when nobody knew there was a choice to be made.

NOR: William Gass comments that you don't revise enough, and that popularity is often based on what is weakest in one's work. Do you have any response to that?

JG: Well, he's probably right. But it has to be said that Bill Gass and I have been teasing each other for 20 years, and then picking on each other publicly and privately. My personal feeling is that Bill Gass revises far too much and becomes so involved with technique and style that he loses his concern for characters and action. But I can't change him, and I'm about ready to live with the way he writes, because he is, after all, a genius, and he does wonderful things. I am one of those writers who, you know, if I were a painter I'd be a guy who stands in the middle of the room and throws paint and tries to get it in roughly the right place. I don't make every line smooth and fix the nose until it looks like your mother's nose. I get the general impression because I'm after enormous effects. I may not get them, it may come off as bombastic foolishness, but I'm trying to get huge emotional and philosophical effects, and if you fuss and fuss with your material, you do two things. One is you rob yourself of time, so that you can't reach the heights you would have reached if you'd hurried a little, and the other is you put off readers because your prose becomes so full of cockleburs that nobody wants to walk through it. So I guess what I would say is that Bill errs in the opposite direction from the one in which he's right about my erring in.

NOR: You have been quoted as saying "You write the book to get control of in yourself things you haven't been able to control and understand in the world . . . Maybe it's an illusory understanding, but I think it helps you to live." Two of your earliest works, *The Resurrection* and *Nickel Mountain*, have been described as "sharing a concern with the affirmation of life in the face of death." Would it be fair to suggest that these works in part represent personal affirmations in the face of your own concerns with mortality?

JG: It would be fair, but incomplete. Part of it is calculated drama. It's true that I am, for various reasons, interested in how people can be blotted out. That's a pretty terrible thing. Obviously, that's what human beings live on, the fact that we know we're here for a short span and can't tell how much the span is. But in my fiction part of it is a dramatic calculation. The central antagonist in all great fiction is death. In my novel *Nickel Mountain* I could have told the central love-story without making death any part of it. The story is essentially about an older man marrying a young girl out of compassion, not really out of love, and then coming to love her, becoming a true husband and father, becoming a fully social and religiously responsible human being. But I chose very early, not in the first draft, but early, to make him a neurotic man who overeats and has a bad heart, so that there's more dramatic urgency to his reaching some kind of conclusion, sanity and balance. The metaphor of death watching at the edge of all our plans is true enough. We don't have to think about it every minute of every day, but it's there, and it can modify our behavior. A man who is going to live forever can do anything he pleases. On the other hand, to tell a story about a man who is going to die just for the dramatic effect of death would be pretty awful. I think that Henry Soames makes the choices he makes because he's afraid of dying, and he becomes a model for other people because in fact we all are dying.

NOR: When did you first attempt to write about the events described in "Redemption"?

JG: Right then. "Redemption" is a story about something that really happened, something I felt guilty about for a long time. All of my novels and short stories before "Redemption" are shot through with a kind of disguised guilt in various ways. In "Redemption" I decided to take it head-on.

NOR: Could you comment on the nature of the redemption in the story?

JG: Well, when you write a story you think you know what it means, but an awful lot of the story you just dredge up out of your unconscious. And then when it's on the page you analyze it and see if you've understood it, and see if it fits with other things. You really come to understand your story when you've revised it 20 times, and you've seen the subtle connections like the connections in dreams, and you realize "Aha! That's what I was doing." Since it comes into the story partly from the unconscious, you can miss what's come to you, you can get it wrong, you can misunderstand, as Lawrence used to do; but my opinion about the story is simply that the central character, in nursing his guilt and thinking himself the worst person who ever lived, and therefore getting a certain sick romantic kick out of his imperfection—a Southern attitude, I claimed earlier—is drawn back into the general human situation. He thinks, early in the story, of people around him as like sheep, a very Nietzschean idea, humanity as mindless herd. He admires his father, who's a pretty lawless man in some ways, a good man obviously, a noble man, one who in his pain and suffering after the death of his child, has abandoned social law. When the father comes back into the fold, the central character, his son, is disgusted. The boy momentarily hates his father because the father is, from the son's point of view, acting like a baby in accepting mundane humanness. Near the end of the story we meet the boy's French horn teacher, a real romantic hero and a lost soul because he can't go back to Russia now that Czarist Russia's been destroyed—a great horn player who can't do anything *but* be a great horn player, and a great teacher, and a raging maniac, a superman. The central character sees, through this man, his own fortunate ordinariness. At the end of the story he is standing on the sidewalk with the herd-like crowd of people walking by, and the herd gently parts to let him in. In "Redemption" it's the sheep who save you, not the great shepherd.

NOR: In your novels you consistently touch upon the ways in which the actions of adults affect the lives of children, and in *On Moral Fiction* you decry writing which "celebrates ideas no father would wittingly teach his children." Does your concern for children act as something of an anchor in your exploration of values?

JG: Well, my wish to deal with children even to the point of writing children's books—in fact now Liz Rosenberg and I are, among others, editors of a new children's magazine, and I have published children's fiction and continue to do so—my wish to deal with children is in a way a part of my quiet campaign against romanticism. The idea of the romantic hero who sort of stands alone, like Clint Eastwood, or whatever, not to mention the Lord Byron, is a terrible, boring idea to me. I believe in society and the pull and push of social interaction, and if you believe in society, you have to believe in society through time, that is to say, society now and in the past and in the future. The timeless, isolated hero is a terrible threat to a child whether or not the child knows it. He childishly abandons his child, his stable world, and goes off in his pirate ship, his truck, his big rig. Americans, for all our childishness, have not been very concerned about children, in a peculiar way. We baby our children, we buy them toys, but American fiction is not rich in stories about families and children. We have lost children who are really little men, like Huck Finn, but not the vulnerable small people society exists to nurture and defend. Television has lots of shows with children in them, but that's just more commercial bullshit, a result of the fact that a lot of kids, not to mention locked-up mothers, watch television. A commercial calculation. But the great American novels very seldom have children. Melville isn't interested. Hawthorne is philosophically interested, but Pearl is the most unconvincing character in *The Scarlet Letter*. I can't think of very many great American novelists—writers of adult novels, that is—who are seriously concerned with children. James, now and then. Another exception, but an ironic one, is John Updike. There are always children, and they're always a nuisance, always getting in the way of the parents' parties and romantic aspirations. I am very much a middle class nineteenth century conservative sort of person, a whig, I guess, and children are central to what I do.

NOR: You have said that the greatest weakness in your fiction is the absence of real sexual love, and that you are dealing more with sexual love in *Shadows*. Could you tell us something about the story?

JG: Not much. You're thinking of a piece done in the *New York Times* by a Mr. Stephen Singular. He asked me about it, "Isn't that a weakness?"—a very unpleasant, aggressive young man—and I said, "Yes, it's a weakness." I didn't mean much by it, just hoping to get rid of a fool. I don't really think that one has to talk about "sexual love," as he calls it. It's something that isn't in my novels much, and I don't

really care about it being in my novels much. It's true that in *Shadows*
there's a love story. *Shadows* is a long novel that won't be out for, at
best, a long time. I'm about 300 pages into it, a sort of decent rough
draft, lots and lots of pages of notes, and so on. I have no sex scenes
planned. I have other things coming out sooner. I won't be bending
over backwards to work in sex scenes there either. I think some
writers who have used sex clearly have become more popular than
they would have been otherwise because they used sex scenes. I
think, for instance, that Jack Barth's earlier novels were appealing to
a wide audience partly because of the sex in them. If they're good,
novelists should get an audience any way they see fit. I think Fowles
is really brilliant on sex. *The French Lieutenant's Woman* is obviously
of prurient interest as well as philosophically profound. I'm not very
interested, though, for myself. In my recent books and the books of
mine that are coming out now . . . I've a book called *Vlemk the Box
Painter*, a peculiar book which comes from a publisher in California.
It's a long, novella-length tale, a love story, but it doesn't have any
sex in it. *Freddy's Book* has marital love in it but no sex.
I guess *October Light* has a little sex, I forget. It has one really filthy
scene, but that's just a joke in the inner novel, making fun of the kind
of novel I'm being encouraged by Mr. Singular to write.

NOR: How would you rate your own works with respect to the
criteria that you set for fiction?

JG: Believe it or not, when I was writing *On Moral Fiction* I didn't
consider whether or not my theory about what fiction ought to do
applied to my own fiction. I just didn't worry about it; I assume one's
opinions and practice come from the same place. I feel very strongly
that fiction, at its best, should work the way *On Moral Fiction* says it
should work. I'm not denying, of course, the legitimate existence of
other kinds of fiction, fictions that violate the rules. I'd only say they
shouldn't be mistaken for great fiction. For instance, Pynchon, I
think, is a brilliant man, but his theory of what fiction ought to do is
diametrically opposed to mine, and while I think he's wonderful and
ought to be read—besides which it's a pleasure—I don't want
anybody confusing him with the great artists of our time. He's a great
stunt-man. I assume at least some of my work does fit the theory.
There is one exception, perhaps, my new book, *Freddy's Book*. I
wrote it after *On Moral Fiction*, and I guess in an unconscious way I

was trying to say what my earlier argument necessarily left out. That is to say, after publishing *On Moral Fiction* and after having gone around doing readings from it, and presenting the position and having people clap and say "Hooray that somebody's finally said that" and so on, I wrote this other book which pretty much violates everything argued in the earlier book. It's my most "immoral" book. It's not quite nihilistic, but it's gloomy and gothic and funny in some of the wrong ways. Certainly Satan and chaos are appealing characters here. That's not so new, of course. Book after book, since *Paradise Lost* and before and after, Satan is always the winner, at least on the applause-meter. No matter what Jesus and God try to do, the snake gets all the lines. I think that the only thing in the book that's really moral is that as you read it you have a good time. It keeps you off the streets.

NOR: Does Satan have Welsh ancestry?

JG: No, actually the Welsh are not that interesting.

Interview with John Gardner

English Department of Pan American University/1981

From *John Gardner: True Art, Moral Art*, ed. Beatrice Mendez-
Egle and James M. Haule. Living Author Series No. 5. Edinburg,
Texas: Pan American University, 1983. Copyright © 1983 by
School of Humanities, Pan American University. Reprinted by
permission.

The following interview with John Gardner was conducted
by several members of the English Department during
Gardner's visit to the Pan American University campus
April 21, 1981.

*Mr. Gardner, there seems to be a double structure in some of your
novels—*Freddy's Book *and* October Light *and* Jason and Medeia.
Why do you favor this device?

I don't know the answer to that. I guess it's different in each case. I
think that in *Jason and Medeia*, I had been teaching Chaucer for a
long time, and I have worked with Apollonios Rhodios and with *The
Argonautica* which is what that's based on. And I've been interested
in so-called meta-fictions—the sort of thing that John Barth does and
so on. And I'm interested in the way you can play with levels of
reality and so on. So that in *Jason and Medeia*, I was very much
concerned with the meta-fictional kind of quality of that narrator.

In *October Light*, that's a completely different kind of thing. I came
to the device really from the theme of the novel; that is to say, what I
wanted to talk about in *October Light* was the way we have models
for things. We can't essentially do anything at all unless we have seen
somebody do it. At least, we can't do it very well. Teaching somebody like Malory, you discover how important it is to have literary
models. Malory didn't know how to do a battle scene. . . . He'd
never seen a good one. He was a genius, and he became the model
for a great many other writers, but he had to work it out all on his
own. What he really had behind him was the thirteenth century
Vulgate Arthurian cycle which is verse. So, when I started writing a

book about how models help and hurt you, whether it's the model that James Page has, myths of Ethan Allen, also made up stories that I collected in Vermont, or his notion of jokes which is always wounding, destroying humor, his character is in an important way shaped by models, heroic or otherwise. And it seems to me, maybe just because I'm a writer, that the most important models people have in civilization are literary models whether they are television heroes or movies, or, as they've been for centuries, people in poems and stories. So that when I started talking about models, it became important to present one inside the book. It would obviously be stupid to use as an inside novel, that is to say the model for the characters reading the book, a book better than the book on the outside. So I decided, necessarily, to use a kind of stupid model. In a way, of course, it is not quite true because I enjoyed writing that parody a lot, and every kind of fiction that I think is awful, I manage to work in and try to weave it all together so it seems like one single kind of fiction. Basically, I think, so does the San Francisco school of fiction.

In other cases, I had other reasons for using a novel within a novel or story within a story. In *In the Suicide Mountains*, I wanted to break up the outside story with little moralizing tales. I wrote *In the Suicide Mountains* just about the same time that I was working on *October Light*, so that there is some influence between the two books.

In any case, I think probably that the over-all answer is that I'm not fundamentally—I don't think of myself or feel fundamentally like—a realistic novelist in a sort of Saul Bellow, John Updike school. And the kind of thing that I favor which really comes out of classical and medieval literature rather than modern tends to be fiction broken up in various ways. The idea of the Aristotelian story, the set of nice long-line story with the actualization of potential that exists in character and situation as Aristotle used to describe plots of tragedies, doesn't appeal to me fundamentally. What happens in Homer is you have this outside story of Achilles and one story after another until finally you get back to the Achilles story. In *The Odyssey*, it's the same kind of thing, the "Telemachiad." . . . Telemachus's story fits in with them, and then there are other little stories like Odysseus telling us about the Trojan war and so on. In *The Argonautica*, it's all like that and so on through all of classical literature. The long-line story isn't a favorite form. There's no such thing as a long-line story in Dante, obviously. Chaucer's most famous for pieces which were very disjunctive. He's not most famous for *Troilus and Criseyde*, although that's probably one of the greatest poems ever written, which does have a long line. But *Canterbury Tales* is just one panel after another. That's what I favor. It's also, of course, what Walt Disney favors—my number one aesthetic influence. When I was a child in my formative years, except for the *Bible*, nothing I ran across was better than what I think was the best Walt Disney. And he always tells a story within a story.

Your works are definitely thought-provoking in the sense of forcing readers to rethink the validity of their values. Is this by design? Is there some influence from the didactic strain in medieval literature?

No, it's not didactic. Certainly not. And it is not by design in the usual sense that I don't sit down and think, "What am I going to teach the reader today?" On the contrary, it's a product of my theory of what fiction essentially is. I think that in good fiction, you tell a story about a person and his friends or enemies. And the way to make that story interesting is to develop what I think of as true suspense as opposed to usual false suspense. What happens in a story full of false suspense is that a character moves through a series of actions, and the author hides certain things from the reader, and the reader's walking along wondering what's going to happen to the character next and the writer every few pages or couple of chapters bushwhacks the reader with some new surprise, new trick. I don't think that kind of suspense is very interesting. It's "Exorcist" suspense to me. The kind of suspense that I am interested in is that which arises when the reader is given all the information, good, solid information. He knows what the character's problem is and what his goal is and what the opposition is and the suspense is, what will he do, what will happen to him if he does that, what will she say, etc.

It's particularly Freddy's Book *I was thinking of, and this fits in with what you're saying.*

I think, I hope it's true of all my books if that's the case. The result is that you have to choose a character who's got a fundamental problem. I think that "theme" in fiction—that thing that's always talked about in literature classes rightly enough—from a writer's point of view is simply the concern of the character. In other words, the character decides that no matter what, he's going to be like Immanuel Kant—always honest—then the question is . . . what happens to the man who is always honest? Is he forced to decide that you can't be? For instance, if you follow Immanuel Kant, and you are living in Nazi Germany, and you have a Jew in your cellar and a member of the SS comes to your door and says, "Is Mr. Burns here?" From Immanuel Kant's point of view, you have to say "yes," and that's pretty awful. On the other hand, lying too much is pretty awful. So that if you take a character who has some obsessive value, some one value that he places higher than all the values, you've naturally got a story and naturally a philosophical book. But I don't choose the theme because I'm interested in the message, whatever the message may turn out to be as I discover in the process of writing, figuring out what I think it is. I choose the story because I think the character is interesting.

Going back to Freddy's Book *in the same relationship, it seems to me that you've got in the knight story—Lars-Goren—definitely a didactic setting in the sense that it is almost a medieval play. He is going to go through the action, and he is going to meet the Devil and engage the Devil and finally beat the Devil. This for me is in a sense didactic because it's got this loyalty. You mentioned loyalty at the beginning, but this is one of his basic traits, and this is what carries him through. This is why he is the strong character he is.*

It's also true that Lars-Goren in that book is essentially an innocent. Just before I wrote that book, I had been reading a lot of George Steiner, particularly his book *Tolstoy or Dostoevsky,* and Steiner talks about Tolstoy's fundamental country affiliation, how he hates Moscow, in fact, and likes the country itself, and he likes country innocence. The problem with that is, especially if you live in America, you recognize that the country as a culture seems at this moment to be dying. It seems that cities, whether we think they're good or bad, are the future. The question is, "what keeps us going if the innocent, the true-hearted man of the country disappears?" In that book, I think Bishop Brask is as important as Lars-Goren. Lars-Goren is simple, country integrity, and Bishop Brask is a man who has become so complicated. He's a genius, but he's lost all heart, and in fact, of course, the Devil—insofar as the Devil is really killed, at least a certain kind of devil in that book is killed, the devil of authority, the devil of tyranny, the devil of that kind of stuff—insofar as he is really killed, he is killed by the two of them together. That is to say, Lars-Goren alone couldn't have done it, and Bishop Brask, of course, would never have tried because he would have no motive. He'd have no reason because he is stymied. . . . So that again, I didn't really mean it didactically. I meant to set up a situation and explore it. It's also true, of course, that in that book there's the additional complication that what I meant to be writing was not a story as I would write it but as a neurotic kid would write it. In other words, the story is meant to be an expression of a kid's attempt, the giant boy's attempt, to cure himself, which is a problem I have been dealing with a lot in my recent fiction. The whole Martin Luther versus Nietzsche argument—Martin Luther's idea of salvation by grace alone, because Martin Luther, being a uremic psychotic, believed that all life, was, to quote him "shit." He used that word constantly. He was just a terrible, foul-mouthed fellow. Anyway, he thought there was no possibility of good works because people are such creeps. Nietzsche, of course, took the other point of view. Once you say "God is dead," you better be able to sublimate on your own. And it seems to me that the Christian world finally fell apart, which is not to say Christianity is dead, but a certain kind of Christian world is dead, with Luther. Luther comes back over and over as he does in *Freddy's Book*. And the answer which the modern world seems to have bought without recognizing this sort of wicked fish hook in the middle of it is the Nietzschean answer, "save yourself"—which is what Freud is doing, what Heidegger did, and so on. So that what I really wanted to do was dramatize a very brilliant, very neurotic, anti-social, rightly anti-social kid's attempt to dramatize his own conflict. How much can he save himself, how much does he need other people? And that's why I end up with those two characters, Lars-Goren and Bishop Brask, and, of course, ultimately, with the reader making the decision in the final lines.

You just called Freddy neurotic. But it seems he's infinitely more appealing as a character than the father who simply has nothing to live for, whereas Freddy certainly has his art works and his book and all the rest of it. Certainly there's an inner life there that's much more valuable.

That's tricky. A writer never can tell what characters which he creates are the loveable or important ones, but I really like the father a lot. The father . . . well . . . is a little crazy, but he really loves his son and is doing the best he can. It's a very difficult situation when you have a brilliant son who's immensely tall and scares people. . . . I think the father has given up his life for his son—I mean, given up his scholarship, given up everything for his son, but he can't do anything, and the reason is that he is not society. What the kid needs is a step out into the world.

The father's not letting him do it.

Right. He's afraid. He loves him too much. . . . Parental smothering, which is very understandable it seems to me, but doesn't help . . . I think the father is the model in Freddy's story of the Devil, although Freddy would be embarrassed to say that consciously. Winesap, the visiting professor, is a sort of neat guy. But in the end, out of his very stupidity, he enables the kid to take the first step in the world. It is by making a mistake and being overheard by the kid that he reveals to the kid that he is human and not frightening. And then the kid gives him the book. That's neat. But I like the father a lot.

You wrote in On Moral Fiction *that we are living in an age of mediocre art. Do you think anything has changed in the world of art or culture since you wrote that?*

I think it is changing. I think probably it is not changing because I wrote the book, although I take some credit for the change. I think that many people were sick and tired of cynical, nihilistic, pornographic art, and I think there were a lot of writers trying to break out of that pattern, and publishers who, always protecting the company, were rejecting good manuscripts because they didn't feel those manuscripts were acceptable somehow according to what I think is basically New York establishment taste, which tends to be cynical, nihilistic. Telling the truth to the New York establishment means saying something awful. If you say a couple lived happily for sixty years together and raised children who felt themselves to be successful and happy children, you are telling some kind of ridiculous fairy tale, although it happens all the time, it seems to me. . . .

I think that a great pressure was building against the mood that human beings are terrible creatures. The only sense in which I would take any credit for having helped the change come about is that I was the one who was able to say it publicly. I know in some specific cases, publishers felt free to publish books because they wanted to test whether or not my feeling about reader's feelings is right and found that I was right. And I know that some writers who felt something like despair trying to write in a different way from the establishment ways then were able to keep going and get published. I think that there is a change. I think that the change was coming anyway. I think that somebody would have said it anyhow, and I think it was useful that somebody who was fairly well known was able to say it. And I must say it is a terrible thing to be the one who says it because you get an awful lot of flack from the establishment for doing it. When *On Moral Fiction* came out it was pretty much raved about all over the country except in New York. Almost without exception, the New York reviews panned it. The few that praised it always felt that in the last paragraph they had to take it back, which was weird.

Anyway, I think that time was coming. I think the 80s are in certain ways more healthfully optimistic than the 70s were. I think we are over certain kinds of guilt and self-incrimination that has to do with the Vietnam War, and so on though not necessarily rightly. I think probably in real life we're as wicked at least as we were during the Vietnam War. It's just that our enemies have changed. We are more destroying ourselves than destroying strangers now. . . . But whether we are better as a people or not, I think that you can't be a healthy, happy civilization if you keep telling yourself how awful you are and if you keep looking at the evil. You've got to look at it; you can't lie. But part of telling the truth is recognizing the optimistic side. And I think there has been a great change. The young writers whose work I admire are very much guarded optimists. Ron Hansen who wrote a book called *The Desperados* is a really wonderful writer, one of the finest that has come along in years, and I think he will be in twenty years one of *the* famous writers in America. A number of young writers . . . show this sort of strong, considered optimism which can make a society strong rather than sick. And I'm glad that I was there to say it, whatever the effect.

You are fairly direct in detailing examples of false or fashionable art in On Moral Fiction. *Has this calling of names brought on any charges of slander or libel? When you say that Vonnegut, for instance, is first class comic book. What happens in cases like that? What is the reaction?*

I'm very fond of Kurt Vonnegut, both as a writer and as a person, and I think he was a little hurt by that although he has told me that he never meant to be a serious writer. He doesn't even like serious writing. His ideal, he told me once, of really fine writing, is the old *Saturday Evening Post* where every week you waited for it, and you read Faulkner, Salinger, Mary Roberts Rinehart, as if it were all one thing. I think that is a usual feeling with writers. In the university we tend to be snobs. We feel like you have to like the great books, and great books can pass by unnoticed. *Gone with the Wind* is, in fact, a great book, no matter what anybody says, and Pearl Buck, no matter what anybody says, is a great, great writer, very powerful. She makes you cry. What more do you want? She doesn't lie to you. If she does, it's because she was wrong about something, and she got it wrong. Nobody can be omniscient. Anyway, in the university there is this tendency toward a sort of snobism which hurts.

Anyhow, to get more directly to the question. I think what happens with writers is that if you criticize them, and your criticism is wise and fair—as mine isn't always. Sometimes I make mistakes. I made a mistake about *Something Happened.* And I still think it's got problems, but my particular criticism of it was wrong—anyhow what happens with writers is if you say something bad about them, and it seems wise and fair, their feelings are hurt, but they're not mad at you because writers are too serious to be mad at you when you tell the truth. Sometimes when a writer is extremely sensitive because of a work he is working on at the time, for instance, if he is working on a book that he is not at all sure of and then you say something bad about him, he gets furious, but he takes it back. I have not developed any enemies that I know of. I wouldn't do it again. I felt it was necessary at that time because I think the argument that I was offering was an important argument. I still think it was an important argument. And I think that an argument without any examples is silly. It's just cowardly and it's not clear. Nobody knows for sure what you mean. So you give examples, and you try not to be unfair in the examples. And I think that that was valuable. But having done that, there is no use in becoming sort of a hit man for the anti-establishment of literature.

In On Moral Fiction *you state that the highest purpose of art is to make people good by choice. Do you still feel this way?*

That's a quotation from Tolstoy. Sure.

And how do you see it working? I guess you'd have to define art for us, how this is going to work to make people good by choice.

Well, I think in a good book or movie or anything else, you present people struggling heroically for what they value, and the reader's natural response to a well-written story about someone heroically struggling for what he believes to be good ends, the reader sympathizes with that character and wants to be like that character, as I say in several different ways in *On Moral Fiction*. Every time a really good movie comes along—like when *On the Waterfront* came along—everybody starts imitating the hero. It was a good hero to imitate. If the hero or the central character in a novel is a whiner who can't get out of bed, who sees nothing but evil in the world, who thinks everybody is a hypocrite, and so on, the people who imitate him are going to destroy themselves in effect because they are wrong about reality. I think that presenting sort of noble models of behavior, which is not to say perfect people—I don't believe in such things— but by presenting noble models of behavior, you give people a model for their own lives, for their own feelings. In a way, you give them permission to feel the nobler things that they do feel without feeling that they are making fools of themselves. I think that all art has always done that. In fact, it often does it when we don't even think about that being an issue. When Shakespeare wrote *Hamlet*, he was obviously writing in the tradition of the revenge tragedy, and the thing about the revengers in tragedies before *Hamlet* is that they're stupid. They're told to go kill somebody, and they do it. And the great thing about Hamlet is that he's not sure. He thinks about it. He worries about it. Is it right to do this? Until finally, when the evidence is overwhelming and he has lost all control, he does what he ought to do, and in that very act, in a way, demeans himself, that is to say, he kills innocent people—So that Hamlet is a strikingly better hero than the heroes he imitates—the older heroes of revenge tragedies. I think that happens over and over in literature. I think that all the great books are great in that way. Certainly *The Odyssey* is. Certainly *The Iliad* is. And there are of course comic or ironic works where that isn't true. In *The Argonautica*, which I think is one of the greatest books ever written, the hero is a dope. But it's a comic work, and you know he is a dope.

I've been struck in reading some of your works by your emphasis on the olfactory. I could say your heroes stink, and many of them literally do. Are you using this as a metaphor?

Everything you use is a metaphor. Everything that goes into a book is a metaphorical characterization, basically, of one or another of the characters. It's true that I think the most important faculty in fiction is visual, but I think that a good writer makes a conscious attempt to get the feel of things, the textures of things. . . . Some writers tend more toward hearing than toward anything else. I guess Thomas Wolfe, you've got to say, has an unusually high quota of sound images, but some kind of image has got to make the dream in the reader's mind vivid.

I think particularly, of course, of Grendel *and* The Sunlight Dialogues *and* Agathon. *All over and over again . . . the odors are unpleasant, and particularly unpleasant odors are associated with those characters.*

Mr. Bloom stinks a little too in *Ulysses.* . . . There is sometimes a bit of an affectionate mode that creeps in, as when we call children "little stinkers," that is a way of humanizing. In a larger sense you would include this as part of the vision that you created, certainly, part of the total dream. It has to have all the senses.

Another question has to do with your story about Anna Karenina—*about the creative process. I have read a story—that Tolstoy was at a railroad station, and that a young woman threw herself in front of a train and that the novel sprang, and I thought of Faulkner's Caddy's dirty panties. Do you get a central vision or a central metaphor, an idea for a novel in that sense?*

No, I don't think it's true that the novel sprang from that memory. That was of course years before the novel was written. It was something stored away in the memory bank of Tolstoy as an important experience in his life, and it may be true that he pored over it and over it and thought about it because it was such a horrible thing. We all think about the things that horrify us, but it nevertheless is the case that when he began to write the first version of *Anna Karenina, Two Marriages,* that was the farthest thing from his mind, at least in the sense that in the first version, *Two Marriages*, it doesn't show up. She doesn't do it. What happened was that as he gradually saw in rewriting and thinking it out more and more carefully that his heroine was going to have to kill herself, his memory bank handed him—probably the unconscious—"Here, Mr. Tolstoy, what about this?" He said, "Terrific, that'll work."

Do you think Faulkner was probably lying?

I don't know about Faulkner. He lies with purpose always. He never tells the truth about how he writes, but the reason, I think, is that all our notes from him on writing are his answers to students, and what he does is tell the student the truth by some myth, some metaphorical version, so that everything he says is true, but none of it is factual. It may be that's how it got started. I don't know.

Your books have a love for Chaucer as a man particular in his caritas—the idea of charity, his forbearance and inclusiveness and generous spirit and that sort of thing. Am I right in thinking that you infuse your own works with this spirit?

I certainly hope so. One can only do the best one can do, but I hope that as a person, I'm as generous as Chaucer was. I think a good artist has to be fair to all his characters. He has to be essentially a generous human being, and Chaucer of course is the absolute model of it. He was more generous to all human beings I think than Shakespeare was. Chaucer never had to take anything back. Shakespeare in *The Tempest* takes back Felonius, that is to say, presents that character that he wasn't quite fair to earlier, quite explicitly by echoes of language, and says, "Now wait a minute; this is the way it really is," shows the dutiful, not very smart, servant who is nevertheless not desiccate, who is a good man. Shakespeare was a generous man; I don't mean to put him down. But I think that every serious writer has got to be generous to all his characters and be fair to everyone. Inevitably you like some characters better than others. I think there's no doubt that Chaucer would rather have the knight to a party than say, the miller. But that doesn't mean you can't understand the miller and sympathize.

I notice that you do draw heavily upon the fable and myth characters in form, and you mention the Walt Disney influence. Why do you think this is the particularly appropriate vehicle for twentieth century readers? Is it personal preference?

Not for all. Yes, personal preference. There are some people whose favorite books are realistic and I think that's fine. Some people like Mexican food and some people like Japanese. My own personal preference is for a sort of cartoon realism, I mean something approaching magical realism. I have written some stories in which I tried really hard to be absolutely realistic just to see if I could do it. I have a new collection of short stories just out this minute called *The Art of Living* and several of the stories in there are very carefully realistic, but my favorite story in the book is something called "Vlemk, the Box Painter," which is about an old Jewish painter of pictures on small boxes who falls in love with a young, beautiful, very Anglo-Saxon princess of the realm, and she tells him when he goes to confess his great love that if he can paint a picture of her on a box so accurate in every detail that it can talk, then she will discuss the matter further and so he does. That is not a very realistic story. It's the world that I am most happy with. The reason is that for me realistic stories spend too much time on just proving that all this is true and on giving you the details of setting and so on, and I don't want to waste that time. I want to go right at it, immediately to what I am talking about. If I can do that by what I would really call kind of expressionistic technique, simplifying like Kafka's "The Hunger Artist"—it's also Walt Disney—just simplify the idea to one single image, a guy in a cage along with a panther, etc., that's terrific. I don't want to waste time.

How does Nickel Mountain *work out with what you are saying about realism?*

Historically, that was the first novel I started, and I worked on it for a long time, and it was pretty non-realistic. I put it away in a drawer, thought it was a failure, and I wrote some things that were definitely not realistic like *Grendel* and *The Wreckage of Agathon* and *Sunlight Dialogues* . . . And I had a lot of trouble with those because I was writing in what was in effect an age of realism. I mean, Kafka was being printed in *Accent* magazine and Andrew Lytle was doing wonderful, crazy, fabulistic things in the South, but mostly the establishment wasn't buying it. And so, I consciously in *Nickel Mountain* tried to write what would pass for perfectly realistic fiction. But because I was young and didn't want to give in completely, I wanted to slip in completely non-realistic things. So there is in *Nickel Mountain* a ghost. There is one moment in *Nickel Mountain* when Callie looks out of the window—she sees ghosts in the room, and she looks out of the window—and the whole valley is full of ghosts. That's

not exactly realism, and I slip in the goat lady. One thing after
another. My object was to write a non-realistic book that would fool
the establishment and that they would take as realistic. I'm pretty
pleased with it. There are some things I don't like about that book as
there are some things I don't like about everything I've done. You
know, you make mistakes. But I really like the fact that it feels realistic
but it is really mythic. I think that's true of *October Light* too, a bit
more obviously. Like you accept James and Sally as realistic
characters but when you look at what they do, it's just absolutely
Walt Disney. James goes over a cliff in his truck, and he's caught in an
apple tree. You can't do that. No stunt man in the world can do that.

*Do you see this swing toward this perhaps not only in your own
work but in things like* Star Wars *and revival of the Arthurian legends
and things like this as a counter reaction to technology?*

Shortly after my books started being published, and not because of
the influence of my books but because the temper of the times was
changing, non-realistic fiction just took over the world. All the famous
writers are non-realists. In fact, now you have to fight very hard to get
a straight realist published—the young writers, the influence of Barth
and Barthelme and Bill Gass not to mention Lytle and all the
Southern gothic people, Eudora Welty even, although she's closer to
realistic. It's been a change. I think it came simultaneously with the
Beatles. There was a swing in literature and suddenly realism was out
and great realists were dismissed as trivial. There is now the intense
interest in science fiction, which sometimes proves to be really
literary, like for instance, *Canticle for Leibowitz* is as good a book as
anybody can write. It's science fiction but . . .

I think popular culture is where serious culture always comes from.
The reason American music is so spectacularly better, American
contemporary composition, than composition elsewhere, is that it is
so much their extreme music. I mean it is true that the Europeans
caught it first. The Europeans were influenced by jazz a long time
before we were . . . and it's the same thing with fiction. Barthelme
can take not only "Phantom of the Opera" but even a Xerox
questionnaire and turn it into kind of interesting fiction. I think that in
countries where popular culture is rejected for serious art, notably
Sweden and Japan, this country is in desperate trouble in literary
terms. In Japan you have two different languages—pop fiction and
serious fiction—and the only serious writer who's come along in a

long time that can be read outside of the very narrow Buddhist sort of culture is Kawabata. . . . Most of the writers that we know and love from Japan are from a culture that they can't teach in the University. Sweden has absolutely strangled on its seriousness. They're good writers. They don't dare do popular things.

In listening to you talk, I sense that you do have some fun writing. I'm not sure how much that is actually fun that I am seeing on the surface and how much of it is serious craftsmanship underneath.

It's all the same.

As I was reading Jason and Medeia I would be reading along very happily just enjoying the story and enjoying the diction and caught up in the very fabric of the writing, and suddenly I'll find a word that sends me diving for a dictionary, and sometimes it is not there, and I was wondering if you could perhaps explain yourself, whether you consider this some of the strangeness or weirdness that you say should be a part of all good writing.

Jason and Medeia is a very special kind of thing. It's in a way not for everybody. It's kind of a game with epic tradition, and one of the things that the epic writers delighted in, not Milton quite so much, but certainly Homer and Apollonios Rhodios and Virgil and Dante and certainly James Joyce, was weird diction. . . . I think that every writer in the epic tradition is consciously talking to every other writer. Before I wrote *Jason and Medeia* I was going to write a book called *The Epic Conversation*. It seems to me that the Homer of *The Iliad* sets down a sort of code of life, and the Homer of *The Odyssey* says, "Yeah, but. . ." *The Odyssey* is an answer, very definitely, to *The Iliad*. Apollonios loves Homer, but in Alexandrian Greece or Egypt, the age of heroes is dead. The hero is the librarian. So Apollonios kids around, mocks, and uses all that pedantry and is wordsy. Terribly difficult to read, worse than Pindar. And then Virgil comes along and obviously everybody knows he divides his epic into two parts which imitate the two Homers, but right in the middle is the Dido story which imitates *The Argonautica*. Obviously Virgil is consciously talking too, and then Dante comes along—the Beowulf poet you'd have to say first—he's probably using commentaries on those things; he probably didn't know the original. Dante using Virgil for a guide. And down to James Joyce constantly and consciously echoing the epic tradition.

When you start writing an epic, I think you commit yourself. Part of

the rules of the game is: Do everything they did. And the fundamental difference between, say, me and Joyce, skipping genius and
all that, is that Joyce is straight across. He is like a lyric poet. He tells
you the truth. However he fools with it, he's straight. He's serious.
And we live—maybe the next generation is going to be doomed by
this—but I do, I live in an age of irony. One cannot listen to noble
sentences without wondering, "What's he after?" When Kennedy
says, "Ask not what your country can do for you, ask what you can
do for your country," you are moved by it, but at the same time, you
say, "That's pretty rhetorical, Buster." It's okay but it smacks of
politicians; it smacks of Congress. So you can't introduce noble
language. One of the things Homer did that was wonderful, Homer
basically wrote (Homer of *The Iliad*) because he wanted to support
the Federation. All these Greek islands and colonies and city-states
and they're all at each other's throats, and meanwhile, they have
more in common than they have with the Barbarians, and Homer's
great act was to tell a story in which he brings in all of those people
and shows that they were once all in one. It wasn't even true. He
made it up. And he introduces *every* god that each of the islands or
city-states values, even when he knows perfectly well, as we can
prove, that this is, in fact, just a mispronunciation of this. He respects
people's gods. And he uses the dialects of all the people, which
makes his poem almost unreadable. It's as if you wrote in phonetic
spelling, a sort of back Texas character's speech, and then somebody
from New Jersey and somebody from Wisconsin and somebody
from San Francisco. It would be almost unreadable on the page in a
hundred years, maybe today even. Well, Homer did that, and then
the Homer of *The Odyssey*—it was the same person or somebody
answering him, it all doesn't matter—imitates that style, and of
course, Apollonios, who was a prankster and an imp and slightly
crazy, goes to extreme lengths. Virgil comes along. He's a nice,
honest, big-city professor, and he just wants to do it right. The
emperor has said, "Virge, I wonder if you would write me an epic like
Homer used to do?" And Virgil says, "Yes, sir." And he freaks out,
"What are the rules?" One of the rules is "Play hard words." And his
Latin isn't as hard as Homer's Greek, but it's not your *everyday*
Latin. . . . Well, when you come to writing *Jason and Medeia*, you
know you can't introduce noble words, so you think, "What kind of

cocklebur can I throw in here?" And half the time what I do is I back-form words from Greek, that is to say "thestral." I don't think there is such a word in English. There are some people named Thester. Often those fancy words that I use are used just as kind of jokes. If you can find them, somebody's been cleverer at a dictionary than anybody I know, because I'm sure I made up half of them. "Ignivomous" I think probably got out of a poem somewhere.

Actually in *Jason and Medeia*, I didn't really mean for things to get serious until the final book. I meant it to be kind of a romp. I assume I'm writing for intelligent, nice, decent, good American people who aren't very thoroughly educated in the classics, and what I want to do ultimately is bring all the myths together, everything from Oedipus to Aeneas to whatever. And so what I do is sort of lay out in Walt Disney terms a story which brings in enough information about everything else that you feel comfortable with in the classical world and then finally shift into high. I shift to Euripides. . . .

Think what Disney could do with Chaucer's description of that chase in the nun's priest's tale.

With anything in Chaucer. My favorite images in Chaucer are things like in the Miller's tale, there's this stupid carpenter who's got this student, Nicholas, living with him, and the door's locked. Nicholas is doing his trick, and the only way the carpenter can see what's happening, this great fat man, is to open up the cat door, and he bends his huge fat body over and cocks his head and looks up through the cat door. And that's obviously Disney. Chaucer couldn't have written that if he didn't see a Disney movie first. He put a lot of Disney into it. Disney liked Chaucer. Interesting.

Were your children's stories written with specific children or adults in mind, and/or adults? The stories are so entertaining that an adult would not fall asleep reading them to a child. Did you think more of children or more of adults as you were writing them?

I had two children, and from the time they were about four—the oldest one about four—on every birthday and every Christmas, I would write them a story, one for each of them. And then they would play with them and crayon all over them. When they were grown up, only a few survived. Most of them were eaten by cats and dogs and cows and made into paper airplanes and so on. Somebody who had to do with publishing was visiting my house one time and saw this pile of goofy papers with typing on them and hand-drawn pictures and stuff and asked what it was and looked at them. And then we put together from the few things that survived twelve or thirteen children's tales that are around still. So I did write them definitely for particular children.

Have you published a book of poetry?

I did publish a book of poetry, but I don't recommend it. There was a period when I wrote a lot of poems. Then a friend, Herbie Allen who published *Vlemk, the Box Painter* in the final edition, asked if I wanted to publish my poems in a book. And I thought, Why not? I knew they weren't any good. They're all right, but they're not very good. Some of them are really junky. Anyhow, he published them and was going to charge like $50 a volume, so I knew nobody would see them anyway, so take the money and run. So I did. Then they came out a little cheaper. So it is possible to write a book of poems, but I don't recommend that anybody do it. I did write one book of poems I really love which is *A Child's Bestiary* (or "Beast"-iary) depending on your point of view. I think that has some really good poems in it. "The Possum" is as good as I can write.

We have a small press here, riverSedge, and we try to publish quality work and have received some recognition in terms of CCR and grants and things like that. There are those who say that a small press is the bastion and first line of defense against the death of art and writing in America. I was wondering what your feelings were about small presses and whether or not you had been published in small presses originally and what your experiences were?

I think it is absolutely true that small presses have been the introducers of most of the writers that we value: Joyce Carol Oates, William Gass, on and on and on the list goes, who started in small magazines. And of course right now there are more small magazines than ever before. More fold every day than ever before, but more started up than ever before, and that's certainly where good young writers are going to show up first. I ran a magazine called *MSS* twenty-one years ago which published first the story of Bill Gass and a lot of people you have heard of. And I'm starting that up again now because I think there is a whole new wave of writers that editors don't know what to do with, particularly what I call "smart girl" fiction, which is a kind of fiction by the second generation feminists. First generation feminists dressed full dyke and shouted loud and fought. The second generation of feminists are people who want to be free to bat their eyelashes, to write a sort of skirt-swinging, elegant prose, but nevertheless write seriously. And they are the most exciting writers to come along since Jane Austen who is of course their spiritual mentor. But I think these writers are really exciting, and they're just the best to come along in years and years. But nobody will publish them. Men get these—and most little magazines are edited by men, even when women are on the editorial board, they defer somehow. That's my experience anyway—but men get these stories, and they have this sort of slick surface that is associated with, say, ladies' fiction, whatever that is, but have real depth and real profundity. The man doesn't know what to do with it. He is embarrassed by the style. The only solution is either to get smart girls as editors or to get people who can get past that. . . . I've met time after time women writers who write in what I call "smart girl" fiction vein, and they just can't get published. Just as twenty years ago Joyce Carol Oates couldn't get published, Bill Gass couldn't get published . . . because they were writing in the sort of nightmarish vein that was not then popular. But I think little presses, like magazines, are immensely important.

I saw that Margaret Atwood got a Guggenheim for her work and I'm excited about that because I think that she probably qualifies as one of your "smart girls."

She's a smart girl. She really is in that vein. She certainly is. She writes that way.

Mr. Gardner, would you like to comment on your new novel that's coming out? Tell us what it's about?

Well, sure. I'm just having typed up and about to receive when I get back home the last chapter of a new novel which is called *Mickelsson's Ghosts.* (I later found out that there is only one Mickelsson family in America, and they call it "Michael-son," but it is too late now because I have been used to the other.) Anyhow, it's a novel about a philosopher who goes insane, who is between marriages and who moves out into the mountains, which is the mountains I happen to live in, and buys a house which is an old fallen-down, huge house, farmhouse with fancy porches, which happens to be haunted. And, his grandfather is psychic, and he's psychic too, but he can't tell reality from his psychic, sick, psychotic hallucinations, and some of his psychotic hallucinations are in fact psychic visions. So that at its most serious level the novel is about the human mind, about how we know what we know if we know anything, but in terms of plot, it's about a mad philosopher trying to deal with ghosts in his house and also ghosts in the past and also ghosts in western-civilizations past. Two characters who show up over and over as ghosts in his mind are Luther and Nietzsche. . . . The part of Pennsylvania where I live has a number of people who are witches in the sort of Pennsylvania Dutch style. And, Northern Pennsylvania where I live is a favorite dumping ground of Mafia truckers who dump radioactive wastes and other things wherever they can hide it. And the only enemies those people have, since the United States government won't do anything about it, is the witches who sabotage bridges and in other ways get rid of these guys. So that it is a complicated mystery-thriller. A plot which is a ghost story and a love story and many other things all rolled into one. My only real doubt about it is that it may be so complicated that it's a screaming bore. I don't know. I can't tell anymore. When you've read a book a thousand times, every word seems a screaming bore. What I've done, of course, is what I always do when I write. I wrote the whole thing, then I put it away for a year, got it out and saw horrible mistakes and fixed all the mistakes I could see and by that time I was so close to it that I was making more mistakes, so I put it away for a year and then got it out again, and I've got it to the point where I don't even want it in the house any more, so that's the point at which you publish things.

   Thank you very much. You've been very generous with your time.

Gardner's Ghosts

Stephen Wigler/1982

From *Rochester Democrat and Chronicle/Upstate Magazine*, 11
July 1982, pp. 15-20. Reprinted by permission of Stephen Wigler.

Every week novelist John Gardner hops on his Harley-Davidson
1200 Electroglide—"a truly authentic hog," he says with pride—to
make the 200-mile trip home to Batavia to do the chores.

Gardner lives in Susquehanna, Pa., and teaches at SUNY
Binghamton, but his family needs him now and for the past 10
months he has split his time between his own life and theirs.

He has arrived earlier this damp June day and his mother says,
"John Jr.'s out in the fields putting in crops." Through the rain and
mist, his prematurely white head can be seen. He's bent over the
ground, planting beans and potatoes.

As he works, before he realizes he's been observed, Gardner is
softly whistling *Someone to Watch Over Me.*

It's raining. His blue turtleneck sweater, work jeans, and shoes—
strangely enough, fashionable tassel-topped loafers—are covered
with mud.

Here is a man who's a study in contrasts and contradictions.

One minute he'll tell you he maybe regrets having written a certain
book. Less than a minute later, he'll tell you that same book "will live
forever."

Gardner has been coming home each week because his 71-
year–old father, John Sr., suffered a paralyzing stroke 10 months ago.
He helps his father with his physical therapy. And he helps his
mother, Priscilla, with work around the once-showplace farm.

He looks around at his parents' farm, and talks about how things
have changed. "When I was a kid there were no houses in sight. We
used to grow hay where that house is. This road is getting to be a real
highway.

"Nothing really changes much. The tamarack tree is the same."

Again, contradictions.

His latest novel, *Mickelsson's Ghosts,* is about a professor at the

State University of New York at Binghamton (as Gardner himself is). He has just been separated from his wife (as Gardner was when he was writing the novel). He's in trouble with the Internal Revenue Service (as Gardner is). He drinks too much (as Gardner admits he used to). He has just bought a beat-up farmhouse in Susquehanna (as Gardner did).

Obviously, the book is based on Gardner himself. But no, the writer insists.

The lead character, he says, is based on his friend, poet and novelist (*Deliverance*) James Dickey.

"He's just like Jim, only he's not a Southerner," says Gardner. "He's always bustling about like a madman."

Gardner can't talk without puffing on a pipe—and his father is sensitive to smoke—so he heads for the toolshed back of the house.

When John Gardner was a boy, says his mother, he used to gather with his brother and sister and cousins in the barn in "a pretend church" to give sermons.

"Actually," corrects Gardner as he points through a haze of pipe smoke, "the 'pretend church' was in the orchard under a snow-apple tree. The orchard is gone and so is the tree.

"And I didn't give that many sermons. My cousin Bill gave most of them. He's the one who really wanted to be a minister. I liked telling stories best."

"It's useful to grow up on a farm," he says. "You spend hours and hours driving around on a tractor. You go crazy if you don't develop your imagination."

"As soon as John Jr. was old enough to listen," says Priscilla Gardner, a tiny 79-year-old woman with a sure, energetic voice, "John Sr. and I began reading to him. We started with Winnie the Pooh stories and it went on from there. John Sr. is a great memorizer and he can recite Shakespeare and Scripture for 4½ hours in a row."

When Gardner was a little boy milking cows in the barn, his mother would sit in a corner reading aloud from Shakespeare. His father would take on parts of different characters, reciting speeches from memory. When John Jr. went to bed at night, his father read poetry to him until he fell asleep.

It was an idyllic existence that was shattered one spring afternoon in 1945, when Gardner was 12. He was plowing the fields. His younger brother, Gilbert, was playing on the cultipacker, a two-ton

implement pulled behind the tractor to crush the soil. Gilbert slipped
off and was killed. John looked back in time to see his brother fall,
but not in time to save him.

There's an only slightly fictionalized account of the accident in
Gardner's short story, "Redemption" (in the collection *The Art of
Living*), says his mother. "He's blamed himself all these years for
what he couldn't possibly have prevented."

John Gardner then began writing stories and poems in earnest. He
attended Washington University in St. Louis, where he majored in
English and married his first wife, Joan, a second cousin whom he
had known since he was 2. It was in St. Louis that he decided he
could be a writer.

"I saw real writers at Washington U. and I realized I could do the
same thing.

"Anyone could," he adds, quickly and quietly.

He walks back to the house, and points across the field.

"There was a huge horse barn. We sold all the cows after my
father's stroke. Now no cows, no horses, we just got memories."

Gardner also says he doesn't have money. Although he has
published more than 30 books in the last 12 years—many of them
best sellers—although he makes a good living as a professor of
creative writing, and although he makes as much as $1,500 for a
single lecture, Gardner says he expects to be in debt for the rest of his
life. He's in *big* trouble with the IRS.

"I didn't keep good records," he explains, "For years, I didn't keep
records of my expenses. I actually don't owe them a thing. But I can't
prove it . . . I owe back taxes for years."

How much in debt is he? $100,000?

"Oh God no," he laughs. "Much, *much* more than that!
Sometimes I think as long as I can survive to write, it's OK. But if
every word you write goes to the IRS, it doesn't make you feel much
like writing. It takes away the incentive."

The conversation is interrupted by the arrival of David Baskervill, a
speech therapist who's trying to help John Sr. learn to speak again.

John Jr. goes into the bedroom to help his father. He dresses him
slowly and patiently and walks him into the living room. Strangely,
Gardner looks older than his father—older and more drawn than a
48-year-old man should look.

"Ooops, I didn't zip you up," he says. He carefully zips the front of his father's pants and heads for the kitchen leaving the living room for Baskervill and his parents.

"I try to keep them on a diet," he says. "I make them cook food without cholesterol and salt. They don't stay on it after I leave."

In addition to 32 published books, John Gardner writes scholarly articles on medieval literature, teaches two courses a term (his contract calls for only one), writes librettos for such composers as Joseph Baber and the Eastman School of Music's Warren Benson, and writes plays for and helps run the Susquehanna Community Choral Society and Laurel Street Theater group.

He also edits *MSS,* a journal for promising young writers, and teaches at Bread Loaf Writers Workshop every summer in Middlebury, Vt.

One can't help but wonder why he does so much—much of it for little or no pay. His health is obviously not good. He had a colostomy for a colon malignancy three years ago. Doctors at Johns Hopkins Medical Center cut a large chunk of his colon out and sewed it back together.

He laughs into the pipe smoke. "I don't sleep too much," he admits.

One reason that John Gardner loves teaching is that he's very good at it. As a novelist, he has his detractors. But he is generally praised as a spellbinding teacher.

Novelist and University of Rochester professor Thomas Gavin, who worked with Gardner at Bread Loaf, recalled listening to him lecture for the first time.

"He arrived at the lecture hall with his white mane of hair and piercing blue eyes. He was 20 minutes late. He said: 'I don't know anything about this crap. I'm a medievalist (Gardner's scholarly specialty is the medieval poet Geoffrey Chaucer).'

"Then he gives a brilliant lecture on fiction techniques," continued Gavin. "He looked dangerous and he spoke brilliantly. That room had a kind of barbaric energy. Yet all that energy was put to the service of ideas I found immensely practical."

Gardner also gave him, says Gavin, far more time than he had to.

"When I came to Bread Loaf the first time, I brought the first part of my first novel and he read it then," says Gavin. "The second summer he read the second part. He asked if he could read the first section again. 'Sometime in the last year, you've learned something about rhythm,' he said. I had unconsciously developed a technique for tightly packing sentences. It was important to me that Gardner had pointed to that."

Gardner has always been deeply involved with the lives of his students. His first important teaching position was at Southern Illinois University in Carbondale in the middle 1960s and early '70s—a time when campuses were burning over the issues of civil rights and the Vietnam War.

He regularly invited Black Power students, SDS members, local residents opposed to the students, and even members of the Ku Klux Klan to his farmhouse to try to get them to talk.

Gardner friends like composer Joseph Baber, now composer-in-residence at the University of Kentucky but then a Carbondale colleague, say some local people were so enraged by what Gardner was doing that he had to move his family to a motel for safety one weekend.

"They were going to burn my house down—a few things like that," Gardner says.

Gardner moved on to a cushier position at prestigious Bennington College in Vermont. He left Bennington in 1976 for a position at Binghamton when his marriage of 23 years ended. Joan continued to teach in a high school in Bennington.

Joseph Baber recalled a Gardner visit to the University of Kentucky when the writer was going through the final stages of his divorce.

"I worried about him," says Baber. "When he's drinking he makes you feel as if there's no reason for going on. He'll start saying things like 'We'll never match up to the great masters.' Then a minute later, he'll say 'I'm the best ever, but nobody will realize it for 300 years.'"

Some critics call Gardner one of the best writers in English; many others don't. He's certainly one of the most controversial—not so much for his fiction as for a critical book published three years ago, *On Moral Fiction,* that attacked fashionable literary styles and such important novelists as Saul Bellow, John Updike, John Barth, and Donald Barthelme.

Gardner accused these writers of playing literary games with words, of creating characters they didn't care about, and, most importantly, of neglecting important human situations. The book caused a still-continuing storm of controversy. And in many of the fashionable literary magazines and journals, where Gardner wasonce praised, he now finds himself attacked.

Gardner admits now to being a little "over-hasty in some of my judgments," not having "read some of the books recently enough," and "not being careful enough in what I said."

In a telephone conversation before the visit to Batavia, he said: "I don't want you to read the book. It's caused me nothing but trouble. I won't talk about it."

Then, almost immediately, he added: "Of course, it's a great book and it will live forever."

Face to face, he says: "I just wanted to make a statement about how fads can ruin writing."

He feels the major problem of much American writing is a prevailing bias toward hopelessness.

"I felt the academy (the intellectual, New York City-oriented crowd) was having an undue effect on what was being published," says Gardner. "When you live in a city like New York, it's really easy to feel the world is rotten."

He says about the writers he attacked: "I really like all those guys. I over-did it. I wasn't careful."

But does he regret the book?

"Absolutely not."

Nevertheless, the reaction to the book may have carried over to the way his latest work, the novel *Mickelsson's Ghosts,* is being reviewed. It has been savagely attacked in *Esquire, New York Review of Books,* and *New York* magazine.

But it also has received a rave review from Anatole Broyard in *The New York Times,* who liked everything but the ending in which more goes on than one believes possible.

Does he read his reviews?

"I get reviews later, read the first and last paragraphs, and see how many are for and against," he jokes.

Gardner stops to listen to what is happening in the next room.

The voice of the speech therapist is asking John Sr. to repeat phrases, slowly, patiently.

John Gardner writes *long* novels. Except for the fable-like *Grendel* (the 1971 retelling of the Beowulf story from the monster's point of

view) and the 1980 fable *Freddy's Book,* Gardner's novels average
well over 500 pages in length. And if his novels, so memorably
populated by believable people, so inventively imagined, have flaws,
it's that they tend to bog down.

"You mean they could be tighter," Gardner offers.

"I never bothered to write spare," he laughs.

The rain has halted and Gardner heads out to the barn where he
once milked cows.

An orange-colored barn cat trots toward him.

"That cat's a survivor," he says scooping it up in his arms. He looks
up at the roof of the barn. Timbers have fallen; light and rainwater
drips in.

The downstairs portion of the barn once housed more than 50
cows. Now there's just one sick calf which belongs to the couple who
rents half of Gardner's parents' home.

Priscilla Gardner remembers when her son told stories to anyone
who would listen in this barn.

" 'Tell us about dragons and dinosaurs,' they asked. And he would.
He loved dragons—still does."

"My mother prettifies it," John Gardner says, "Mostly what I made
up was tales of wicked fiends and beautiful maidens. The fiends were
so bad that you had to kill them five times over."

Fiends and monsters still populate the fiction of John Gardner.
Grendel is about a monster. The protagonists of *Freddy's Book* and
Nickel Mountain are monstrous-looking. The Sunlight Man in *The
Sunlight Dialogues* has been monstrously deformed by a fire. James
L. Page, the hero of *October Light,* has monstrous attributes. There
are witches and monstrous-looking people in *Mickelsson's Ghosts.*
And, of course, the protagonists of the operas written with Joseph
Baber, *Frankenstein* and *Rumpelstiltskin,* are monsters.

Yet all of Gardner's monsters strive to be human, and are
somehow likeable. Gardner himself, with his long white hair which
used to hang below his shoulders and his dishevelled clothing, often
looked a bit like a troll.

"I probably didn't notice it, but yeah," admits Gardner.

"I do see people as monsters, clowns, and human beings," he
says. "What's so wonderful about clowns is that they try to be human
beings and can't make it. When you watch a clown, you think, 'that's

what I really am.' It's true of monsters, too. That's what they really
want—to be human. It's hard to join. It's a very exclusive club."

Gardner has traveled an uneasy road to literary fame. He finished
his first novel in 1958 and wrote several others after that. Everything
he wrote—short stories, novels, and poetry—was rejected until *The
Resurrection* was published in 1966.

Then came more rejections until *Grendel* was published in 1971.

"I just kept on writing, and I wondered what was wrong," he says.

"He had never published anything," says his friend Baber, "but he
kept telling me 'I'm the best writer in this country.'

"I was completely under his spell. The wife of Thomas Kinsella
(the Irish poet and a colleague at Carbondale) kept telling me: 'He
always talks, but the great books never get written.'

"But John would show me single pages from the novels and
poems he was working on: 'See,' he'd tell me, 'look at what I can
do.' They'd be terrific and I'd fall under his spell again."

Grendel is a high school classic on the order of *Catcher in the Rye,
Cat's Cradle,* and *Lord of the Flies.* And college professors, like the
University of Rochester's Russell Peck, say it's not uncommon to find
college students who have read everything that Gardner has written.
"This is something," says Peck, "you don't find about other writers
like Updike and Bellow."

"It must be the kids are smarter than the guys at the *New York
Review of Books, Esquire,* and *New York,*" says Gardner.

"You couldn't ask for anything more confused than an intelligent
adolescent," says William O'Malley, a Jesuit priest who has been
teaching *Grendel* for years at McQuaid Jesuit High School. "Kids
love Gardner's fiction." O'Malley calls Gardner "a religious writer,"
and says that what his students "resonate to" is "a glimmer of the
truth."

John Gardner is generally regarded as a very conservative novelist.
Part of this reputation comes from the stance he takes against
experimental novelists like John Barth and Donald Barthelme. The
way Gardner talks about current writing in *On Moral Fiction,* one
might think that really good novels stopped with Tolstoy, Dostoyevsky
and Dickens.

Even his books have an old-fashioned look. All of them—with the
exception of *Mickelsson's Ghosts*—are illustrated by drawings, as

books were in the 18th and 19th centuries. Even *Mickelsson's Ghosts*
has illustrative photographs of the Susquehanna countryside, taken
by his 22-year-old photographer son Joel.

"I just like pictures in books," says Gardner. "But it only works in
certain types of books. I wouldn't want Updike or [Henry] James
illustrated. But my books have a lot of fantasy. And however careful I
am about the psychic life of my characters, they're sort of like
cartoons."

Gardner has actually done quite a bit of innovative work.

He's never repeated characters from one novel to the next. He
never repeats structural devices. *Grendel* is a mythic fable. *The
Sunlight Dialogues* is a small-town novel set in Batavia. *October Light*
is a pastoral with a built-in narrative discontinuity because part of the
novel is a novel-within-the-novel—a side-splitting parody of pornog-
raphy that one of the characters is reading. And *Freddy's Book* is a
narrative experiment of another kind—with a first-person narrative
introduction to a tale that ends without bringing back the original
narrator.

"I've certainly done a lot of experimental stuff," says Gardner, with
a touch of bitterness. "But I'm certainly not perceived that way."

If Gardner is old-fashioned, it's his values—his belief in family, in
the redeeming power of love, and, ultimately, in faith in God—or
something very like Him.

His current work-in-progress is called *Shadows*. As Gardner
describes it, it will be both his most experimental in his techniques,
and his most conservative in its values.

"I'll take all the standard elements of a mystery novel and slow
them down," says Gardner. "I'll take all the conventions of the
mystery and take them seriously. If Lew Archer really took a glass of
scotch every time he walked into a room, he'd see white flashes. If
everybody—including the detective—could have committed the
murder, then there'd be mass paranoia. The reader would be one
nervous person. The real trick is how do you work back to faith from
that. The easy answer would be to be born again. But I know that
answer and it's not interesting to me."

Gardner was born into the Presbyterian faith, but he no longer
considers himself a Presbyterian.

"Not any more," he says. "They [the Presbyterians] now do the

kind of stuff the Baptists do, but that's OK. Presbyterians used to be a
real historical church that believed in the historical Jesus. It was the
church with a big library, steeped in history and tradition. It was the
Jewish church of Christianity. The church that believed in ethical
choices. Now it's the fashionable church. They talk about heaven, but
never mention hell."

But if Gardner is not a member of a formal church, he is still a
deeply religious person, says Joseph Baber.

"When my wife died, he wrote me a long, hysterically entertaining
letter," says Baber. "He said something about art and Christianity—
or something like it—stand or fall together. If Christianity isn't true,
then art isn't, he said. Artistic choices are moral choices. If one thing
is better than another, then there's a hierarchy of values. He believes
deeply in God as the end of the hierarchy of values."

Faith is important, says Gardner, because "people who live a
condition of faith are a lot happier than those who don't. Joyce Carol
Oates told me once that every time she drives a car she fears every
car she sees will hit her. That's pretty scary."

Gardner is now separated from his second wife, poet Liz
Rosenberg, who edits *MSS.* with him, and whom he met when she
was his student at Bennington College.

"We're still friendly," says Gardner.

Will he marry again?

"Who knows," he says.

A pause.

"Probably."

Gardner wanders back to the farmhouse.

The speech therapy is over and Priscilla Gardner is standing in the
kitchen with a jar of freshly canned tomatoes.

"I used to can 100 quarts each of tomatoes and corn each year,"
she says. "I wanted to feed my family, but now I don't have much of
a family to feed."

Says Gardner, "She just talks on the telephone now and reads
dirty books."

"If my son writes them I do," she says.

Suddenly, without warning, the interview is concluded.

"I hope you guys don't mind," says Gardner, "but there's
something I have to do with my father."

What?

"I'm going to read to him."

What?

"*The Magic City*," he says with a big smile. (It's a children's book by E. Nesbitt.) "It's the *most* wonderful book."

John Gardner Sr. once read stories to his son; now John Jr. reads them to his father.

"It seems fair," says Gardner.

John Gardner, Flat Out

Curt Suplee/1982

From *The Washington Post*, 25 July 1982, pp. H1, H8-H9. Copyright © 1982 by *The Washington Post*. Reprinted by permission.

NEW YORK—A match flares angrily within the thick cloud of pipe smoke over the cocktail table. A pudgy, grimy hand reaches out to enwrap a martini, and draws it up to the roiling nimbus—through which the glum face of John Gardner now dimly appears. The martini glass tips, the floating lemon peel bobs once violently, and the elfin grimace recedes into the fog.

"I'm absolutely loved in the Midwest and West," says the cloud. "In Kansas City, Los Angeles, Chicago, I'm *God.*"

But this is Manhattan, a murky barroom in the shadow of the Plaza, and "these people in New York," says the 49–year-old novelist, critic and embattled oracle, "have decided that John Gardner is no good."

No good? The man who dazzled the critics with *Grendel, The Sunlight Dialogues,* and *October Light?* Who enraged the establishment with his brutal but powerful critical polemic, *On Moral Fiction?* Who still rampages across the literary landscape like the motorcycle racer he used to be, fabled from Binghamton to the Bread Loaf Writers' Conference and beyond for his tireless generosity to students—and for his tireless debauchery as well, a bleary juggernaut running on brains, charisma and gin? And over whom now the cloud lifts to reveal a boyish face somewhere between Prince Valiant and Mickey Rooney with the deep-wrinkled eyes of a Welsh crocodile. A mean red scar from a recent fall cuts across his nose and eyebrow.

No good? In truth, that's the majority East Coast opinion on his new novel, *Mickelsson's Ghost,* and Gardner says he is "badly hurt." But then, he expected that in New York, where animosities are still smoldering over *On Moral Fiction.*

"John has the capacity to revise himself almost instantly," says Gail Godwin, who has known him for years at Bread Loaf. And this afternoon, he will say variously: a) he should never have written it; b)

282

he's glad he wrote it because it changed the shape of American fiction; c) the idea was inevitable anyway; d) the tone was deliberately caustic to get attention; and e) "I don't think there's any anger. I think I was gentle. Think what I could have said!"

In calling for books with "true morality—life affirming, just and compassionate behavior," art which "clarifies life, establishes models of human action" and "carefully judges our right and wrong directions," he railied with arguable justice against the modish nihilism and flip despair of contemporary fiction. (Much to Gardner's embarrassment, he was praised by the New York branch of Moral Majority.)

But he also saw fit to condemn most American writers as "quite bad." Doctorow was "fraudulent," Barthelme "enfeebled," Pynchon full of "winking, mugging despair." Mailer, Vonnegut and Heller embodied "cant, cynicism or dramatic gimmickry," and Barth was a "philosophical fake." Even the qualified "exceptions" took a licking. Bellow's was a "subtler kind of failure" (essayistic "self- indulgence"), Updike doesn't revise enough" and his "books don't say what he means them to say," and Malamud, although a "great artist," still "keeps blowing it in his novels."

Reaction was caustic and immediate. Barth called it "a shrill pitch to the literary right wing." Updike found it "cavalier," Heller saw "dull carping criticism," Mailer threatened that "we'll meet in heaven." And Malamud said, "whenever Gardner hands you a chocolate cake, it's full of worms." Gardner remained adamant: "I am absolutely sure that my ideas will prevail."

"Look," Gardner says now, his manic terror sinking into a plaintive *sotto* drone. "I wrote that book in 1964. I had not yet been published. I was furious—just enraged at those guys with big reputations—and I wrote a vituperative, angry book." An editor friend told him, " 'You're crazy. It's not just that you'll hurt people's feelings—it's that you'll live to regret it.' Ten years later, right after I left [his first wife] Joan and my heart was breaking and I was sick, I went through the book and updated it, tried to tone it down.

"I thought those guys I don't like were not really liked by readers either. I thought it was just a New York establishment con." But now he knows that "I really hurt some people, people who loved that kind of thing," and he's "ashamed" of his remarks about Barth: "I should have known from his style that if there's anybody in the world who wants to be authentic, it's John Barth. Actually, I'm the only person in the world who loves *Letters.*"

Musing, he stabs a finger deep into his pipe bowl. It comes up blackened to the second knuckle. Except for cigarette breaks, the pipe fumes constantly, and the incessant restoking turns his hands filthy.

"Most of it I got wrong. Like I misunderstood Heller. I'm ashamed of my mistakes, and it's full of them. I never looked up a single quote. In fact, I got a letter from John Cheever saying, 'John, I really liked your quotation, but that's not what I said.' I never look it up. That's one of the reasons I'm accused of plagiarism." He was, and justly, for borrowing passages in *The Life and Times of Chaucer* (1977). But like any other English teacher, "I have in my head hundreds of paragraphs from writers, and I treasure them. And sometimes," he says, voice soft with shame, "I think I made 'em up."

Well, as long as he's recanting—doesn't *Mickelsson* owe a good deal to Bellow's *Herzog* in plan? "Yeah, I grew up and began to understand Bellow." (He now calls him "the greatest artist in America," although John Fowles "is probably the greatest artist in English" and Sol Yurick "probably the smartest man writing fiction." But "if you want real gut pain with full intellectual control, it's Cynthia Ozick.") And doesn't *Mickelsson* owe much too, to Updike in its prose texture? "Yeah, I'm comin' around to Updike. You know I'm slow."

Not that slow. In fact, the new novel is one of his best, striving toward his vision of fiction as "a vivid and continuous dream," deeply serious yet surprisingly exciting. "What I basically was trying to do," he says in his upstate nasal whine, "was a thriller which is thrilling on every level—intellectually, spiritually and physically."

And autobiographically? Gardner, professor of writing at the State University of New York at Binghamton, veteran of two failed marriages, two dozen books and a volatile reputation, pursued by the IRS for nearly half a million dollars in back taxes and determined to write a best-seller to make money, now lives with a former student in a 150-year-old farmhouse in Susquehanna, Pa.

His fictional protagonist, Peter Mickelsson, a fiftyish philosophy professor at SUNY/Binghamton, bibulous loner and nonstop smoker, faces a fading national name, a nasty divorce fight, an avalanche of unpaid bills and hostile investigation from the IRS. So he buys an old haunted farmhouse in Susquehanna, runs up more debts, courts a voluptuous colleague while involved with a teen-age prostitute whose pregnancy drives him to crime, and gradually nuts out in progressively depressive seclusion until the spirits and mysterious Mormon terrorists bring the story to a bloody crescendo.

"Mickelsson is a man who hates the '80s," Gardner says, exhaling another lung-clotting blast. "In every sphere he's fighting the prevailing trends. But it is also about midlife crisis. He's not just a man who's come to the peak of his career and begun to slide. He's a man who's destroying his career. He wants to start over. And so on a sort of unconscious level he does everything in his power to wreck himself. It's mad—it's obvious in the book that he's crazy—but it's sort of heroic," he says, like Ahab or Lear. "At the emotionally deepest level of the book for me—and of course, I am Mickelsson in a sense, although I don't think I'm *that* crazy—but I've written novels in certain kinds of ways all my life. And I've tried to tear everything that I've done apart and do something different."

That he has. Gardner is known chiefly for sprawling, often ponderous, metaphysical novels structured around a dialectic between two characters who become thesis and antithesis, the principal action cerebral, the principal conflict between freedom (with its potential for evil) and order (with its tendency to repression). By comparison, *Mickelsson* is a highbrow potboiler.

"My old-fashioned model of a novel was a kind of 19th century steamboat with a lot of frills. Now it's a 747." And it takes a wide-bodied and fast-moving narrative to carry all Gardner's themes, among them the totalitarian threats in modern culture (metaphorically embodied in the Mormons and tax men) and a grand theological synthesis. "The two sorts of ghosts in the thing are Nietzsche and Luther: Luther's saying none of your works mean anything; and Nietzsche's saying works are everything. And if you get those things together, you have courtly love. The lover does the most that he can possibly do, and then the grace of the lady saves him."

Saving grace. Gardner is full of it, a hypnotically charming raconteur, ricocheting between brazen cheer and mild humility, strewing anxious literary compliments with prodigal largesse from Joyce Carol Oates to Heinrich Boll, taking a shot when there's an opening. He's still mad at "the New York circuit" with its "cynicism and ennui," especially *The New Yorker's* tiny-domestic-despair school of fiction. "Making sure that the reader understands that nothing is happening in the story," Gardner growls, "is a way of saying that, 'We people who have Steuben glass and so on probably oughtn't to be reading at all.' The technique of the story is the message: That one can sensitively perceive, but there is in fact nothing to be perceived."

And he's proud of his clout. "I get all these letters from publishers saying, 'We were afraid to publish so-and-so. But since you are the spokesman for Middle America, we tried this book.'" It helped Oates's career, he believes, and made possible the success of John Irving and D.M. Thomas, among others.

Was he ever personally attacked when *On Moral Fiction* came out? "No, but I dream of it. I'm still a motorcycle kid. I wish some reviewer would come and hit me." What? "I mean, hit me *first*. I would have a dead reviewer and I would get off." It's an intriguing analogy, criticism and motorcycle racing: arrogant and self-dooming, taunting the cosmos until . . .

"Flat out!" he says suddenly, apropos of nothing in particular, everything in general. "Do you know where the expression comes from—motorcycle racing! When you get near the finish line, and you're out ahead, you'd just put your hands down on the bars like this," and he plops on the table, elbows spread, "and then you'd stick your head under. You couldn't see anything! But you'd pick up four or five miles an hour that way."

Head down. Flat out. A word that comes up a lot when you ask people whether John Gardner is "self-destructive." ("He inspires a maternal feeling in a certain kind of woman," says one old friend.) And it makes a certain sense as the martini count approaches double-digits, the pronunciation turns muddy, and the pipe drops occasionally from his mouth ("gotta get these teeth fixed!"). Makes sense, too, if you go back to Batavia, N.Y. in the mid-'40s.

Born in 1933, Gardner grew up in a Welsh family, with a grandmother who, he writes, taught him that angels were "as real as trees or hay wagons" and "made my world mythic." "In all my work," he says now, "I'm trying to break down the distinction between reality and fiction, to make the world fiction, to get back to the *real* real world, where all the myths are true."

His mother was a high-school literature teacher, his father a dairy farmer, prodigious recounter of folk stories ("I knew by the time I was 5 that the best thing in the world to be was a storyteller") and a mesmerizing lay preacher. "His sermons were poems, just gorgeous things. I take after my mother. My father's an intellectual, smart and cool, and he reads a lot. My mother can never decide what she thinks about anything, she's always confused, immensely loving and sometimes hating, kind of a lady of passion. Thesis, antithesis: He grew up "in a balance" between gossip and abstraction, "and then for 14 hours a day, you're all by yourself on a tractor, mulling things over, making up stories."

That was where his brother died. Gardner was 12 and driving the tractor when his 7-year-old brother was crushed by the machinery. He "could have prevented his brother's death," Gardner writes in a story called "Redemption," but was "unable to think, or rather, thought unclearly, and so watched it happen, as he would again and again watch it happen in his mind, with nearly undiminished intensity and clarity all his life."

"After my brother died," Gardner says now, "my parents didn't know what to do with me and they let me drift." He drifted into writing, but the gloom remained as he grew older. "I was terrific at guilt. And I did everything in my power to get guiltier." This included racing his Harleys—big flathead hogs that could crush you against a fence—and "looking for rules" in literature.

By 19, he was married; by 25 he had a doctorate in languages and was writing fiction furiously; by 29, he had been fired from two different universities for organizing faculty, baiting authority. Throughout the long academic migrancy that would take him to Southern Illinois, Bennington, Skidmore, Williams, George Mason and Binghamton, he kept writing, often fighting suicidal despondency. The early novels were not lucrative. *The Resurrection* (1966) sold fewer than 1,000 copies and *The Wreckage of Agathon* (1970), though a critical success, was no windfall. So when he met Telly Savalas, who asked him to try writing a movie, Gardner headed for Hollywood. "They said, 'Bring a movie, John.' So I brought a movie. And then before

the guy heard my story, he said, 'John, before you tell me what
you've got in mind, let me say that we've done the marketing
research and we know the American people don't like movies about
farmers. And they don't like movies about snow. And the American
people don't like movies where the central characters are foreigners.'
And he went on—he had about 20 things.

"But the movie I came with was a Vietnamese family's first winter
in Iowa."

Still, two of his projects were made. "I don't usually admit it," and
will not reveal the titles. "I took my name off because they changed
everything and I didn't like it."

But then *he* changed everything. First *Grendel* (1971) was a hit,
and Gardner was making public appearances. "In those days I would
wear a crushed velvet robe—I'm shameless, right!—with a huge,
silver chain. I felt that *every* time I did a reading, I was cheating the
people because they came hoping for something very exciting. I
wanted them to think that their $5 or $7 or whatever was worthwhile.
So I wore this robe, so that when they went home, at least they could
say, 'I went to the most boring reading in history—but *boy*, did that
guy dress funny!' "

Then in 1972, *The Sunlight Dialogues* became a best seller. Nearly
half a million dollars rolled in. "Man, I was really rich!" Gardner says,
eyes popping wide in recall. *Nickel Mountain* (1973) was warmly
received, *October Light* (1976) won the National Book Critics Circle
Award. He survived surgery for cancer of the colon, and still kept up
an artistic momentum that would exhaust many a younger man.

Then the big hammer came down. *On Moral Fiction* made
Gardner a celebrity—and plenty of long-lasting enemies. One major
novelist whom Gardner calls a friend and praises highly in person
refuses to return the compliment: "Maybe he said that—but when he
puts it in print it comes out backwards."

And the IRS went after him for back taxes. A compromise
settlement is expected next month. If he is found responsible for the
whole sum, he says, "I'll never be able to pay in my lifetime." Not
even if they seized his 30-acre farm in Susquehanna, where he lives
with Susan Thornton, 32, whom he met at Bread Loaf. There's not
much to take, he says, "beyond our goats and our pigs and our
cranberries" and the big Harley ("I drive like an old lady—a *fast* old

lady"). Not even a television set: The reception is too poor, and Gardner is bereft. "I'm out of it! It's a real part of American life, and I can't write about it. I haven't seen Walter Cronkite since his hair got gray."

Meanwhile, it's salvation by works. He teaches novel-writing, obliged to read reams. "All my writers become famous," he says, citing John Irving, Toni Morrison, Tim O'Brien, Roberta Gupta and Ron Hansen. "In fact, some of the best porno writers in America are my kids." He writes radio plays and librettos. (His *Rumpelstiltskin* is the annual Christmas production of the Philadelphia Opera Society.) He edits *MSS* ("absolutely flat-out the finest literary magazine going"). And along with his estranged wife Liz, he is active in local theater. He's now directing *You're a Good Man, Charlie Brown*. And revising it to accommodate the moral needs of rural Pennsylvania: "There's one scene where Peppermint Patty comes in with a limp jump rope in her hand, looking sad. Charlie Brown says, 'What's wrong?' And she says, "It's all so *futile!*" " Gardner groans in ecstasy of disgust. "Do you know how that would play in Susquehanna? They'd kill her!"

And, of course, the novels. His next is tentatively titled *Shadows.* Gardner has predicted it will "be either the most pompous, stupid thing in the world, or it'll be a mindbreaker." It "uses the technique of a Ross McDonald mystery, but slowed way down." Over hundreds of pages, the murders mount until everyone begins to "suspect everybody else of horrible crimes, it leads you to feel total paranoia, you distrust everybody in your world." About two-thirds of the way through, the criminals will be revealed, leaving a secondary problem: "If you don't trust *anybody*, how do you find you way back to faith?" And who are these anybodies? "Many major characters are people I know," and authors like William Gass, John Barth and John Updike will find themselves portrayed in fictional guise, so that "after about the third reading, people who really care about modern writers will say, 'Gee!—that's a lot like Pynchon!' "

But "I'm not writing now. I'm hurt," into one of the depressions in which he holes up with scores of "cheap books." (He is a prodigious fan of Stephen King.) "You know, I think I'm really a great artist," he says, tortured by lukewarm reviews "while some woman's book that is a Hallmark card of a novel is praised to the skies."

But this is the man who once told a group of Bread Loaf students, "I used to be afraid of a lot of things—but then I faced death, and now I'm not even afraid of that." So let's have another drink. Another pipe-load. There'll be another novel, another time around the track, and Gardner is grinning now, the cloud dispelled. *Flat out!* "It's the same thing as motorcycle racing. You believe in something and you push it and you just don't worry about what's going to happen . . . Like you believe in your machine and you believe in your crew, and then you try to get in front of everybody so they can't hit you."

John Gardner's Last Interview

Bruce Beans/1982

From: *Today: The [Philadelphia] Inquirer Magazine,* 17 October 1982, pp. 1, 18-21. Reprinted by permission.

John Gardner must have known it would end there someday. He had even written about the cemetery just outside of Batavia, N.Y., surrounded by a sea of Genesee County cornfields.

Of course, as novelists often do in order to get at their own particular sense of the truth, he moved things around—rooting up an iron fence from a cemetery that was actually in town, near a steel-boiler plant, and bringing it out to this cemetery; and erecting two red barns across the road. But when he opened his first published novel, *The Resurrection,* in an upstate New York graveyard, he no doubt had thought of Grand View Cemetery.

It was here on a startlingly clear mid-September morning, on which the flame-orange of the maple leaves viewed with the brilliant blue of the cloudless sky, that the novelist was buried beside his brother Gilbert in a scene that again could have come from one of his own novels.

Indeed, the manner and timing of his death last month were things that could have come from his Roman-candle-like imagination, but at the same time there's also reason to suspect that he wouldn't have written it the way it happened. There was too much of the kind of melodrama he despised.

For one thing, the reader of Gardner's work had not been prepared, as he would have been in a well-constructed novel, for the manner of Gardner's death. It was too far-fetched. Gardner, who was 49 when he died, had ridden motorcycles since he was a teenager, and never had had a serious accident. "I ride for pleasure, not thrills," he said.

It was no doubt for pleasure that Gardner had left his 30-acre farm just outside of Susquehanna, Pa., to savor another clear late summer day in the Endless Mountains of Northeastern Pennsylvania. But three miles to the north, where Route 92 follows the wide, solemn

291

Susquehanna River toward the New York state line, he inexplicably
lost control after rounding a left-hand curve. The cycle—he called it
his "hog," a raw-powered Harley-Davidson Electroglide 1200—bit a
shallow trench into the dirt shoulder on the right side of the asphalt
road for 20 yards. Then the bike rolled to the left. As it hit the
pavement, the handlebars plunged into Gardner's stomach, and
although the skin was not broken, the injury caused massive
abdominal bleeding. He died in an ambulance seconds before it
could deliver him to a nearby hospital.

Another criticism of his death as literature is that it was an unfairly
easy way of resolving a complicated plot. It clearly violated one of the
rules Gardner always gave to his students: "Never do anything cheap
with the reader. Don't kill a kid." And don't, he may have added, idly
kill off the protagonist as he faces the crucial moments of his life.

Gardner's death came just four days before he was to be married
for the third time (he had just been divorced from his second wife),
and just as his financial advisers were hoping to resolve a dispute
with the Internal Revenue Service, which contended that he owed
$500,000 in back taxes as a result of what Gardner called "sloppy
bookkeeping." (That obligation is now expected to consume his
entire estate.)

Perhaps most tragically, he died with his reputation under attack—
or possibly counterattack. He had launched his own assault on the
icons of contemporary literature in his book *On Moral Fiction,* which
left no one unscathed. Most current literature, he charged, was
"either trivial or false." It didn't do what he thought literature should
do.

"A lot of times when I was a kid and I was deeply unhappy," he
said in an interview several weeks before his death, "I would go read
Dickens and I would feel better. I think great works of art make you
whole. I want to be the kind of artist that makes life worthwhile, that's
what *On Moral Fiction* is all about, whatever it sounds like it's about."

Gardner subsequently took back or modified many of the things
he'd said about specific writers, but he stuck to his judgment that
today the literary establishment has "judged cynical or nihilistic
writers as characteristic of the age, and therefore significant and thus
supports, even celebrates ideas no father would wittingly teach his
children. . . . " He felt it had become offensive to suggest publicly
that anything might turn out well in this world. Many writers, Gardner

wrote, were self-indulgent game-players "more in love with the sound of words than creating fictional worlds."

The work was not terribly popular in literary circles. "Gardner is a pretentious young man, talks a lot and has little of intelligence to say," said Joseph Heller, author of *Catch-22*, who was one of Gardner's targets. Gardner, for one, thought the negative reviews of his most recent books, *Mickelsson's Ghosts,* were in part retribution for *Moral Fiction.*

In assessing his own work, he alternated quickly during the interview between charming modesty and mountainous egotism with the erratic swiftness of the barn swallows that careen over his farm pond. "In writing, as in boxing, there are different weights," he said. "You may not be very good in your class, but you're in it. I may be the fattest, flabbiest heavyweight to ever come along, but I *am* a heavyweight. I stand with [Saul] Bellow and John Fowles and nobody else."

Suddenly Gardner rolled his head back and stuck out his tongue like a dragon in mock agony. "Ooh . . . yah!" he whooped. "I'm just thinking about how all this will sound: 'John Gardner says he is a heavyweight. . . .' " But, when not beset by self-doubt, which corroded his soul and sensibility, he believed it.

Even his admirers were left wondering, though, after his death, whether he would have fulfilled the promise shown in the books he had written, which were peopled with bigger-than-life characters and infused with clashing philosophical ideas. These included *Grendel*, a retelling of the Beowulf legend through the eyes of the monster, which is now a campus classic. He also received applause from critics—and best-seller status—for *The Sunlight Dialogues* (1972), *Nickel Mountain* (1973) and *October Light*, which won the National Book Critics Circle Award as the best novel of 1976.

Even if he wouldn't have written the story of his death quite the way it happened, there were some intriguing prefigurations of Gardner's funeral in his novels. Looking around inside the white nave of the First Presbyterian Church on East Main Street in Batavia, a mourner might have half expected to see Police Chief Fred Clumly in one of the pews. Clumly was one of Gardner's characters in *The Sunlight Dialogues,* a book set in Batavia that was his biggest seller. Gardner had written about Clumly.

"Fred Clumly enjoyed funerals. It was a sad thing to see all one's

old friends and relatives slipping away, one after the other, leaving
their grown sons and daughters weeping, soberly dabbing at their
eyes with their neat white hankies. . . . But it was pleasant, too, in a
mysterious way he couldn't and didn't really want to find words for.
There stood the whole family—three, four generations—the living
testimonial to the man's having been. . . . "

At the start of Gardner's funeral, the church was filled with the
softly textured sounds of a French horn duet—a tape of Gardner and
his son Joel playing "Amazing Grace." Joel, 22, a photographer, sat
in the first pew nearest his father's pine coffin. He was as fair as his
father and dressed in the kind of dark Icelandic wool sweater that
became one of his father's trademarks. In the same pew sat Gardner's
other child, Joel's sister Lucy, 20, a delicately-beautiful straw blonde
whose face bore an unmistakable resemblance to her father's. The
life-threatening kidney disease she is battling had been one of her
father's greatest sources of anguish.

Both of his children had an arm around their mother, Joan
Gardner, a rounded, red-haired woman who had been Gardner's first
wife. They were second cousins and had known each other from the
time they were 2 years old. They had married at 19, and the marriage
had lasted 23 years—until Joan Gardner had grown weary of trying
to "live on the edge" with her husband. She was now living happily
in anonymity as a high school music teacher in Bennington, Vt.

Gardner had blamed himself for their divorce, and at times he felt
he had been meant to be married to her for the rest of his life. He
spoke of her in loving terms, remembering how she had looked as a
child. "She was unspeakably beautiful," he recalled. "When she was
13, she had red hair that touched the floor. Her hands were small;
she couldn't play Liszt—but Bach, Beethoven and Mozart like
nobody you've ever heard."

Behind his first wife and his children sat Gardner's parents: John
Sr., 71, a dairy farmer until a stroke crippled his right side a year ago,
and Priscilla, 79, a short, delightful woman who had taught high
school English. Nearby sat Jim Gardner, a brother, who is a local
truck driver, and Sandy, Gardner's sister, who teaches school in
Detroit.

Behind Gardner's parents sat Liz Rosenberg, 27. Gardner's second
wife: their amicable divorce had become final just three days before
Gardner's death. A critic and poet who teaches at the State University

of New York-Binghamton—where Gardner had been the creative writing director for the last four years—Rosenberg, a bright, vibrant brunette, had been a student of Gardner's at Bennington College seven years ago.

Gardner enjoyed recounting how she had run away to J.D. Salinger's home when she was 14 because she wanted him to teach her how to write. And he darkened when he remembered how Salinger, the reclusive novelist, "acted as if he hardly knew her" when she waited for him last year at his post office in New Hampshire. "Good thing I wasn't there," he said with his eyes twinkling, half enjoying the thought. "That would have been some literary murder."

"She doesn't want to be without me, and I don't want to be without her," Gardner had said several weeks earlier. But "she's a thousand volts: Susan is peace. And I want peace. I really do. I need it for my work, for my life."

He was referring to Susan Thornton, a distraught woman who sat to the far left of the front pew, supported by one of Gardner's white-haired aunts. A plain-featured 32-year-old from Rochester whom Gardner had taught at the Bread Loaf (Vt.) Writers' Conference, she had spent what was to have been the day of her marriage to Gardner attending his wake.

Gardner had concluded his account of Chief Clumly's view of the fictional funeral by writing, "And there it was, a man's whole life drawn together at last. Stilled to a charm, honored and respected, and the minister took off his black hat and prayed, and Clumly prayed, with tears in his eyes and his police cap over his fallen chest. And so, with dignity, the man's life closed, like the book in the minister's hands."

In the interview, Gardner had said: "I love Clumly. He's the hero of the novel. A lot of things I had Clumly say I giggled at when I wrote them. I thought they were wonderful and funny and sweet and sincere, and in another way just plain whacko. . . . I don't think death is the final order. I find death is practically an illusion."

Gardner had faced the imminent possibility of dying five years ago, when he was told by surgeons at Johns Hopkins University Hospital in Baltimore that he had cancer of the colon, and that his chances of surviving a then-experimental operation were extremely small.

"I figured . . . I would die." Gardner said. "I thought, 'Wow, that's interesting. Now I'm going to find out.' I just can't explain it in a way that doesn't sound phony, but it didn't bother me. . . . My chief concern [then] was the enormous distress that my loved ones would feel. I was very worried about the reaction of my mother and father. I was scared to death about Liz because at that time I hadn't yet talked her into the afterlife. I was worried about Lucy and Joel, Joan, everybody. I felt in a funny way I had betrayed them."

Gardner had said this in the middle of a long conversation. By 5 a.m., his discourse was beginning to take on the same fatigued, late-night dreaminess to which Gardner succumbed when he wrote most creatively. The mood was broken only by his repeated trips to the kitchen to mix more martinis, and a couple of trips to the front porch of his 150-year-old farmhouse to relieve himself of their effect.

Inside again, Gardner, like one of his medieval monsters rooting through a cave, rummaged upstairs and rifled through a raincoat looking for matches to keep the incense of his pipe perpetually swirling about his head along with the flies. "My whole life," he lamented, "is a search for matches."

Slightly paunchy, with gentle, wrinkled eyes, a soft, slightly nasal upstate New York twang, and a pewter-white mane worthy of Merlin, John Gardner was a living engine of ambition who was seen in different ways by different people. He once said of a friend, "Like any genius, he can't find a box big enough for himself." He might have been talking about himself.

Certainly others had trouble categorizing him. "John was an extremely complex personality, almost like a character out of a Dostoevsky novel," said novelist Joyce Carol Oates after she had heard of Gardner's death, "There's hardly an adjective not applicable."

To begin with, there was the exterior Gardner, who, in his leather jacket, could seem as tough as a motorcycle hood. Gardner was proud of a scar—the result of a fall in his driveway this past summer—that sliced across his forehead and the bridge of his nose. He had refused stitches, he explained, because "I think you should wear your life on your face."

But underneath was a gentle country boy as fragile as an eggshell, a likable Eagle Scout who bear-hugged his neighbors. He spent many weekends during what would turn out to be the last year of his

life making the four-hour trip to Batavia to help his crippled father
with swimming therapy. He also read aloud to him from *Treasure
Island* and other books.

Gardner could also be the temperamental artist, raging for two
hours before accepting Liz Rosenberg's criticism of his manuscripts.
He brought to everything he did a passion that at times bordered on
madness. When he decided in the mid-1970s to leave his first wife,
Joan, who was living with another man in the same house, he had so
thoroughly convinced himself she would kill him that he was afraid to
say goodbye to her.

His books were as difficult to pigeonhole as his personality. He was
a medieval scholar who was influenced by Tolstoy, Dickens—and
Disney. His 32 works included short stories, novels, children's tales,
poetry, criticism, and analyses of medieval literature such as a
biography of Chaucer for which he was accused of plagiarism. He
also wrote uncredited screenplays, plays, and the libretto for
Rumpelstiltskin, a children's opera that was put on at Christmas time
by the Philadelphia Opera Company for the past three years.

And "for sport, like other people play bridge," he was a major
figure in Susquehanna's amateur Laurel Street Theater. Last July he
and Liz Rosenberg co-directed *You're a Good Man, Charlie Brown*
there in a production for which they had written new music.

Lastly, he was a flamboyant lecturer who used to wear a velvet
robe and gold medallion to his readings, and a charismatic teacher
who was generous with his time. "Sometimes," his mother said with
a sigh last summer, "it seems to me that he's trying to live the lives of
two people."

In a way, he was. Gardner grappled with that impossibility for most
of his life, ever since a cruel April day in 1945 on his family's 180-acre
dairy farm near Batavia.

Not yet 12, Gardner was atop a tractor pulling a cultipacker—a
two-ton, iron-wheeled implement that smoothed the freshly plowed
soil, and atop which his brother Gilbert, 6, was riding. Looking back
when his sister Sandy screamed, Gardner saw Gilbert crushed up to
his pelvis underneath the cultipacker. He did not stop.

"I don't really know if I could have," Gardner said. Then he
paused, straining not so much to recall the accident—he could see his
mangled brother as well as the visitor who sat across from him—but

for the right words. " . . . I know . . . that when I looked back my brother was more than half crushed and I didn't choose to stop. I probably should have, but if I tried to stop I couldn't have, and if I had stopped I know I couldn't have gotten it off of him. I think the truth is he would've been dead either way, and I think I just did it the quick way."

Nonetheless, Gardner blamed himself for killing his brother and for the despondency that enveloped his parents, particularly his father. "It was a terribly tragic event in Bud's life," said his mother, using a family nickname for Gardner. "He blamed himself, but nobody could have prevented that accident, only God, and He doesn't work that way."

The guilt haunted Gardner for years. Nightmares of the accident made him scream in his sleep. During the day, he would experience what psychiatrists call "afterflashes"—incredibly vivid hallucinations of the accident. "I had spent all my life avoiding those afterflashes or trying to duck them, but they'd come and start playing themselves right out to the end." Gardner said, "It was unhealthy. When you're driving along and you start to see something in your mind that becomes so powerful you can't see the road, that's dangerous."

Finally, at the urging of a psychiatrist, in 1977 he wrote and published "Redemption," a highly autobiographical short story about the accident. Afterward, he suffered only two more afterflashes.

It was his brother's death that probably made Gardner a writer. Long before the accident, he had sat in the family's barn in the evening listening to his mother read novels and Shakespeare's plays while his father, milking the cows, took on some of the parts. A lay preacher with an astounding memory, John Gardner Sr. would also recite long stretches of poetry, and, out in the fields, would sing along with the Texaco opera broadcasts.

Becoming withdrawn after the accident, Gardner began to play to that parental audience. "My parents valued music and words about as much as they probably valued anything," he said, "and if I wrote a story or a poem, that my parents really liked, their approval was instantaneous. Obviously, when you hate yourself, it's always good to have somebody praise you."

Parking the tractor in fields he was supposed to be plowing, Gardner would sit underneath it for hours scribbling poems, tales and thriller novels that he would read to his grandmother or to his cousins in the barn after chores were done. By the time he was 19, he had written a story that was the genesis for *Nickel Mountain,* a moving pastoral novel that would become a best-seller 21 years later.

He also became so good at playing the French horn that, after high school, he was offered a music scholarship. He turned it down because he felt he would never attain greatness as a musician. Gardner actually began college as a chemistry major, but by the time he graduated from Washington University in St. Louis, his knack for languages and creative writing had won out over his interest in chemical theory.

In 1958, armed with a Ph.D. in writing, he embarked on a long odyssey through academic America, which took him to San Francisco State between 1961 and 1964. He found himself traveling in two circles, one consisting of sophisticated academics, and the other composed of the hip crowd gathered around Lawrence Ferlinghetti and Allen Ginsberg, the poets. (Gardner launched a literary magazine, called *MSS.,* out of Ferlinghetti's City Lights bookstore.)

But Gardner felt like an outsider in both. "I thought I was going crazy," he says. "I was torn between being a writer like the City Lights crowd, who were into things I thought were wonderful but not mine—drugs, the social revolution and all kinds of things I didn't want to do, although I didn't disagree.

"On the other hand, people were going to new plays I thought were unspeakably awful, praising novelists I couldn't read, and I just had to get away from all the talk about writing. It wasn't my talk."

Another problem is that he was being ignored as a writer. He published the first work of authors such as Joyce Carol Oates and William Gass in his magazine, but could not find a publisher for his own work.

Gardner finally escaped San Francisco for a teaching job in Carbondale, Ill., a move he thinks may have saved his sanity but cost him his marriage because it required Joan Gardner to give up a promising career as a concert pianist. "She couldn't handle the move to Carbondale," he said somberly. "She was heartbroken. She felt it was my fault that she had lost her career, which was true. She was making $24,000, I was making just $12,000. If I had known about male chauvinism then, I would've somehow survived. I just thought, 'I can't stand it, I gotta go.' It was idiotic."

In California and Illinois, Gardner said, he sometimes contemplated suicide, "but when you know that your kids, who you really love, would inevitably be hurt and statistically are likely to commit suicide, you grab hold of yourself." Instead, he marinated himself in gin.

Eventually, Gardner felt he had to return to the East, and to a rural setting. He did so, moving first to Bennington, then to Susquehanna. "I think a writer who leaves his roots leaves any hope of writing importantly," he said. "When I lived in San Francisco, I felt out of touch with my material and felt half that way in Illinois. But when I came back East . . . like, I know what people are thinking if I just watch the twitch of their cheek. And that just wasn't true in San Francisco, where, for all I know, it's the style this week.

"I think big cities like New York or Chicago tend to foster a certain cynicism that's different from a rural upbringing," he said. "But then, I'd quickly have to say that some of the meanest, most nihilistic, cynical, stupid people I ever knew were country people, and some of the gentlest and wisest were city people. . . . "

Gardner had first come to Susquehanna County as a teenager, joy riding on his motorcycle after racing it at Watkins Glen, N.Y. He loved the raw beauty of the mountains where Joseph Smith started Mormonism 150 years ago.

"I never dreamed I'd end up here," Gardner said during a drive earlier in the evening. "I love everything about this country. I love the way the hills slope into the hills, I love the darkness. They just found a witches' coven across the New York state line . . . mutilated animals, strange clothes. It's a strange place. It's wonderful."

The farm, which Gardner moved to a year after he came to SUNY-Binghamton, is a mile into the hills south of Susquehanna. The unpretentious farmhouse, which includes an exposed-beam dining room plastered by Gardner, is guarded by five stately sugar maples. Both it and a handsome gazebo Gardner built last summer—and split-cedar shingled roof and cross-hatched lattice trim—look out across a valley of pine and aspen to a steep maple mountainside. Behind the house, hayfields climb sharply to thick woods, from which herds of deer slip out to browse at twilight.

On the farm, Gardner tried to coax vegetables from the rocky soil, kept a German Shepherd named Teddy and raised a few pigs and goats. But mainly he wrote.

He worked on an IBM self-correcting Selectric III, at a desk fashioned from a wide door set on sawhorses in a cluttered first-floor study. There he battled blank pages and muscle aches for 18 hours a day, he said. In the course of five or 10 years, he said, he would go through 30 different drafts of a novel, until the prose "is so full of detail and richness that it sounds like a piece of my mother's gossip."

Gardner's advice to students was to write "a story so good and interesting that it can compete if an exciting 20-person Romanian circus comes to town. I start out wanting to tell a wonderful, suspenseful story—I care about that more than anything else. And then, after I work out a good tight story, I try to figure out, 'How do I make that large, something that will be unforgettable?' Because I don't want it just to be a very fine circus act, I want it to be *Moby Dick.*"

Gardner also brought the zeal of a missionary to his teaching. "I believe in the holiness . . . forgive me," he said, trying to wave away his pomposity, " . . . of what I do. I *must* teach because I'm good at it and I'm Presbyterian and we believe in duty. We have a word for it—stewardship."

He had demonstrated that five years ago at Johns Hopkins when, with an intravenous unit in his arm and a typewriter on his bed, Gardner continued working on a yet-to-be-published writers' guide—hours before he thought he was going to die as a result of the colon operation.

The last book published before his death was *Mickelsson's Ghosts.* It involved a SUNY-Binghamton professor living on the outskirts of Susquehanna who is hounded by torn love loyalties, bills and the IRS. But, Gardner insisted repeatedly, "I am not Peter Mickelsson, NO WAY!" He said the character was based on the same friend who inspired an unfinished Gardner oil painting of an ailing bear of a man who broods over Gardner's typewriter—James Dickey, who wrote *Deliverance.*

"Jim's a genius, like nobody of our time has claim to that word." Gardner said. "But he drinks a lot, behaves badly and a lot of people take offense. He feels such a degree of self-hatred that his way of having a friend is to p--- on him and see if you still like him.

"With Mickelsson, I wanted to write a book about greatness—

greatness is agony and I wanted to make a real hero who deals with current issues, pollution, ecology, fundamentalism." The novel has a disquieting tone: unexplained murders and talk of witchcraft, UFOs, prescience and other phenomena that undermine our grasp of reality.

Gardner, not surprisingly, was a collector of odd facts, a fan of Stephen King and the *National Enquirer*, who appreciatively used the word *weird* a lot.

Mickelsson's Ghosts received a few glowing reviews. Novelist Larry Woiwode called it "the kind of book that can alter one's way of looking at life." But for the most part, the complex tale of a once-distinguished philosophy professor deep in the throes of a mid-life crisis was savaged by the worst pans Gardner received during his 11 years of national prominence. "A whopping piece of academic bull slinging," wrote *Esquire*'s James Wolcott.

"I think the fact is, it's a great novel," Gardner said. "It's being judged, to a great extent, by people who are cross at *On Moral Fiction*."

Despite this show of self-assurance, the fact is that the negative reviews so depressed Gardner that earlier last summer he told Liz Rosenberg and other confidants that he was through as a novelist.

"It's partly a feeling he has of drawing towards 50 and that he hasn't written a really great book, although he's written some good ones . . ." Rosenberg said. "Besides not having much confidence in himself—he goes through this gloom and depression for months in between books—this time it's compounded by the way he keeps getting smacked in the head because of *On Moral Fiction*."

However, his former wife, for one, didn't believe him. "I've never seen someone so addicted to writing," she said.

He would write again, he conceded in late July, but said he was too drained at the moment to attack his 750-page manuscript of *Shadows,* a love story and murder mystery in which Gardner was attempting to push the conventions of the thriller novel to their limits. He had started it 10 years ago, and hoped it would be his masterpiece. In the meantime, his desk was covered with pages of what he intended to be the definitive translation of the *Gilgamesh,* the Mesopotamian flood epic written about 2,000 B.C.

"You know, it just *bugs* me," Gardner said, ruing the flaws of some contemporary best-sellers. "Bob Gottlieb [Gardner's editor] says,

'John, you're a golden album. A thousand years from now we'll be selling your books.'

"I want it NOW!" Gardner roared, seizing the air with his right fist. "Is that too much to ask?"

Index

G